Routledge Questions & Answers Series

Civil Liberties & Human Rights

2013–2014

D0224647

Routledge Q&A series

Each Routledge Q&A contains approximately 50 questions on topics commonly found on exam papers, with comprehensive suggested answers. The titles are written by lecturers who are also examiners, so the student gains an important insight into exactly what examiners are looking for in an answer. This makes them excellent revision and practice guides. With over 500,000 copies of the Routledge Q&As sold to date, accept no other substitute.

New editions publishing in 2013:

Civil Liberties & Human Rights
Company Law
Commercial Law
Constitutional & Administrative Law
Contract Law
Criminal Law
Employment Law
English Legal System
Equity & Trusts
European Union Law

Evidence
Family Law
Jurisprudence
Land Law
Medical Law
Torts

Published in 2012:

Business Law 2012–2013
Intellectual Property Law 2012–2013

For a full listing, visit http://cw.routledge.com/textbooks/revision

Routledge Questions & Answers Series

Civil Liberties & Human Rights

2013–2014

Helen Fenwick and Richard Glancey

Routledge
Taylor & Francis Group

LONDON AND NEW YORK

Sixth edition published 2013
by Routledge
2 Park Square, Milton Park, Abingdon, Oxon OX14 4RN

Simultaneously published in the USA and Canada
by Routledge
711 Third Avenue, New York, NY 10017

Routledge is an imprint of the Taylor & Francis Group, an informa business

© 2013 Helen Fenwick

First and second editions prepared by Helen Fenwick, third edition prepared by Helen Fenwick and Howard Davis and published by Cavendish Publishing Limited.

The right of Helen Fenwick to be identified as author of this work has been asserted by her in accordance with sections 77 and 78 of the Copyright, Designs and Patents Act 1988.

First edition published by Cavendish Publishing 1994
Fifth edition published by Routledge 2011

British Library Cataloguing in Publication Data
A catalogue record for this book is available from the British Library

Library of Congress Cataloging in Publication Data
Fenwick, Helen.
  Q&A civil liberties and human rights / Helen Fenwick and Richard Glancey.—6th ed.
    p. cm.
  "Simultaneously published in the USA and Canada."
  ISBN 978-0-415-63365-9 (pbk)—ISBN 978-0-203-08409-0 (ebk)
  1. Civil rights—Great Britain—Examinations, questions, etc.   2. Human rights—Great Britain—
  Examinations, questions, etc.   I. Glancey, Richard.   II. Title.   III. Title: Q & A civil liberties and human
  rights.   IV. Title: Q and A civil liberties and human rights.   V. Title: Question and answer civil liberties and
  human rights.
  KD4080.F465 2013
  342.4108'5076—dc23

                                                                                        2012020644

ISBN: 978–0–415–63365–9 (pbk)
ISBN: 978–0–203–08409–0 (ebk)

Typeset in TheSans
by RefineCatch Limited, Bungay, Suffolk

Printed and bound in Great Britain by the MPG Books Group

Contents

Table of Cases

Table of Legislation

STATUTES

SECONDARY LEGISLATION

INTERNATIONAL LEGISLATION

DIRECTIVES

REGULATIONS

US LEGISLATION

Guide to the Companion Website

http://cw.routledge.com/textbooks/revision

Visit the Routledge Q&A website to discover even more study tips and advice on getting those top marks.

On the Routledge revision website you will find the following resources designed to enhance your revision on all areas of undergraduate law.

The Good, The Fair, & The Ugly

Good essays are the gateway to top marks. This interactive tutorial provides sample essays together with voice-over commentary and tips for successful exam essays, written by our Q&A authors themselves.

Multiple Choice Questions

Knowledge is the foundation of every good essay. Focusing on key examination themes, these MCQs have been written to test your knowledge and understanding of each subject in the book.

Bonus Q&As

Having studied our exam advice, put your revision into practice and test your essay writing skills with our additional online questions and answers.

Don't forget to check out even more revision guides and exam tools from Routledge!

Lawcards

Lawcards are your complete, pocket-sized guides to key examinable areas of the undergraduate law.

Routledge Student Statutes

Comprehensive selections; clear, easy-to-use layout; alphabetical, chronological, and thematic indexes; and a competitive price make *Routledge Student Statutes* the statute book of choice for the serious law student.

Introduction

This book is intended to be of help to students studying Civil Liberties and Human Rights courses who feel that they have acquired a body of knowledge, but do not feel confident about using it effectively in exams. The book sets out to demonstrate how to apply the knowledge to the question and how to structure the answer. Students, especially first-year students, often find the technique of answering problem questions particularly hard to grasp, so this book contains a large number of answers to such questions. This technique is rarely taught in law schools and the student who comes from studying science or maths A levels may find it particularly tricky. Equally, a student who has studied English literature may find it difficult to adapt to the impersonal, logical, concise style that problem answers demand. It is hoped that this book will be particularly useful at exam time, but may also prove useful throughout the year. It provides examples of the kind of questions that are usually asked in end-of-year examinations, along with suggested solutions. Each chapter deals with one of the main topics covered in Civil Liberties/Human Rights or Public Law courses and contains typical questions on that area. The aim is not to include questions covering every aspect of a course, but to pick out the areas that tend to be examined because they are particularly contentious or topical. Many courses contain a certain amount of material that is not examined, although it is important as providing background knowledge.

PROBLEM AND ESSAY QUESTIONS

Some areas tend to be examined only by essays, some mainly – although not invariably – by problems, and some by either. The questions chosen reflect this mix, and the introductions at the beginning of each chapter discuss the type of question usually asked. It is important not to choose a topic and then assume that it will appear on the exam paper in a particular form unless it is in an area where, for example, a problem question is never set. If it might appear as an essay or a problem, revision should be geared to either possibility: a very thorough knowledge of the area should be acquired, but also an awareness of critical opinion in relation to it.

LENGTH OF ANSWERS

The answers in this book are about the length of an essay that a good student would expect to write in an exam. Some are somewhat longer and these will also provide useful guidance for students writing assessed essays, which typically are around 2,000 words. In relation to exam questions, there are a number of reasons for including lengthy answers: some students can write long answers – about 1,800 words – under exam conditions; some students who cannot, nevertheless write two very good and lengthy essays and one reasonable but much shorter one. Such students tend to do quite well, although it must be emphasised that it is much better to aim to spread the time evenly between all three essays. Therefore, some answers indicate what might be done if very thorough coverage of a topic were to be undertaken.

AIM HIGHER/COMMON PITFALLS

Certain essays also provide points that could be made to obtain extra marks as well as pointing out common mistakes students sometimes make.

EXPRESSING A POINT OF VIEW

Students sometimes ask, especially in an area such as Civil Liberties, which can be quite topical and politically controversial, whether they should argue for any particular point of view in an essay. It will be noticed that the essays in this book tend to do this. In general, the good student does argue for one side, but he or she always uses sound arguments to support his or her view. Further, a good student does not ignore the opposing arguments; they are considered and, if possible, their weaknesses are exposed. Of course, it would not be appropriate to do this in a problem question or in some essay questions but, where an invitation to do so is held out, it is a good idea to accept it rather than sit on the fence.

EXAM PAPERS

Exam papers normally on these courses include one question on each of the main areas. For example, a typical paper might include problem questions on public order, or police powers, and essay questions on the Human Rights Act or freedom of expression. Therefore, the questions have to be fairly wide-ranging in order to cover a reasonable amount of ground on each topic. Some answers in this book therefore have to cover some of the same material, especially where it is particularly central to the topic in question.

SUGGESTIONS FOR EXAM TECHNIQUE

Below are some suggestions that might improve exam technique; some failings are pointed out that are very commonly found on exam scripts.

(1) When tackling a problem question, do not write out the facts in the answer. Quite a number of students write out chunks of the facts as they answer the question – perhaps to help themselves to pick out the important issues. It is better to avoid this and merely to refer to the significant facts.

(2) Use an impersonal style in both problem and essay answers. In an essay, you should rarely need to use the word 'I' and, in our view, it should not be used at all in a problem answer. (Of course, examiners may differ in their views on this point.)

Instead, you could say 'it is therefore submitted that' or 'it is arguable that'; avoid saying 'I believe that' or 'I feel that'.

(3) In answers to problem questions, try to explain at the beginning of each section of your answer what point you are trying to establish. You might say, for example: 'In order to show that liability under s 1 will arise, three tests must be satisfied.' You should then consider all three, citing the relevant case-law, come to a conclusion on each, and then come to a final conclusion as to whether or not liability will arise. If you are really unsure whether or not it will arise (which will often be the case – there is not much point in asking a question to which there is one very clear and obvious answer), then consider what you have written in relation to the three tests. Perhaps one of them is clearly satisfied, one is probably satisfied and the other (arising under, for example, s 1(8)) probably is not. You might then say: 'As the facts give little support to an argument that s 1(8) is satisfied, it is concluded that liability is unlikely to be established.'

(4) If you make a point, *always* if at all possible substantiate it by citing a case or a statutory provision. If it cannot be supported in that way, as it is speculative, seek to support it by citing academic writing.

(5) It cannot be emphasised enough that the main points raised by a question have to be covered before interesting, but less obvious, issues can be explored.

Common Pitfalls ✗

The most common mistake made when using Questions & Answers books for revision is to memorise the model answers provided and try to reproduce them in exams. This approach is a sure-fire pitfall, likely to result in a poor overall mark because your answer will not be specific enough to the particular question on your exam paper, and there is also a danger that reproducing an answer in this way would be treated as plagiarism. You must instead be sure to read the question carefully, to identify the issues and problems it is asking you to address and to answer it directly in your exam. If you take our examiners' advice and use your Q&A to focus on your question-answering skills and understanding of the law applied, you will be ready for whatever your exam paper has to offer!

Freedom of Expression

1

INTRODUCTION

Freedom of expression is obviously a key element in a civil liberties course and therefore it may arise in more than one question on the exam paper. Examiners tend to set general essays in this area; the emphasis is usually on the degree to which a balance is struck between freedom of expression and a variety of other interests. However, problem questions are sometimes set, particularly in the area of contempt of court.

There is a large amount of overlap between this area and that of freedom of information, since freedom of information may broadly be viewed as one aspect of freedom of expression. The case of *Shayler* (2002), considered in Chapter 2, could readily be viewed as relating to both freedoms. Therefore, what may be termed 'freedom of information issues' may well be treated as aspects of freedom of expression. However, the overlap is not complete: in some circumstances, information may be sought where there is no speaker willing to disclose it and, therefore, such instances tend to fall only within the area of freedom of information. Moreover, although **Art 10** of the **European Convention on Human Rights (ECHR)** covers the right to *receive* information it does not include the right to *access* information. Thus in cases like *Leander v Sweden* (1987) the European Court has rejected freedom of information claims based on **Art 10** while recognising a limited right of access in some situations under **Art 8**. The current interest in further media regulation to protect privacy may well be reflected in civil liberties examinations; as such, you may well be called upon to consider the conflict between freedom of expression and privacy. In this book, that issue is covered in the chapter on privacy but, of course, the freedom of expression dimension is taken into account.

It is now essential in your answers to take the **ECHR** into account, especially **Art 10**, which provides the guarantee of freedom of expression. The **Convention** was received into UK law when the **Human Rights Act (HRA) 1998** came fully into force in October 2000. Until that time, **Art 10** and other **Convention** Articles relevant in this area were not directly applicable in UK courts, but the judiciary referred to the **Convention** more and more in resolving ambiguity in statutes in the run up to the inception of the **HRA**. The **HRA** has now been in force for over fifteen years and there are some significant decisions in the field of freedom of expression (such as *ProLife Alliance v BBC* (2003), *AG v Punch* (2003), *Nilsen v Governor HMP Full Sutton* (2005), *Campbell v MGN* (2004) and *R (on the* *application of Animal Defenders International) v Secretary of State for Culture Media & Sport (2008)* 1 AC 1312). **Section 3** requires that: 'So far as it is possible to do so, primary and subordinate legislation must be read and given effect in a way which is compatible with the Convention rights . . .'. **Section 3(2)(b)** reads: 'this section does not affect the validity, continuing operation or enforcement of any incompatible primary legislation'. This goes beyond the previous obligation to resolve ambiguity in statutes (see Chapter 9 for further information about the impact of the **Human Rights Act**).

All statutes affecting freedom of expression and media freedom therefore have to be interpreted so as to be in harmony with the **Convention** if that is at all possible. Under **s 6** of the **HRA**, **Convention** guarantees are binding only against public authorities. These are defined to include bodies which have a partly public function. The definition is therefore quite wide, but means that private bodies, including most of the media (apart from the 'public bodies', such as the BBC, Ofcom and the Press Complaints Commission) can violate **Convention** rights unless a part of the common law, which will also be interpreted in conformity with the **Convention**, bears on the matter.

Thus, exam questions will reflect this extremely significant development and will require an awareness of the **Art 10** jurisprudence and of the impact of the **HRA** on freedom of expression. It is also important to remember that the common law contains significant protection for freedom of expression and that this has been emphasised since the passage of the **Human Rights Act** (see for example *R v Home Secretary Ex parte Simms* (1999)).

Checklist ✔

You should be familiar with the following areas:

- **Art 10** of the **ECHR**, other relevant rights such as **Art 6**, **Art 10** jurisprudence and the **HRA 1998**;

- common law free speech jurisprudence pre-**HRA** (see, for example, *Reynolds v Times Newspapers* (1999), *Derbyshire CC v Times Newspapers* (1993), *R v Secretary of State for the Home Department ex p Simms* (1999));

- decisions taking account of the **HRA** and **Art 10** such as *ProLife Alliance v BBC* (2003), *AG v Punch* (2003), *Campbell v MGN* (2004);

- key aspects of the **Contempt of Court Act 1981** and common law contempt;

- the doctrine of breach of confidence;

- key aspects of the **Broadcasting Acts 1990** and **1996**, and the **Communications Act 2003** ('taste and decency', impartiality provisions);

- the **Obscene Publications Act 1959** as amended; common law indecency: *Gibson* (1990);

- the **Cinemas Act 1985**; the **Video Recordings Act 1984**, as amended;
- blasphemy;
- hate crimes, including amendments in the **Racial and Religious Hatred Act 2006**.

QUESTION 1

Critically evaluate the current regime governing the regulation and censorship of cinema films and videos in relation to the demands of **Art 10** of the **European Convention on Human Rights** as received into domestic law under the **Human Rights Act**.

How to Answer this Question

This is a reasonably straightforward essay question about the role of the British Board of Film Classification in regulating and censoring cinema films and videos. Bear in mind the implications flowing from the fact that the **ECHR** has been afforded further effect in domestic law under the **HRA 1998**: you need to consider the key provisions of the **HRA** as they relate to the regulation and censorship of films and videos; you also need to examine the relevant Strasbourg jurisprudence. The mere fact that **Art 10** of the **ECHR** has been received into domestic law under the **HRA** does not necessarily mean that change is needed.

Essentially, the following areas should be considered:

- ❖ **Art 10** of the **ECHR** and the **HRA 1998**;
- ❖ relevant Strasbourg jurisprudence under **Art 10**;
- ❖ classification and censorship of cinema films;
- ❖ the legal framework relating to films and videos;
- ❖ conclusions regarding compatibility of the regulatory regime and **Art 10** of the **ECHR**.

Answer Structure

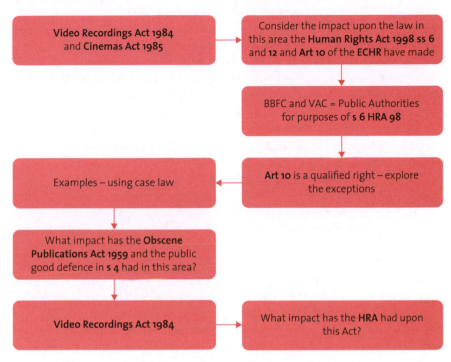

Video Recordings Act 1984 and **Cinemas Act 1985**	Consider the impact upon the law in this area the **Human Rights Act 1998 ss 6** and **12** and **Art 10** of the **ECHR** have made

BBFC and VAC = Public Authorities for purposes of **s 6 HRA 98**

Examples – using case law ← **Art 10** is a qualified right – explore the exceptions

What impact has the **Obscene Publications Act 1959** and the public good defence in **s 4** had in this area?

Video Recordings Act 1984 → What impact has the **HRA** had upon this Act?

Aim Higher ★

If you are able to show an appreciation of the practical context or operation of the law your answer is likely to be viewed favourably by the examiner. Sometimes the bare legal rules provide only a partial picture and you need to explore non legal matters to provide a thorough picture of the issues. See, for example, in the answer below, the discussion about the practical operation of the film classification system of regulation and the likelihood of this leading to self-censorship for commercial motives.

ANSWER

The legislation governing censorship of films and videos (the **Video Recordings Act 1984** as amended and the **Cinemas Act 1985**) must be read by the courts in a manner which gives effect, so far as is possible, to the **Convention** rights (**s 3** of the **HRA**). Further, the **HRA** gives particular regard to the importance of freedom of expression in **s 12**, although this has been interpreted by the courts as not giving **Art 10** any trump status. Under **s 6** of the **HRA** media bodies such as the British Board of Film Classification (BBFC) and the Video Appeals Committee of the BBFC (VAC) are likely to be public authorities obliged to respect **Convention** rights. It is argued that the independent regulation of film and video, which clearly affects the rights of those involved in production and distribution, is a function of a public nature under **s 6** of the **HRA**.[1] Assuming that they are public authorities, these bodies must ensure that **Art 10** is not infringed in their decision making. Ultimately, decisions of media regulators or of other media bodies that are also public authorities can be challenged in the courts, which should seek to ensure that **Art 10** is being complied with. Thus, it is submitted that restrictions on freedom of expression in this context may undergo fresh scrutiny, with a possible change in the balance against restraints on the showing of explicit material.[2] Nevertheless, there have not so far been any successful challenges to decisions of the BBFC or VAC.

The regulation of films does not necessarily in itself infringe **Art 10. Article 10(1)** specifically provides that the Article 'shall not prevent States from requiring the licensing of broadcasting, television or cinema enterprises'. It is significant that this provision arises in the *first* paragraph of **Art 10**, thereby providing a limitation of the primary right that on its face is not subject to the test of **para 2**. However, a very restrictive approach to this sentence has been adopted. It has been found to mean that a licensing system is allowed for on grounds not restricted to those enumerated in **para 2**; the State may determine who is to have a licence to broadcast. But in general, other decisions of the regulatory bodies are not covered by the last sentence of **para 1** and must be considered within **para 2** (*Groppera Radio AG v Switzerland* (1990)). Thus, content requirements must be considered under **para 2**. Certain forms of expression which may be said to be of no value may fall outside the scope of **Art 10(1)** and it is arguable that, for example, material gratuitously offensive to religious sensibilities (*Otto-Preminger Institut v Austria* (1994), *Norwood v United Kingdom* (2005)) or depictions of genitals in pornographic magazines intended merely for entertainment (*Groppera Radio AG v Switzerland* (1990)) may fall outside its scope. On the other hand, 'hardcore' pornography has been found by the Commission to fall within **Art 10(1)** (*Hoare v UK* (1997)).

Political speech receives a more robust degree of protection than other types of expression. By contrast, in cases involving artistic speech, an exactly opposite pattern emerges: applicants have tended to be unsuccessful and a deferential approach to the judgments of the national authorities as to its obscene or blasphemous nature has been adopted (*Müller v Switzerland* (1991), *Handyside v UK* (1976), *Otto-Preminger Institut v Austria* (1994), *Gay News v UK* (1982)).[3] In *Otto-Preminger Institut v Austria* (1994), the

---

1   The ability to apply **s 6 HRA** to the BBFC and VAC demonstrates good understanding to the examiner.
2   This will impress the examiner as it shows an ability to provide context to freedom of expression law.
3   Credit will be given for this demonstration of an understanding of deference in this area, which is backed up with authority.

court found that a State may restrict expressions which may offend a particular population, although, otherwise, freedom of expression includes freedom to disseminate unpopular, shocking and disturbing information and ideas.

Currently, in the UK, censorship of cinema films operates in practice on two levels: first, the BBFC, a self-censoring body set up by the film industry itself in 1912, may insist on cuts before issuing a certificate allowing a film to be screened or may refuse to issue a certificate at all. Films are classified by age: 'U' films are open to anybody, as, in effect, are 'PG' (parental guidance) classified films. After that are '12'/'12A', '15' and '18' certificate films. 'R18' films (restricted viewing) may be viewed only on segregated premises. An 'R18' certificate means that the BBFC considers that the film would survive an **Obscene Publications Act 1959** prosecution; it will refuse a certificate if a film is thought to fall foul of the Act. In coming to its decision, the BBFC will take the 'public good' defence under **s 4(1A)** of the **1959 Act**, as amended, into account. This defence provides that a film or soundtrack can be justified as being for the public good 'on the ground that it is in the interests of drama, opera, ballet or any other art or of literature or learning'. Therefore, the BBFC may grant a certificate on the grounds of artistic merit to a film that contains some obscene matter. Clearly, most film distributors have no interest in achieving only a restricted publication for a film and are, therefore, prepared to make cuts to achieve a wider circulation. Thus, the system of control may be driven largely by commercial motives: a distributor may make quite stringent cuts in order to ensure that, for example, a film receives a '15' certificate and so reaches a wider audience.

The second level of censorship is operated by local authorities under the **Cinemas Act 1985**, which continues the old power arising under the **Cinematograph Act 1909**. The local authority will usually follow the BBFC's advice; authorities are reluctant to devote resources to viewing films and will tend to rely on the Board's judgment. Thus, although technically the BBFC wields no power in this area, in reality its judgments are likely to be determinative. Authorities may, on occasion, choose to grant or not to grant a licence to a film regardless of its decision. This dual system of censorship was criticised by the Williams Committee in 1979 partly on the ground of the anomalies caused by having two overlapping levels and partly due to the inconsistency between local authorities. The **Video Recordings Act (VRA) 1984** was introduced after a campaign about the dangers posed by video 'nasties' to children. Under the **VRA 1984**, the BBFC was established as the authority charged with classifying videos for viewing in the home. Videos are classified and therefore censored in almost the same way as films, and under **s 9** of the **1984 Act** it is an offence to supply a video without a classification certificate, unless it is exempt on grounds of its concern with education, sport, music or religion. Under **s 2(2)**, the exemption will not apply if the video portrays human sexual activity or gross violence or is likely to stimulate or encourage this. Further, the exemptions will not apply if a video depicts techniques likely to encourage the commission of offences.

The BBFC must have 'special regard' to harm which may be caused to 'potential viewers or through their behaviour to society' by the manner in which the film deals with criminal behaviour, illegal drugs, violent behaviour or incidents, horrific incidents or behaviour, or human sexual activity. These criteria are non-exhaustive. The kind of harm envisaged to a child or to society is not specified and nor is the degree of seriousness envisaged. There is a right of appeal from the decisions of the BBFC to the VAC, under **s 4**, which operates as a tribunal.[4]

The stance of the BBFC is obviously influenced by the composition of the Board, but its effect on film and video makers has been criticised as militating against creativity. It has been suggested by Robertson that a cosy relationship has developed that is insufficiently challenging – the acceptable boundaries are not fully explored in the name of artistic integrity and creative freedom. The age-based classification system encourages commercial judgments rather than artistic considerations to dominate; the most pressing consideration is to find the widest audience, which may mean instituting cuts in order to obtain a '15' certificate. These factors lead to a heavier censorship of films in the UK than in Europe or the US.

It seems possible that the inception of the **HRA** could have some impact on this situation. For example, a film maker whose film was refused a classification without certain cuts could seek to challenge the decision of the BBFC or, in the case of a video, that of the VAC, upholding the BBFC's decision. The VAC and BBFC are, assuming that they are public authorities, bound by the **Convention** rights under **s 6** of the **HRA**. Therefore, they should ensure that their decisions do not breach **Art 10** or any other relevant Article. One potential problem for aggrieved film makers is that the courts are likely to defer to a significant extent to the specialist regulatory bodies as has been the case with press regulation: *R (Ford) v Press Complaints Commission* (2001).

The **1984 Act**, as amended, must be interpreted compatibly with the **Convention** rights. Given that a number of its terms are very open-ended, there is room for a range of interpretations. In actions against the BBFC, the court would have to give effect to **s 12** of the **HRA**. Although this requires particular regard to be given to the importance of **Art 10** this has been interpreted in cases such as *Campbell v MGN* (2004) to include not just the right but also the restrictions in **Art 10(2)**. Thus it affords no special status to freedom of expression.

The stance taken by Strasbourg in relation to films likely to offend religious sensibilities was indicated in the leading decision, *Otto-Preminger* (1994). The film in question was not likely to be viewed by children, but was found to be offensive to religious sensibilities. The seizure and forfeiture of the film was not found to breach **Art 10**. Further guidance derives

....
4   This demonstrates a good understanding of how the BBFC operates.

from the decision of the Court of Human Rights in *Wingrove v UK* (1996). This judgment concerned a decision of the BBFC, upheld by the VAC, to refuse a certificate to the short, explicit film *Visions of Ecstasy*. The Court found that the decision to refuse a certificate was within the national authorities' margin of appreciation. The film, which was to be promulgated as a short video, was viewed as offensive to religious sensibilities and as quite likely to come to the attention of children, since it could be viewed in the home. No breach of **Art 10** was found.

In the case of a sexually explicit or violent film, the problem would be, as indicated above, that the Strasbourg jurisprudence appears to support quite far-reaching restrictions. However, where the risk of children viewing the film is very slight due to the use of age restrictions relating to films to be shown in the cinema, *and* the question of offending religious sensibilities does not arise, it is suggested that the jurisprudence can be viewed as supporting the availability of even very explicit films. This contention derives from the principles underlying the jurisprudence, which, as indicated above, relate to the familiar free speech justifications, including that of self-fulfilment.

It is concluded that where the question of offence to religious sensibilities does not arise it would be consonant with the general Strasbourg freedom of expression jurisprudence to leave little scope under **Art 10(2)** for interferences with the freedom of expression of film makers in respect of films targeted at adults. Different considerations would apply to videos, owing to the possibility that they might be viewed by children, although this argument should be considered carefully in terms of its impact on adults. The question of the harm that might be caused should also be considered, bearing in mind the lack of evidence regarding a connection between behaviour seen on film and actual behaviour. The mere invocation of the possibility that children might view a video should not be enough. Guidance on this matter might usefully be sought from other jurisdictions, since it is not a matter that Strasbourg has inquired into in any depth.

QUESTION 2

In what ways does **Art 10** of the **European Convention on Human Rights**, as given effect by the European Court of Human Rights, require States to strike an effective balance between those forms of political speech that should be permitted in a democratic society, and those which can legitimately be restricted?

How to Answer this Question

This question requires a critical approach to the case law of the European Court of Human Rights on **Art 10** and also a sense of how the principles developed by the Court may be significant for aspects of the law in the UK. It also requires an understanding of a number of issues in relation to which political expression can legitimately be curtailed and of the general approach the European Court of Human Rights has adopted to such issues. There is no definitive list and any answer is bound to be selective.

The essential matters to be discussed are:

❖   the structure of **Art 10** of the **European Convention on Human Rights (ECHR)**;
❖   its general impact under the **HRA 1998**;
❖   the main principles governing the approach of the Court of Human Rights to political speech;
❖   examples of **Art 10** jurisprudence which impact upon circumstances in which political speech is restricted.

Answer Structure

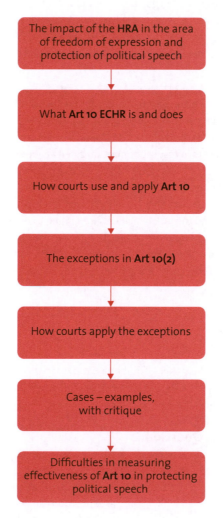

The impact of the **HRA** in the area of freedom of expression and protection of political speech

↓

What **Art 10 ECHR** is and does

↓

How courts use and apply **Art 10**

↓

The exceptions in **Art 10(2)**

↓

How courts apply the exceptions

↓

Cases – examples, with critique

↓

Difficulties in measuring effectiveness of **Art 10** in protecting political speech

ANSWER

The common law recognises freedom of expression and media freedom as fundamental values capable of influencing the way the law develops and the way judicial discretion, such as in respect of remedies, is exercised. Since the coming into effect of the **HRA 1998, Art 10** of the **ECHR** ('freedom of expression') now provides an additional and significant basis for ensuring that speech, particularly political speech, receives proper protection under the law. UK courts' understanding of **Art 10** now influences the way Acts of Parliament are interpreted and it is a standard against which the legality of the actions of public authorities (as defined by **s 6** of the **HRA**) is measured. **Art 10** may also influence the way private law develops as the courts give effect to being, themselves, public authorities who are required to act compatibly with the scheduled **Convention** rights. This has been seen in relation to the absorbing of **Arts 8 and 10** into the existing tort of breach of confidence in cases such as *Campbell v MGN* (2004).[5]

As with **Arts 8, 9 and 11, Art 10** has two paragraphs. **Article 10(1)** identifies a general right to freedom of expression and it specifically mentions that this includes the freedom to hold opinions and to receive and impart information and ideas without interference from a public authority. **Article 10(2)** identifies the exclusive circumstances under which the freedom in **Art 10(1)** can be restricted. It also notes that the exercise of freedom of expression carries with it duties and responsibilities.

In resolving freedom of expression issues, the courts must first decide whether the issue is within the terms of **Art 10(1)**. Freedom of expression has been broadly interpreted by the Strasbourg Court to include matters that go beyond simple speech. Acts of political protest, for example, are likely to be covered by the term, as in *Steel v UK* (1999), and so the law on public order will need to be formulated, as far as possible, to take the right to freedom of expression into account. It should be noted that both commercial speech, such as advertising, and artistic expression are included in the reach of **Art 10(1)**. Both these forms of expression are capable of having political significance, and since, as we

5   This is a good introduction, setting out some good knowledge about the impact of the **HRA** in this area.

shall see, political speech receives the highest degree of protection under **Art 10**, the question may well arise whether political aspects outweigh any commercial or artistic aspects in any particular case.[6]

Article 10(2) lays down the exclusive circumstances under which expression, including political speech, can be made subject to any 'formalities, conditions, restrictions or penalties'. Of course, the terms of **Art 10(2)** have to be interpreted by judges and nothing in **Art 10** indicates what, if any, priority is to be given to expression among the other rights and freedoms the **Convention** aims to secure.

First, any restrictions, etc., on freedom of expression must be 'prescribed by law': the restriction must have a basis in law and its application be reasonably foreseeable. Unlike in the context of privacy under **Art 8**, this provision has not caused significant problems for English law regarding freedom of expression. Even vague, common law offences, such as outraging public decency, seem to pass the test, as in *S and G v UK* (1991), where the prosecution of those responsible for an art exhibition which included the display of freeze-dried foetuses was found not to violate **Art 10**.

Secondly, restrictions on freedom of expression can only be imposed if they are intended to serve one or more of the purposes listed in **Art 10(2)**. Most of the major areas of English law where freedom of expression is limited can be brought within these purposes. They include, for example, restrictions aimed at protecting national security (including official secrets legislation) or at preventing the disclosure of confidential material (including breach of confidence injunctions) or at maintaining the authority and impartiality of the judiciary (such as convictions for contempt of court). Protecting the 'rights of others' is a purpose that could play a wide-ranging, justifying role.

The most important requirement of **Art 10(2)** is, thirdly, that any restriction of freedom of expression must be 'necessary in a democratic society', and this means that any particular restriction must be a proportionate means of meeting a pressing social need. It is in this context that the judgments of the courts can be controversial, particularly in a political context.[7] The job of the court, giving effect to **Art 10**, is to ensure a fair balance between the rights of individuals to freedom of expression and the public interest, such as it is, in restricting or suppressing speech.

Various guidelines can be discerned. The European Court of Human Rights has been clear that political speech is to be given the highest priority, more than artistic or commercial speech, in the sense that any public interest purporting to justify restriction must be

---

6   This shows good application of **Art 10** to the issues raised by the question.
7   Good understanding of the court's decisions in relation to **Art 10** in this capacity is needed to make comments such as this.

particularly strong and persuasive (the leading case is *Lingens v Austria* (1986)). Freedom of political speech is a requirement of a democratic society, which the **Convention** views as the form of society under which the protection of human rights is most likely to be secured. In this context, political speech is broadly defined to include information about, and discussion of, matters of general public concern in society and is not confined to matters of State politics or the concerns of political parties. Free expression in a democracy also requires that the protection of the law should extend to unpopular expression that others, perhaps the majority or those in social, economic or political power, may find offensive, shocking or disturbing (*Handyside v United Kingdom* (1976)). In this context, the European Court of Human Rights has also sought to defend media freedom. Reporting and comment may be vigorous and hostile to those affected. Furthermore, the Court upholds the general principle that journalists should be able to report allegations and should not be subject to criminal penalty merely because they are unable to prove the truth of what they report. This is a matter of great importance for effective investigative journalism (*Thorgeirson v Iceland* (1992), *Karman v Russia* (2006)).

The effectiveness of **Art 10**, as interpreted by the Court of Human Rights, in the context of political speech is hard to measure. As a matter of principle the Court is of the view that there is little scope for restrictions on political speech in a democratic society and the margin of appreciation is correspondingly small in relation to political matters. Any judgment will, of course, depend upon the point of view adopted for evaluation. **ECHR** cases are highly dependent on their individual facts and circumstances. Nevertheless, the Court's approach to some difficult questions about political speech can be considered. Its position tends to be complex. It does not take an absolutist position in favour of freedom of expression, but will strike down disproportionate or over-rigid restrictions on speech even if they are aimed at a legitimate, democratic purpose.[8]

In a good example of the divergent views in this area, the House of Lords upheld a general ban on television political advertising in the **Communications Act 2003** on the basis of the powerful and pervasive nature of television. In so doing it criticised an earlier Court of Human Rights decision which found similar restrictions to be incompatible with the protection afforded in **Art 10** (*R (Animal Defenders International) v Secretary of State for Culture, Media and Sport* (2008), reviewing *Vgt Verein Gegen Tierfabriken v Switzerland* (2002)).

A major issue about political speech relates to the question of the degree to which a tolerant society should permit intolerant speech. The inclusion of offensive and unpopular expression within the sphere which is protected by **Art 10** means that the banning of, for example, racist speech is likely to require convincing justification.

....

8   Such arguments as this paragraph sets out in relation to the Courts' role are given great weight as it offers some balance to the argument.

Protecting the rights of others and preventing disorder and crime are legitimate purposes for restricting speech, but bans must also be proportionate. In *Jersild v Denmark* (1994), for instance, the conviction of a journalist for producing a programme, whose intention was anti-racist, but in which racists were allowed to speak for themselves, was held to be disproportionate. Of course, under **Art 17**, racist organisations will not be able to assert any **Convention** rights which they can then use to violate the rights of others such as denial of the fact of the Holocaust (*Lehiduex and Isorni v France* (1998)); or equating Muslims with terrorists (*Norwood v United Kingdom* (2006)).

Article 10 permits speech and expression to be restricted 'for the protection of morals'. In *Handyside v UK* (1979–80), the Court of Human Rights allowed a wide margin of appreciation to States in this context. The problem is that matters impinging on moral questions can also be of political importance and a wide margin of appreciation may not allow sufficient protection to be given to this political dimension. This may be important in the UK where, for example, broadcasting organisations are required by law not to broadcast matter which offends against good taste and decency. The point was illustrated in *R (ProLife Alliance) v BBC* (2003), where the House of Lords upheld the right of the BBC to ban a party political broadcast (which was anti-abortion and contained graphic, disturbing images of aborted foetuses) on the grounds that it offended good taste. The Court of Appeal, whose judgment was overturned, had seen the matter as one of illegal censorship.

The question of political violence and the advocacy of causes associated with violence is a pressing one in the climate of the 'war against terrorism'. States are permitted to restrain political speech if it is an incitement to violence but, at the same time, need to recognise that, in a democratic society, the population is entitled to be informed and for difficult issues to be discussed. In *United Communist Party of Turkey v Turkey* (1998), for example, the Court upheld the linked rights of freedom of expression and freedom of association in respect of advocacy and campaigning for major constitutional change taking place against a background of political violence, albeit not violence that could be attributed to the applicants. The border between advocacy and incitement is, of course, hard to identify. In *Baskaya and Okçuoglu v Turkey* (2001), where the conviction of a university professor and journalist for publishing a book on the Kurdish problem was held to violate **Art 10**, the Court nevertheless seemed to accept that, in the context of political violence, a greater margin of appreciation, even on the suppression of political speech, was acceptable. The way the border between legitimate advocacy in a context of violence and incitement to violence is drawn by the courts as they review the activities of State authorities is clearly a matter of importance and relevant in the UK today as regards some of the offences in the **Terrorism Act 2000** which relate to the activities of members of proscribed organisations.

In conclusion, we can see that the Strasbourg Court does not take an absolutist approach. Nevertheless, given the importance of political speech in the **Convention** scheme, restrictions on political speech can only be justified if it is clear that the purpose served and the need for any particular restriction are very compelling. Justifications for restricting political speech must, above all, be demonstrated to meet a social need of the most pressing kind. Restrictions on matters mentioned such as incitements to violence or racist politics are widely accepted in principle. As the issues about elections and political advertising show, however, there remain areas of reasonable disagreement about political speech where the **Convention** position may be at odds with alternative views about how best to promote fair democratic procedures in terms of which human rights can flourish.

QUESTION 3

'The **Obscene Publications Act 1959** strikes a balance between freedom of expression and the interest in maintaining proper standards of taste and decency, which can be viewed as in accordance with the demands of **Art 10** of the **European Convention on Human Rights**.'

▶ **Discuss.**

How to Answer this Question

This is a reasonably straightforward essay question. It is important to consider the statute only and not the common law in this area. Obviously, the question could be 'attacked', in the sense that you might argue that no balance at all should be struck between, for example, freedom of expression on the one hand and maintaining proper standards of taste and decency: freedom of expression should entirely outweigh the other value, since it is too broad and vague to justify restrictions. You could argue that allowing freedom of expression to outweigh that other value entirely would be in accordance with **Art 10**. Another approach would be to argue that the **1959 Act** has nothing to do with taste and decency but rather is aimed at preventing harm broadly construed. Your answer should recognise that the **European Convention on Human Rights (ECHR)** has been afforded further effect in domestic law under the **HRA 1998**; **Convention** case law can thus be applied directly in domestic law to help understand the meaning of the **Convention** and to interpret statutes and the common law. This goes significantly further than merely resolving statutory ambiguity as in the pre-**HRA** era.

Essentially, the following areas should be considered:

- ❖ **Art 10** of the **ECHR** and the **HRA**;
- ❖ relevant Strasbourg jurisprudence;
- ❖ offences under the **Obscene Publications Acts**;
- ❖ the forfeiture regime under the **1959 Act**;
- ❖ conclusions regarding compatibility of the statutory provisions and **Art 10** of the **ECHR**.

Answer Structure

Human Rights Act 1998, ss 3, 6 and 12 in particular and the ECHR

The **Obscene Publications Act 1959** and **s 3 HRA 98** – fact **OPA** must be read compatibly with **ECHR** rights so far as possible to do so

Examples of **Art 10** cases relevant to **Obscene Publications Act**

Examples of **Obscene Publications Act** cases

Exploration and critique of the 'deprave and corrupt' test

Common Pitfalls ✖

In the pressure of the exam room environment it is often easy to forget things that you have revised very carefully. A common problem is students forgetting the name of a significant case. If this happens to you do not panic. Simply leave a short blank space and write the proposition of law or other point arising from the case. If, by the time you get to the end of your answer, you still cannot recall the case name just write 'recent authority suggests', 'decisions have established' or something similar. This will not be ideal but you will still have made the legal point and you will not have wasted valuable minutes struggling to recall the elusive case.

ANSWER

At the present time, it is arguably necessary for public authorities and the courts to take a stronger stance than previously in favour of freedom of expression, due to the impact of the **HRA 1998**, which incorporates the **Convention**, including the guarantee of freedom of expression under **Art 10** of the **Convention**, into domestic law.[9] The **Obscene Publications Act 1959**, as amended, must be read by the courts in a manner which gives effect, so far as is possible, to the **Convention** rights (**s 3** of the **HRA**); if this is not possible, a declaration of incompatibility may be issued (**s 4**), and remedial action may be taken as a result (**s 10**). Further, the **HRA** requires particular regard to the importance of freedom of expression in **s 12**, although this does not give **Art 10** a trump status. Public authorities are bound by the **Convention** rights under **s 6** unless **s 6(2)** applies. The term covers all the bodies including courts who are involved in prosecutions, seizures and forfeitures under the **1959 Act**. All these bodies must ensure that **Art 10** is not infringed in their decision making. The courts could, if necessary, use **s 3** of the **HRA** to modify overly restrictive statutory provisions, or the court could decide that, as a public authority, it could itself apply the Act in such a way as to avoid infringing **Art 10**. Restrictions on freedom of expression created by the **1959 Act** must now undergo fresh scrutiny when **Convention** rights are engaged, although there is little in the **Convention** case law that suggests the courts will demand a more permissive approach to the publication of explicit material.

The impact of the **HRA** in this context depends on the interpretation of **Art 10**. Certain forms of expression which may be said to be of no value may fall outside the scope of **Art 10(1)** and it is arguable that, for example, material gratuitously offensive to religious sensibilities (*Otto-Preminger Institut v Austria* (1994)) or depictions of genitals in pornographic magazines intended merely for entertainment (*Groppera Radio AG v Switzerland* (1990)) may fall outside its scope. On the other hand, 'hardcore' pornography has been found by the Commission to fall within **Art 10(1)** (*Hoare v UK* (1997)).[10]

Assuming that most explicit material falls within **Art 10(1)**, how high a level of protection does it receive? Cases involving artistic speech have been found to deserve a lower level of protection than those involving political expression. A deferential approach to the judgments of the national authorities as to alleged obscene or blasphemous content has been adopted (*Müller v Switzerland* (1991), *Handyside v UK* (1976), *Otto-Preminger Institut v Austria* (1994), *Gay News v UK* (1982)). In *Otto-Preminger Institut v Austria* (1994), the Court found that a State may restrict expressions which may offend a particular population, although, otherwise, freedom of expression includes freedom to disseminate unpopular, shocking and disturbing information and ideas. The film in question was not likely to be viewed by children, but was found to be offensive to religious sensibilities. The seizure and forfeiture of the film was not found to breach **Art 10**. Further guidance derives from the decision of the Court of Human Rights in *Wingrove v UK* (1996). This judgment concerned a decision of the BBFC, upheld by the VAC, to refuse a certificate to the short, explicit film *Visions of Ecstasy*. The Court found that the decision to refuse a certificate

....

9   This is a good, strong opening statement which shows good appreciation of the effect of the **HRA** in this area.

10 The examiner will give credit to arguments such as this which highlight problems and difficulties with different forms of expression.

was within the national authority's margin of appreciation. The film, which was to be promulgated as a short video, was viewed as offensive to religious sensibilities and as quite likely to come to the attention of children since it could be viewed in the home. No breach of **Art 10** was found.

However, even in respect of artistic expression, which appears to have a lower place in the hierarchy of expression, there are no decisions defending restrictions on the freedom of expression of adults, except in respect of hardcore pornography where the distributor cannot ultimately control access to the material (*Hoare v UK* (1997)), or where a risk to children is also present, or in the context of offending religious sensibilities. This stance is in accordance with the principles underlying the jurisprudence, which relate to the familiar free speech justifications, including that of self-fulfilment.

It is concluded that where the question of offence to religious sensibilities does not arise, it would be consonant with the general Strasbourg freedom of expression jurisprudence to leave little scope under **Art 10(2)** for interferences with the freedom of expression of publishers of explicit material targeted at adults.[11] The case of *Scherer v Switzerland* (1993) supports the contention that restraints on the material that can be offered to a willing adult audience should be minimal. Different considerations would apply to material aimed at children or teenagers and the possibility that children might access the material would be relevant. Against this background we need to consider the compatibility of the domestic obscenity legislation which, as will be seen, does impose fairly strict controls over material thought to be harmful.

The **Obscene Publications Act** covers all media under **s 1(2)**, once the **Broadcasting Act (BA) 1990** brought radio and television within its ambit.[12] The Act creates criminal offences of publishing obscene material or possessing obscene material for publication for gain. Publication is given a very broad definition including selling, offering, lending, playing, and transmitting. It would, for example, cover lending a magazine, selling a video, or forwarding an email. There need be no financial motivation and no intention or awareness that the content is obscene. The law has been limited in its application to the following subjects: prostitution (*Shaw v DPP* (1962)), pornography (*DPP v Whyte* (1972)), drug use (*R v Skirving* (1985)) and violence (*DPP v A and BC Chewing Gum Ltd* (1968)).

The Act makes a specific attempt at creating a balance between protecting morality on the one hand and safeguarding freedom of speech on the other. The provisions aimed at achieving this balance are **s 1(1)** and **s 4**. **Section 1(1)** prohibits publication of material which tends to deprave and corrupt its likely audience. The meaning of this test has caused the

----

11   This is another strong statement in relation to the application of freedom of expression law which shows a good grasp of the area.

12   Comments such as this, in relation to the **BA 1990**, all stack up and impress examiners by showing general knowledge in the area.

courts some difficulty: the House of Lords held in *Knuller v DPP* (1973) that it did not connote something which might lead to social evil in the sense that the material in question would be likely to cause a person to act in an anti-social fashion. The House of Lords found that such a test would be too narrow and would fail to catch a great deal of material. Nevertheless it is clear that the tendency must be viewed against the impact on its likely audience, not in the abstract. Thus material aimed at children is more likely to have such a tendency than material aimed at adults and material that tends to disgust and repel will not meet the deprave and corrupt level: *R v Caldar and Boyars* (1969). The test has been criticised by Stone as lacking theoretical coherence and practical utility.

The deprave and corrupt test is balanced by the 'public good' defence contained in **s 4**. This defence requires a jury to ask first whether an article is obscene and, if so, to consider whether its scientific, literary, artistic, educational or other merits outweigh its obscenity. This test was included as a means of giving protection to freedom of expression in relation to publications of cultural benefit. However, it has been criticised by Robertson as requiring a jury to embark on the very difficult task of weighing an intrinsic quality against a predicted change for the worse in the minds of the group of persons likely to encounter the article. However, the application of these tests at the present time, as seen in the trial for obscenity of the book *Inside Linda Lovelace* in 1976, suggests that no book of any conceivable literary merit will be prosecuted for obscenity. Other publications, however, are a different matter: under **s 3** of the Act, magazines and other material such as videos can be seized in forfeiture proceedings, which may mean that the full safeguards provided by the Act can be bypassed: there will be no jury trial and a full consideration may not be given to the possible literary or other merits of such material. It seems, therefore, that the protection afforded by the Act to freedom of speech depends more on the willingness of the prosecuting authorities to refrain from bringing prosecutions or on the tolerance of magistrates, rather than on the law itself.

Given the wide margin of appreciation afforded to the domestic authorities in the relevant decisions, little guidance as to the requirements of **Art 10** in this context is available, especially where the material is directed at a willing adult audience. The domestic judiciary are, therefore, theoretically free to take a different stance. The decisions considered above at Strasbourg on the **1959 Act** (*Handyside*, *Hoare*) indicate that the statutory regime relating to publication of an obscene article under **s 2** is broadly in harmony with **Art 10** of the **European Convention**. Nevertheless, a specific decision might not meet the proportionality requirements if scrutinised more intensively than at Strasbourg. However, in the first challenge to the **1959 Act** under **Art 10** (*R v Perrin* (2002)) the Court of Appeal held that the criminalisation of publishing obscene material served a legitimate purpose and that the law was sufficiently precise for the interference to be prescribed by law under **Art 10(2)**. Despite a lengthy summary of the parties' submissions the reasoning was very sparse, but it is clear that the Court was of the view that the criminal offence was a proportionate response to the legislature's concerns over the publication of hard core pornography. It does not indicate a more demanding test than in Strasbourg. Changing attitudes in society towards hard core pornography also need to be taken into account in this area. In *R v Peacock* (2012) the jury found the defendant not guilty of the offence under **s 1** where the material concerned was hard core homosexual pornography which included male fisting and urination. It is hard to believe a jury 20 or even 10 years ago would have decided in such a way.[13] This is comparable to the 'living instrument' doctrine we see the ECtHR at Strasbourg applying to the **Convention**.

The UK forfeiture regime has not itself been tested at Strasbourg. The **HRA** requirements may be especially pertinent in relation to forfeiture: the magistrates conducting the proceedings are, of course, bound by **Art 10** and therefore would be expected to approach the task with greater rigour. In particular, it is arguably necessary to examine each item, even where a large scale seizure has occurred, rather than considering a sample of items only (see *Snaresbrook Crown Court ex p Commissioner of the Metropolis* (1984)). However, since, in practice, a vast amount of material is condemned as obscene in legal actions for forfeiture, the practical difficulties facing magistrates make it possible, especially initially, that the impact of the **HRA** will be more theoretical than real. It seems probable that, in practice, magistrates will not examine each item and will give only cursory attention, if any, to considering the application of the somewhat elusive Strasbourg case law. However, if on occasion publishers seek to contest **s 3** orders before a jury, the proportionality of the measures adopted may receive more attention.

The Strasbourg cases discussed appear to show that freedom of expression could have been given greater guarantees in UK courts, since the margin of appreciation doctrine – so influential in this particular area – is inapplicable. Therefore, it is arguable that the **HRA** could provide an impetus towards liberality. The chance that this will occur was never high, especially as in relation to the protection of morality, the Strasbourg jurisprudence leaves room for a number of interpretations domestically. The *Perrin* case effectively undermines any hopes of a pro-active judicial approach towards freedom of expression in this area. It seems that the provisions of the **1959 Act** and their application in practice are compatible with **Art 10** and strike a balance which is broadly consistent with its demands (following *Handyside*).

QUESTION 4

To what extent do you consider that the **Contempt of Court Act 1981** has succeeded in creating a balance between freedom of speech and the administration of justice that is in accordance with **Art 10** of the **European Convention on Human Rights** as scheduled in the **Human Rights Act 1998**?

---

13   This shows an ability to provide context to obscenity laws, and examiners like to see an ability to step back and appreciate such contextual issues.

How to Answer this Question

This is a reasonably straightforward essay question if you are familiar with the reforms in this area undertaken after the *Sunday Times* decision by means of the **Contempt of Court Act 1981**. The following matters should be discussed:

❖ the need to show a substantial risk of serious prejudice under **s 2(2)** of the **Contempt of Court Act 1981**;

❖ the concept of 'active' proceedings under **s 2(3)** of and **Sched 1** to the **1981 Act**;

❖ discussions in good faith under **s 5**;

❖ the survival of common law contempt and its relationship with the **1981 Act**;

❖ intention to prejudice the administration of justice;

❖ the concept of imminence in common law contempt;

❖ the possibility of establishing a 'trial by newspaper';

❖ contempt of court and the Strasbourg jurisprudence.

Answer Structure

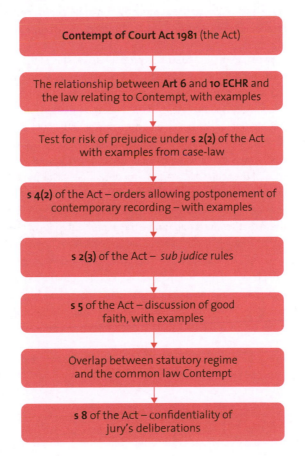

Contempt of Court Act 1981 (the Act)

The relationship between **Art 6** and **10 ECHR** and the law relating to Contempt, with examples

Test for risk of prejudice under **s 2(2)** of the Act with examples from case-law

s 4(2) of the Act – orders allowing postponement of contemporary recording – with examples

s 2(3) of the Act – *sub judice* rules

s 5 of the Act – discussion of good faith, with examples

Overlap between statutory regime and the common law Contempt

s 8 of the Act – confidentiality of jury's deliberations

Common Pitfalls ✗

The skill of a good lawyer is the way he or she can make often complex rules and principles clear and accessible. The same is true of students writing about the law. A common problem you need to avoid is trying too hard to impress the examiner by using convoluted language and sentence structure. This is likely to backfire and obscure, rather than illuminate, your answer. As a general rule, keep your language clear and use explanations that are as simple and straightforward as the complexity of the provisions will allow.

ANSWER

The **Contempt of Court Act 1981** brought about various reforms which were intended to give greater weight to freedom of speech in order to bring about harmonisation between UK contempt law and **Art 10** of the **ECHR**. In particular, it created a stricter test for risk of prejudice, which gave less weight to the administration of justice, it created a shorter *sub judice* period and it allowed discussions in good faith of public affairs to escape liability.[14]

The basic **Convention** requirement is to strike a proper relationship of balance between freedom of expression in **Art 10**, and the right to a fair trial in **Art 6**. **Article 10** permits restrictions on freedom of expression aimed at maintaining the 'integrity and impartiality of the judiciary'. The leading Strasbourg case is *Worm v Austria* (1998), in which a journalist had been convicted for contempt for publishing an article implying the guilt of a politician who, at the time of publication, was on trial. The Court held that the conviction was not a violation of **Art 10** and upheld the view that it was legitimate to restrain the media in order to maintain the function of the courts as the forum for deciding legal disputes and criminal trials, and to ensure that everyone, including prominent persons, has their right to a fair trial protected.[15] Articles and programmes prejudging particular issues before the courts can be restricted, as can those that seriously undermine the general integrity of the courts. At the same time, the Court of Human Rights, as in earlier cases such as *Sunday Times v UK* (1979), stressed that the needs of a free press in a democratic society included permitting vigorous debate on matters of public interest and these could include both the judiciary and court system and also matters forming the context of cases before the courts. In *AG v Guardian Newspapers Ltd* (1999), the Divisional Court said that the **Contempt of Court Act 1981** could be applied in a manner that is compatible with these **Convention** principles.

The test for risk of prejudice arises under **s 2(2)** and requires that a substantial risk of serious prejudice must be shown. According to the Court of Appeal in *AG v News Group*

---

14   This is a good introduction which sums up some of the major points in relation to the **Contempt of Court Act 1981**.

15   This important case has been well explained and set out. Sometimes it is necessary to go into more detail with some cases.

Newspapers (1987), both limbs of this test must be satisfied; showing a slight risk of serious prejudice or a substantial risk of slight prejudice would not be sufficient. In *AG v English* (1983), Lord Diplock interpreted 'substantial risk' as excluding a 'risk which is only remote', which implies that fairly slight risks are sufficient. Later cases, however, have created a test which, it is submitted, requires there to be a fairly or reasonably substantial risk. It is therefore suggested that it has moved the balance somewhat away from the administration of justice towards freedom of speech.[16]

Under **s 4(2)** of the **1981 Act**, a judge may make an order postponing contemporaneous reporting of any public legal proceedings if such an order 'appears necessary for avoiding a substantial risk of prejudice to the administration of justice in those proceedings'. This is quite a wide provision, more extensive than at common law, which on its face provides little protection for media freedom. Generally, such orders are likely to be compatible with **Art 10** (see, for example, *Hodgson and Others v UK* (1998)) if they address the necessity for a reporting restriction to prevent a risk that is 'not insubstantial' (*Telegraph Group plc v Sherwood* (2001)).

The test for the *sub judice* period which arises under **s 2(3)** is more clearly defined than the test at common law and, therefore, proceedings are 'active' (or *sub judice*) for shorter periods. Thus, the test is intended to have a liberalising effect and, since it produces greater certainty about the time from which the contempt jurisdiction runs, it is easier to show consistency with the pervasive 'legality' principle in human rights law.[17]

Even where a publication is published in the active period and satisfies **s 2(2)**, it may still escape liability if the prosecution cannot show that it does not amount to 'a discussion in good faith of public affairs or other matters of general public interest', or that, 'the risk of impediment or prejudice to particular legal proceedings is not merely incidental to the discussion' (**s 5**). In other words, media discussions of various issues are less stifled under the Act than they were previously under the common law.

Section 5 does not give the media *carte blanche* to discuss issues arising from or relating to any particular case during the 'active' period. For example, an article which is focused predominantly on the alleged bad character of the defendant and does not raise a major independent matter of public interest is likely to fall outside the scope of **s 5** (*AG v Guardian Newspapers Ltd* (1999)). The ruling in *AG v English* (1983) gave an emphasis to freedom of speech in the context of prejudice that was incidental to the main theme of an article. Indeed, it may go beyond what **Art 10** requires since it permitted the publication of an article which created a substantial risk of serious prejudice to a trial. **Section 5** does not,

---

16 This exploration of 'substantial risk' ends with some good reference back to the set question, which it is crucial to do.

17 This reference to the wider pervasive theme of legality shows a deep understanding of the law in this area and general knowledge.

in its own terms, limit what can be published by the fair trial requirement in **Art 6**, and **s 3** of the **HRA 1998** may require this to be interpreted into the section.

Due largely to the operation of **s 5** the strict liability rule seems to have created a fairer balance than was the case at common law between freedom of speech and protection for the administration of justice. However, the uncertainty as to the application of **s 5** where the article focuses on the case itself means that **s 5** will allow some legitimate debate in the press to be stifled and, therefore, it might be argued that further relaxation is needed, such as a general public interest defence.

It may be argued that the tests under the **1981 Act**, especially the **s 5** test, have tended to afford recognition to the free speech principle, but the possibility of escaping from the 'balance' created by the Act by using the common law has been preserved by **s 6(c)**. Common law contempt presents an alternative in all instances in which proceedings are not active, assuming, of course, that the *mens rea* requirement can be satisfied. Even more controversially, common law contempt may be an alternative in instances where proceedings are active, but liability under the Act cannot be established; again, the provisions of **s 5** could be undermined.

In the *Hislop* (1991) case, it appeared that a finding of intention to prejudice the administration of justice necessary to found liability for contempt at common law would probably preclude a finding of good faith under **s 5** In the majority of cases, a finding of good faith under **s 5** would preclude a finding of intention to prejudice proceedings. A situation is imaginable in which a newspaper recognised a strong risk that proceedings would be prejudiced, and did not desire such prejudice but felt that publication was justified by an overriding need to bring iniquity to public attention (as may have been the case in *AG v Newspaper Publishing plc* (1990)). **Section 5** might cover such a situation, thereby preventing liability under statute. However, liability could still arise at common law if the necessary intention can be proved. This would allow a newspaper to be punished for contempt where proceedings were active and where publication of material covered by an injunction fell within **s 5** Thus, in this sense, common law contempt clearly has the ability to undermine the statutory protection for freedom of speech. Also, it may be noted that the upholding of an interlocutory injunction by the House of Lords in *AG v Punch* (2003) indicates that there is little inclination on the part of the senior judiciary to narrow down the common law tests in favour of freedom of expression in the post-**HRA** era.

Similarly, common law contempt in respect of 'active' proceedings is possible in other circumstances. **Section 2(2)** might not be satisfied on the basis that, although some risk of prejudice arose, it could not be termed serious enough. In such an instance, there appears to be no reason why the common law could not be used instead, on the basis that the test of showing 'a real risk of prejudice' is less difficult to satisfy. If so, it would be possible to circumvent the more stringent **s 2(2)** requirement. Of course, it would be necessary to prove an intention to prejudice the administration of justice.

Thus, due to the possible difference between the test under **s 2(2)** and the equivalent common law test of 'real risk of prejudice', the safeguards for media freedom in **s 5** could be avoided even when there was a good faith discussion. However, the point is open to argument and it could be argued that using **s 6** of the **HRA** and **Art 10**, the courts should not allow the safeguard of **s 5** to be circumvented in this manner.[18]

The impact of **s 8** of the **1981 Act** on freedom of expression has been the source of extensive judicial analysis over recent years. In principle it is compatible with the **Art 10** of the **Convention** to prevent disclosure of jury room deliberations (*Gregory v United Kingdom* (1997)). Protecting the integrity of the jury provided sufficient justification for limiting the freedom of expression of jurors by the criminal law. However, in *R v Mirza* (2004), the House of Lords recognised that there was a broad interest in ensuring concerns about miscarriages of justice were investigated. Thus it was accepted that the court itself could not be in contempt of court for investigating allegations about jury room conduct and by logical extension, a juror who disclosed such conduct would not be guilty under **s 8**. In *AG v Scotcher* (2005) the House of Lords extended this to indirect routes such as court clerks, jury bailiffs etc. but would not accept that **Art 10** required an interpretation of **s 8** that would permit the disclosure in good faith to persons outside the court system (in that case the convicted person's mother). It is argued that the balance here is entirely appropriate, permitting serious concerns to be raised and investigated but only in the appropriate forums.

It may be concluded that some broadening of **s 5**, development of a public interest defence at common law and tightening up parts of the common law test, especially the test for imminence, might be desirable. Scope for such changes is given by the **HRA**, which obliges the courts under **s 6** to develop the common law in line with the requirements of **Art 10** of the **ECHR**, and thus to give greater weight than in the past to freedom of expression. Perhaps this would enable the media to discuss matters of public interest focusing mainly on the particular case. However, the **ECHR** also requires the protection of the right to a fair trial and does not forbid, and may require, the restriction of speech about a matter involving a strong public interest, on the grounds of its specific impact on fair trial rights (see, for example, the Commission's approach in *BBC Scotland v UK* (1998)).

QUESTION 5

To what extent do you consider the criminalisation of the possession of extreme pornography is a necessary and proportionate restriction on free expression in response to deficiencies in the control of obscene publications?

---

18 Some very good discussion and comparison between the statutory provisions and the common law, which ends with some good analysis.

How to Answer this Question

This is a straightforward essay question which gives you significant flexibility as to how you will produce your answer. The two key limiting factors are, of course, the new provisions on extreme pornography – these should form the substantive backbone of your essay – and the justification for these rules based in analysis of possible deficiencies in the operation of the obscene publication legislation. So long as you keep these two matters central to your answer you have the freedom to develop arguments in a number of different directions, either in favour or against the measures. Your analysis should focus on whether the new law is necessary and proportionate. This is likely to involve **Convention** rights arguments but may also lead you to wider policy analysis. Your answer may cover:

- ❖ the Home Office consultation, 'On the Possession of Extreme Pornographic Material';
- ❖ government justifications for banning extreme pornography;
- ❖ the **Criminal Justice and Immigration Act 2008** provisions: what is extreme pornography? What offences and defences are created?
- ❖ compatibility of the provisions with **Art 10** of the **Convention**;
- ❖ necessity and proportionality of the measures.

Answer Structure

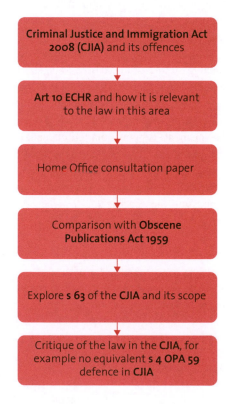

> **Criminal Justice and Immigration Act 2008 (CJIA)** and its offences

> **Art 10 ECHR** and how it is relevant to the law in this area

> Home Office consultation paper

> Comparison with **Obscene Publications Act 1959**

> Explore **s 63** of the **CJIA** and its scope

> Critique of the law in the **CJIA**, for example no equivalent **s 4 OPA 59** defence in **CJIA**

ANSWER

The extreme pornography provisions of the **Criminal Justice and Immigration Act 2008** constitute the first serious attempt to criminalise the mere possession as opposed to the publication of extreme images. The new law alters substantially the relationship between the State and the individual regarding the freedom of adults to decide what they wish to read, watch or listen. As such it interferes with the right of citizens to receive information and ideas which is an important aspect of **Art 10** of the **European Convention**. This calls for clear evidence of a pressing need to interfere and that the measures used are proportionate. It will be argued that this evidence is lacking in this area. While the jurisprudence of the Court of Human Rights is unlikely to prove a barrier to successful enforcement of these laws, the policy argument in favour of their introduction is far from clear and convincing.

The origins of the law reform can be traced to the Home Office consultation, 'On the Possession of Extreme Pornographic Material'[19] (2005) which asserted there was public concern over the availability of extreme pornography which was already illegal to publish under the **Obscene Publications Act 1959** but that it was very difficult to prosecute those responsible due to the global nature of the Internet. Publishers could hide their identities or base themselves outside of the jurisdiction of UK courts. The principles of the reform were diverse, including a desire to prevent harm to participant victims, protect society, particularly children from exposure to such material and to restrict access to images which may encourage interest in violent or deviant sexual behaviour. Essentially, the Government sought to address problems with control of the supply of extreme pornography by placing prohibitions on the demand side.

Despite explicitly acknowledging that there was no clear evidence that access to extreme pornographic material caused criminal activity, the Government asserted a 'moral and public protection' case for intervening. It is argued that in the absence of an evidence

---

19   This knowledge of background material to the creation of the **2008 Act** will impress the examiner.

base suggestive of harm, the resort to public protection justification is unhelpful and misleading.[20]

The original proposals were remarkably wide, covering the actual performance or realistic depiction of a range of activities which included at its widest, 'serious violence in a sexual context'. The clauses were criticised by the Joint Committee on Human Rights for being insufficiently precise to meet the **Convention** test of 'prescribed by law' due to the inherent subjectivity of the concept 'extreme' (Joint Committee 5th Report, 2007–8).[21] As will be seen, the definition crystallised during its parliamentary passage so that the resulting law was less widely drawn.

In addressing the human rights impact of the proposals the Government asserted that although the freedom to view what one liked in the privacy of one's own home was restricted, the material they intended to target was at the very extreme end of the spectrum which most people would find abhorrent. Moreover, the proposals were not intended to restrict political or artistic expression or limit debates about matters of public interest.

Section 63 of the Act creates an offence with a maximum three-year sentence of possession of an 'extreme pornographic image'. This is an image that is both 'pornographic' (i.e. produced for sexual arousal) and 'extreme' (i.e. grossly offensive, disgusting or otherwise of an obscene character AND realistically portrays various extreme situations). These situations are: an act which threatens a person's life; serious injury to a person's anus, breasts or genitals; sexual interference with a human corpse or intercourse or oral sex with an animal.

As noted, this definition is tighter than the original proposal in that there is no reference to general violence in a sexual context. Rather, specific instances of harm must be depicted before the image can be said to be extreme. Indeed this led McGlynn to criticise the law as a 'pale imitation of that originally proposed' which was a missed opportunity that lost sight of the real harm of extreme pornography. It is submitted on the contrary that while the increased precision is to be welcomed, in fact that law still represents a major restriction on individual freedom which is not warranted by the available evidence.

The provisions do not apply where the image is part of a classified work (e.g. 18/18R movie or game) so this provides protection for a wide range of mainstream material. However, this is not the case where images are extracted from a classified work for sexual arousal, e.g. through video editing or creation of montage images. Furthermore, it is a defence if the accused can prove a legitimate reason for being in possession of the image, or that he

---

20 This analysis of the justifications for the **2008 Act** will impress the examiner.
21 References to wider reading, such as this reference to the Joint Committee's report, are great ways to impress examiners, as they can only be made if you have researched the area effectively.

had not seen the image and did not know, nor had any cause to suspect, it to be an extreme pornographic image, or was sent the image without request and did not keep it for an unreasonable time. There is also a defence to protect consensual participants so that people who possess images of themselves will not normally be guilty of an offence.

There is no defence equivalent to the **s 4 Obscene Publications Act 1959** public good defence. This may seem unsurprising in a law that explicitly prohibits material on the basis of its extreme nature. Although the circumstances in which it would be possible to argue for artistic merit of material that met the legal definition of extreme pornography, it is argued that it should remain possible for defendants to argue that the creative merits of the material should preclude a conviction. Indeed, part of the Government's human rights justification was that this law did not undermine political or artistic expression.[22]

In any prosecution, it would of course be open to an accused to ask a court to have regard to **Art 10** of the **Convention**. Arguably the right to receive information and ideas expressed in **Art 10(1)** covers the viewing of images that may be deemed to be extreme and pornographic (*Hoare v UK* (1997)). As regards **Art 10(2)**, although artistic expression is generally viewed as lower in the hierarchy of expression, there are few decisions defending restrictions on the freedom of expression of adults, absent the risk of widespread distribution or to protect children. In view of the wide margin of appreciation afforded to the domestic authorities, little guidance as to the requirements of **Art 10** in this context is available, especially where the material is consumed by consenting adults. The case of *Scherer v Switzerland* (1993) arguably supports the contention that restraints on the material for a willing adult audience should be minimal. Whether the new law goes beyond such minimal restraints remains to be seen. In theory under the **Human Rights Act** the domestic courts would be able to adopt a more interventionist approach and require clearer evidence of the proportionality of the measure, although there is little evidence thus far of this being likely in the field of pornography (*R v Perrin* (2002)).

The perceived problem of the **Obscene Publications Act 1959** was one of enforcement. It is undoubtedly true that the internet age has made it more difficult to successfully prosecute publishers of obscene material. First, the publisher itself is remote from the place of publication (an image downloaded onto a computer could have been produced anywhere in the world). Secondly, the place where the transaction takes place is less overt – there is no need for a physical transfer of property when the vast majority of images are stored electronically. Nevertheless, it is highly questionable whether the purported solution of targeting the demand side of the problem is workable or equitable. There is nothing intrinsically wrong with such an approach – it has been long established in relation to possession of child pornography. However, it is argued that there is a clear distinction here in that all the participants (producers, performers and consumers) may

---

22 This shows good analysis of the **2008 Act** in relation to the **1959 Act** which goes to the heart of the set question.

be consenting adults. It is at least arguable that this is or can be a victimless crime. Moreover, the high volume and private nature of downloading from the internet means that enforcement is likely to be tokenistic without any real impact on the production or consumption of extreme material.

In conclusion, it is argued that a conceptual Rubicon has been crossed with this law. Trying to control the private leisure interests of consenting adults by use of the criminal law has rarely been attempted before and certainly not in the realm of non-child pornography. Although the law is fairly specific in nature and relates to extreme imagery, it criminalises ostensibly harmless behaviour without clear evidence that this leads to other harmful consequences. Indeed the notion of harm is elusive in these provisions. The mischief the law seeks to address is unclear and the measures of enforcement are potentially draconian. The proposals were described by the Campaign Against Censorship as 'Orwellian victimless crime enforced by Thought Police'. This may be overstating the position but it is certainly a step in the wrong direction that was not warranted by the perceived defects of the existing law.

QUESTION 6

Assess the extent to which 'hate crime' legislation in England and Wales strikes the appropriate balance between the protection of vulnerable groups and the preservation of the right to freedom of expression.

How to Answer this Question

This is a typical style of essay requiring you to consider competing rights and the concept of balancing individual and group/community rights and interests. In this case the question requires detailed knowledge of 'hate crime' and assessment of the impact this has on freedom of expression. 'Hate crime' is not a precise phrase and your answer should briefly address the scope of legislation it covers. Although there are only two categories (race and religion) which are protected by specific offences, other vulnerable groups are protected through other means (for example, gay people are protected by sentencing guidelines which make homophobic motivation an aggravating factor). A good answer should reflect the breadth of the legislative response to hate crime.

You should be familiar with recent legislative reforms such as the **Racial and Religious Hatred Act 2006** and the ongoing debate over criminalising speech *per se*. You should be willing to weave domestic and **Convention** case law into your answer to illustrate your argument.

Essentially the following matters should be considered:

❖   analysis of the statement in the question;
❖   what are hate crimes?

- ❖   what interests are at stake?
- ❖   how does the legislation impact on freedom of expression?
- ❖   how does the legislation protect vulnerable groups?
- ❖   **Public Order Act 1986**;
- ❖   **Racial and Religious Hatred Act 2006**;
- ❖   aggravated offences;
- ❖   hate crime as a sentencing issue.

Answer Structure

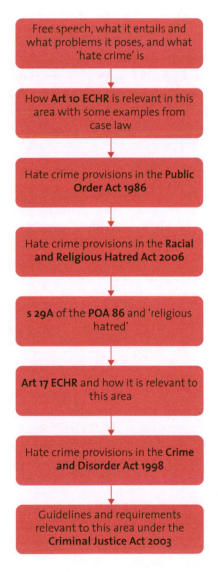

Free speech, what it entails and what problems it poses, and what 'hate crime' is

How **Art 10 ECHR** is relevant in this area with some examples from case law

Hate crime provisions in the **Public Order Act 1986**

Hate crime provisions in the **Racial and Religious Hatred Act 2006**

s 29A of the **POA 86** and 'religious hatred'

Art 17 ECHR and how it is relevant to this area

Hate crime provisions in the **Crime and Disorder Act 1998**

Guidelines and requirements relevant to this area under the **Criminal Justice Act 2003**

Aim Higher   ★

Selective use of hypothetical examples can be very helpful to illustrate the ambit and extent of the law, particularly where there is no case authority interpreting the point at issue. See the use of the example in the answer below about pamphlets abusing the Muslim faith to appreciate how examples may assist you to explain complex legal provisions.

ANSWER

'Sticks and stones may break my bones but names can never hurt me.' This nursery phrase is apt to illustrate one approach towards the problem of hatred in society: that it should be ignored, in the knowledge that words alone cannot harm people. However, such an approach has been said to be simplistic, in that it fails to appreciate the real harm that can arise as a consequence of hate speech. Tolerance of hatred, it can be argued, engenders a culture of disregard for the legitimate interests of individuals or groups who may be targeted and can lead directly to harmful acts against such people. Moreover, a liberal society demands that the State stigmatises those who offend against its values.[23]

'Hate crimes' are one response to these problems. Such offences seek to criminalise certain manifestations of hatred. In so doing they inevitably impede the ability of some people to freely express their views. This is where the concept of balance comes into play. Freedom of expression is seen as a fundamental human right, of crucial importance not just to individuals but to the furtherance of pluralistic, democratic societies. In *Handyside v United Kingdom* (1976) the European Court of Human Rights highlighted the necessity for tolerance. It said that **Art 10** was applicable not only to inoffensive speech, but also to ideas that 'offend, shock or disturb'. This principle has been accepted by the domestic courts, for example, Sedley LJ in *Redmond-Bate v DPP* (2000) suggested free expression extended to 'the irritating, the contentious, the eccentric, the heretical, the unwelcome and the provocative'.[24]

Any restriction on free speech must therefore have a cogent justification. The core rationale for hate crimes is the protection of certain people against being targeted for vilification on the basis of their position as part of a minority group, their status or beliefs. The principle of protecting individuals and groups in this way is well established, and clearly falls within the parameters of **Art 10(2)**, but there remains extensive debate over the extent of limits on free speech and the type of group deserving of protection.

23   This background and context to hate crime is good material to include in the introduction.
24   This is a good quote from Sedley LJ as it is relevant to the question. Do not use quotes just for the sake of it; they need to be relevant, as this quote demonstrates.

This essay seeks to assess whether the restrictions on freedom of expression inherent in current hate crime laws are justified by the potential benefits to groups who may otherwise be abused. It considers the key hate crime offences based on race and religion. It also considers broader provisions to target hatred as a motivation in offending by the creation of aggravated offences and aggravated sentencing guidelines.

The main legislative provision is the **Public Order Act (POA) 1986**. **Part 3** of the Act contains provisions criminalising various conduct loosely described as incitement to racial hatred. The Act has been amended on a number of occasions, most recently (and controversially) by the **Racial and Religious Hatred Act 2006**,[25] which added a raft of similar offences to protect against incitement to religious hatred (**Part 3A** of the Act). All offences are triable either way, with a maximum of seven years' imprisonment on indictment. Confusingly, the race offences differ from the religion offences in several important ways, due mainly to amendments made during the 2006 Bill's tortuous passage through Parliament.

The race offences are anchored to the concept of racial hatred, defined in **s 17** of the Act as 'hatred against any group of persons defined by reference to colour, race, nationality (including citizenship), or ethnic or national origins'. **Sections 18–22** prohibit words or behaviour, displays, written material, performance of plays, or the showing/broadcasting of films, videos or records where the behaviour or material is threatening, abusive or insulting and the defendant intends or is likely to stir up racial hatred.

The Act also prohibits in **s 23** the possession of material that falls within the type described above, although the possession must be with a view to publication, broadly defined.

The religion offences are linked to the concept of religious hatred defined in **s 29A** as 'hatred against a group of persons defined by reference to religious belief or lack of religious belief'. The Act did not attempt to define religion, so courts will have to decide on a case-by-case basis whether a particular group qualifies for protection.

The religion offences follow a similar set of activities as the race offences. However, there are significant differences in relation to the elements of the offences. Importantly, the *actus reus* of the offences is limited to conduct which is 'threatening'. Abusive and insulting content is insufficient. Secondly, in contrast to the race offences, the defendant must intend to stir up religious hatred. Likelihood of stirring up hatred is insufficient. These differences clearly make the race offences much broader in application than the religion offences. For example, pamphlets that abused the Muslim faith and linked Islam with terrorism would not contravene the provisions unless they could be said to be

---

25 Keeping up to date with the law, as this reference to the updating of the **POA 1986** shows, is essential in order to obtain high marks.

threatening and unless the defendant *intended* to cause religious hatred by the publication. If the target of the pamphlets was not Muslims but Iraqis, then abuse alone would suffice, and intention would not be necessary if the pamphlets were likely to stir up racial hatred.

At first sight the differences may be seen as the arbitrary products of Westminster political compromise. Nevertheless, the amendments do provide a useful focal point for assessing the interests at stake and whether the balance between free expression and protection of vulnerable groups is appropriate.[26]

The major focus of controversy in respect of the **2006 Act** was the argument that religious affiliation was by its nature a voluntary act. Although religious belief is often deeply held it is always just that: belief. The idea that faith should be protected from external vilification can be seen as anathema to the notion of evangelism that is common in many religions. Once it is accepted that religion is voluntary and can change then the idea of competition, criticism and animosity between adherents becomes much more understandable.

By contrast, racial make-up is a permanent part of a person's identity in a way that religion could never be. People cannot choose their race, ethnicity or national origin. These differences perhaps explain why the religion-based offences are narrower than race-based offences. Religion or lack of religion constitutes a weaker claim to protection from vilification than does race, ethnicity etc. Similarly, the claim to freedom of expression of those who might be charged with criminal offences is arguably stronger in relation to religion than it is in relation to race. Religion can be seen as an idea which must stand or fall on its own merits in the marketplace of ideas, whereas race is an identity and as such cannot be subject to a marketplace analysis.

Once it is accepted that freedom of expression is not absolute, then it becomes permissible to restrict free expression for legitimate reasons where the restriction is proportionate. **Article 10(2)** of the **Convention** explicitly recognises the 'rights and reputations of others' as legitimate reasons for interference, and the European Court has repeatedly acknowledged this as a justification for preventing or punishing free speech (see e.g. *Jersild v Denmark* (1995)).

A further justification for interference can be seen in **Art 17** of the **European Convention** which prevents the rights being used to protect acts aimed at the destruction of other people's **Convention** rights. In *Norwood v United Kingdom* (2005) the European Court said that **Art 17** was aimed at preventing those with totalitarian aims from exploiting their

---

26 This analysis in relation to the religious offences is an example of how to fit in good analysis to a question.

own rights to destroy others' rights. As such it applied to an applicant who had been convicted of religiously aggravated harassment, alarm or distress by displaying a poster linking the whole of the Muslim faith with the 9/11 attacks. He thus could not rely on the protection under **Art 10**.

We have seen that the criminal law is structured so as to provide somewhat broader protection for those attacked on the basis of their race as compared to religion or belief. To this extent free expression may be interfered with to a greater extent in the context of racist speech than faith-based attacks. In view of the permanence of race as a concept, the vulnerability of racial groups, and the real problems caused to them by the propagation of racist ideas, it is submitted that it is clearly acceptable to prohibit the extreme manifestation of racist attitudes and in this sense the **Public Order Act** strikes the appropriate balance between free expression and protection of minorities. For the reasons stated above, it is also submitted that Parliament has succeeded in appropriately restricting the scope of the religion-based offences. There is somewhat less justification for protection and more justification for freedom of expression in this field than in respect of race.

In summary, the balance between freedom of expression and protection of vulnerable groups is achieved first by criminalising only extreme versions of hate speech. This protects genuine political discourse, academic comment etc. Secondly, it is achieved by requiring a clear and direct link to the proliferation of hate through the requirement for intention (or likelihood) of stirring up hatred. The law takes into account the different nature of the protected groups in a logical and appropriate manner.

A further safeguard lies in the fact that no prosecution may be brought without the consent of the Attorney General. This reflects the view that prosecutions under these provisions may often be politically sensitive or controversial and there ought to be control over the use of private prosecutions.

It may seem strange that there are only two specifically protected groups – race and religion – in the current hate crime framework. There are other groups, for example the gay community, disabled people and the elderly, who may also be at risk of being targeted because of their status as members of such a group. There is no offence of using threatening behaviour with intent to stir up hatred against such people. They have to seek protection in general public order or harassment law, for example *Hammond v DPP DC* (2004), where the Divisional Court upheld a conviction under **s 5 Public Order Act 1986** (causing harassment, alarm or distress) for displaying a homophobic placard.[27]

----

27 This analysis, highlighting the deficiencies of the hate crime regime, will be given high marks by the examiner.

Similarly, racial and religious groups are specifically protected by the creation of racially and religiously aggravated offences under **ss 28–32** of the **Crime and Disorder Act 1998**. This Act created aggravated forms of various assault, criminal damage and public order offences if the offender showed or was motivated by racial or religious hostility. Again other minority or vulnerable groups do not benefit from the protection of these crimes.

However, some additional protection appears in the form of sentencing guidelines under the **Criminal Justice Act 2003** and from the Sentencing Council. **Section 145** of the **2003 Act** requires the court to view racial or religious motivation as aggravating sentencing factors for offenders. **Section 146** creates a similar requirement for offending which shows or is motivated by sexual orientation or disability hostility. The Sentencing Council guidelines on the **2003 Act** reflect these requirements. Thus far this is the only specific protection such groups have from hate crime.

In conclusion, the current balance between freedom of expression and protection of vulnerable groups is adequate but further consideration ought to be given to whether there ought to be more general hate crime legislation prohibiting the use of extreme forms of hate speech against any group subject to a defence of reasonableness.

QUESTION 7

(a) Relatives of old people in the Sunnymede Old People's Home become suspicious after a number of the residents become ill. Evidence of neglect comes to light and certain of the relatives decide to sue the Home. The owners of the Home enter into negotiations with the relatives' legal representatives, with a view to settling out of court. Meanwhile, the *Daily Argus*, a national newspaper, intends to publish the following article (article (a)) on its 'Personal Lives' page:

Caring for old people in the modern times

Joan Smith set out one day last June to visit her mother in the Sunnymede Old People's Home in Southton. It was a lovely day and she was looking forward to the visit. But when she arrived, she was appalled by the state of the Home. Some of the residents were sitting around unwashed in nightclothes, others were still in bed, although it was midday and they were able to get up. They all looked bored, listless and passive. The floors were filthy, as were the beds. For lunch, Joan's mother was offered a small bowl of soup. Joan was absolutely devastated and is now desperately trying to get her mother into another Home. But how can these conditions exist? Do we want to neglect our old people in this way? It is time the Government woke up to this problem and instituted a rigorous system of inspection for these Homes. Otherwise, people like Joan's mother will continue to suffer.

▶ **Advise the Daily Argus whether contempt proceedings in respect of this article would be likely to succeed.**

(b) A year later, criminal charges are brought against the officer in charge of the Sunnymede Home, Mrs Sly, for assaults allegedly committed by her on a resident of the Home. At this point, the *Daily Screech*, a national tabloid newspaper with a large circulation, intends to publish the following article (article (b)):

'Care' Workers?

How do you get a job in an Old People's Home? Does your background have to be investigated? Do you have to have good qualifications? The answer to both these questions appears to be 'no' if the case of Mrs Sly, a 'care' worker who has just been charged with assaulting an old person, is anything to go by. Mrs Sly has had four posts in Old People's Homes in the last five years. She was dismissed from the second one after a disciplinary hearing, which found that she had neglected old people in her charge. How is it that she went on to obtain two more posts? It is time that the appointment of workers to these Homes was looked into carefully; their background should be fully investigated. At present, there seems to be no control at all: this is a scandal which the *Daily Screech* is determined to root out.

▶ **Advise the *Daily Screech* whether contempt proceedings in respect of this article would be likely to succeed.**

How to Answer this Question

Contempt of court is an area that lends itself very readily to setting problem questions. A problem question should not be attempted unless a student is very familiar with the area and, crucially, can determine when proceedings are 'active'. It is essential to take account of the **HRA 1998** and relevant **Convention** jurisprudence in the answer, since the discussion concerns a potential interference with freedom of expression. Essentially, the following matters should be discussed:

PART (a)

- ❖ the concept of 'active' proceedings under **s 2(3)** and **Sched 1** to the Act;
- ❖ intention to prejudice the administration of justice under common law contempt;
- ❖ the concept of imminence in common law contempt;
- ❖ creating a 'real risk of prejudice';
- ❖ the possibility of narrowing down common law contempt by reliance on **s 6** of the **HRA**.

PART (b)

- ❖ the concept of 'active' proceedings under **s 2(3)** of and **Sched 1** to the Act;
- ❖ the creation of a substantial risk of serious prejudice under **s 2(2)** of the **Contempt of Court Act 1981**;

❖   discussions in good faith under **s 5** and the effect of **Art 10** under the **HRA**,
    relevance of **s 3** of the **HRA**;
❖   intention to prejudice the administration of justice under common law contempt.

Applying the Law

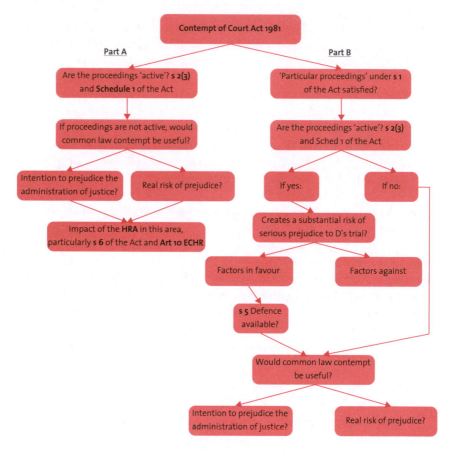

This diagram shows how to apply the **Contempt of Court Act 1981** to parts (a) and (b) of the
question.

Common Pitfalls ✗

The most common error students are guilty of when dealing with problem
questions is failing to apply the law to the facts of the question. It is all too
easy to explain the law in great detail while neglecting to remember that
you are requested to advise one or more parties regarding their legal rights,
liability etc. If you do this your answer looks like an essay and you will have

failed to display the fact management and problem solving skills expected by the marker. For an example of application see the following section in the answer below: 'The article is not couched in particularly vitriolic language, although it does convey potentially inadmissible character evidence about D's previous disciplinary record, which is likely to create an unfavourable impression.' This shows that the student has given thought to how the facts of the case might affect the operation of the law.

ANSWER

This question concerns the rules governing contempt of court arising under the **Contempt of Court Act 1981** (hereafter 'the Act') and at common law. In advising the newspapers, it is necessary to take account of the **HRA** and relevant **Convention** jurisprudence since the discussion concerns a potential interference with freedom of expression. The two newspaper articles will be considered separately.

Liability in respect of article (a) will not arise under the Act, since the proceedings are not 'active'. This test arises under **s 2(3)** and the starting and ending points for civil proceedings are defined in **Sched 1**. The starting point for civil proceedings occurs when the case is set down for a hearing in the High Court or a date for the hearing is fixed (**Sched 1, ss 12** and **13**). Since the civil proceedings in question are only at the negotiating stage, this starting point has not yet arisen. Indeed it is not clear that the civil claim has even been issued.[28]

However, liability may arise at common law in respect of article (a). **Section 6(c)** of the Act preserves liability for contempt at common law if intention to prejudice the administration of justice can be shown. Prejudice to the administration of justice clearly includes prejudice to particular proceedings. Once the requirement of intent is satisfied, it is easier to establish contempt at common law, rather than under the Act, as it is only necessary to show 'a real risk of prejudice' and proceedings need only be imminent, not 'active'. However, the court is a public authority under **s 6** of the **HRA** and therefore must seek to ensure that the common law is compatible with the demands of **Art 10** (see in a different context *Douglas v Hello!* (2001)), bearing in mind that the law of contempt also plays a role in protecting the guarantee of a fair trial under **Art 6(1)**.

The test for intention to prejudice the administration of justice was established in *AG v Newspaper Publishing plc* (1990) and *AG v News Group Newspapers plc* (1988). It was reaffirmed in *AG v Punch* (2003). It was made clear that 'intention' connotes specific

---

28 This application of the law about 'active proceedings' is very concise. Where there are multiple issues to consider this is the best approach to take.

intent and therefore cannot include recklessness.[29] The test may be summed up as follows: did the defendant either wish to prejudice proceedings or foresee that such prejudice was a virtually inevitable consequence of publishing the material in question?

Article (a) *may* create a risk of prejudice to the future proceedings, although this is not likely – there is no explicit link between the article and the proceedings, and no hearing is likely for a long time. Although Sunnymede is identified and portrayed in an unfavourable light this seems a long way from causing prejudice to the proceedings. However, even if the editor of the *Argus* recognises this risk (which is unclear), it cannot be said that prejudice is virtually certain to be created, since the proceedings are such a long way off. It would thus be very difficult to establish intention to prejudice. Desire to prejudice proceedings cannot be established since the feature allowing an inference of such desire to be drawn in the *AG v News Group Newspapers plc* case – the personal involvement of *The Sun* – is not apparently present in the case of the *Daily Argus*.

It is questionable whether the interference with freedom of expression that a broad test to imminence represents could be said to be 'prescribed by law' under **Art 10(2)**, due to the lack of precision and therefore of foreseeability present in this area of the common law. In the instant case, it is highly likely, following this discussion, that the test of imminence cannot be met. First, if the test were to be narrowed down under **s 6** of the **HRA**, it would become even less likely that it could be met. Even if it were not narrowed down as suggested, it could not be met since the requirement of intent was not established and therefore the extension of the test undertaken in the *AG v News Group Newspapers plc* case would be inapplicable. The only way of meeting this test would be to argue that although the proceedings are a long way off, they can be viewed as imminent following *Savundranayagan* and that **s 6** of the **HRA** does not require a narrowing down of this test.[30]

Further, as alluded to above, it is also suggested that the *actus reus* of common law contempt cannot be established since the risk of prejudice is very uncertain: the proceedings will not occur for some time and the article may therefore be forgotten by those involved in the case. (Had it appeared that the article might well create a real risk of prejudice, and had the first test for intention been satisfied, it would have been necessary to consider in more detail the question whether proceedings were 'imminent'. This test would probably be readily satisfied as *dicta* in *AG v Newspapers* and, in the *Sport* case, suggested that even 'imminence' need not be established once the *mens rea* is shown.) Moreover, no jury will be involved, since the action seems to be either in tort (for negligence) or in contract and, although a judge or witnesses might be prejudiced by this article, it is suggested that this is less likely.

....

29 This is very good exposition of the common law regime as it uses cases and then explains the law in a simple and straightforward way.

30 This is an example of some excellent application of the law in relation to interfering with freedom of expression.

In *Hislop and Pressdram* (1991), it was found that the defendants, who were one party in an action for defamation, had interfered with the administration of justice because they had brought improper pressure to bear on the other party, Sonia Sutcliffe, by publishing material in *Private Eye* intended to deter her from pursuing the action. However, the pressure placed on Sunnymede Old People's Home as a litigant is much less apparent: legal proceedings are not even mentioned, the focus of the article being the need for better regulation by Government. It is therefore argued that a real risk of prejudice does not arise on this argument either.

Liability in respect of article (b) may arise under the Act. The first question to be determined is whether the publication in question could have an effect on any 'particular proceedings' under **s1** of the Act. The article makes reference to Mrs Sly; therefore, the strict liability rule under **s1** of the Act may apply if the following three tests are satisfied.[31]

First, proceedings must be active under **s 2(3)** of and **Sched 1** to the Act. Mrs Sly (hereinafter 'D') has been charged and proceedings are therefore active under **Sched 1, s 4(a)**.

Secondly, it must be shown that the article creates a substantial risk of serious prejudice to D's trial (**s 2(2)** of the Act). According to the Court of Appeal in *AG v News Group Newspapers plc*, both limbs of this test must be satisfied. As regards the first limb, can it be shown that there is a substantial risk that a person involved in D's trial, such as a juror, would: (a) encounter the article; (b) remember it; and (c) be affected by it so that he or she could not put it out of his or her mind during the trial? As this is a national newspaper with a large circulation, it is possible that jurors and others may encounter the article. It was found in *AG v Independent Television News Ltd* (1994) that a small circulation would clearly be one factor predisposing a court to determine that prejudice to proceedings did not occur. Relevant factors will include the prominence of the article and the novelty of its content (*AG v Mirror Group Newspapers* (1997)). As to this the revelation of D's previous disciplinary record may impact on the reader. The length of time between publication and trial is also very significant. In *AG v News Group Newspapers plc* (1986), a gap of 10 months was held to obviate the risk of prejudice. On the other hand, in *AG v BBC* (1996), a risk was held to exist despite a gap of six months. It is unclear what interval of time will elapse between charging Mrs Sly and the trial. The Court of Appeal in *AG v Mirror Group Newspapers* noted that the residual impact of a prejudicial article could be reduced by the effects of the jury's listening to evidence over a prolonged period, and the judge's directions. In this case, therefore, it could be argued that, although there is a risk that a juror might see and remember the article, it is of a relatively mild nature and might therefore be blotted out by the immediacy of the trial. The article is not couched in particularly vitriolic language, although it does

----

31 Where there are multiple issues to consider, signposting your structure to the examiner, as happens here in relation to liability under the statutory regime, helps them to have confidence in your abilities and leads to higher marks.

convey potentially inadmissible character evidence about D's previous disciplinary record, which is likely to create an unfavourable impression.

The stronger argument appears to be to the effect that the requirement for prejudice in **s 2(2)** is not fulfilled. However, since this is not absolutely certain, it must next be established that **s 5** does not apply. Following *AG v English* (1983), the test to be applied seems to be – looking at the actual words written (as opposed to considering what could have been omitted) – is the article written in good faith and concerned with a question of general legitimate public interest which creates an incidental risk of prejudice to a particular case? It is possible on this basis to argue that **s 5** does apply on the basis that the conditions in Old People's Homes are clearly a matter of genuine public interest, the article appears to be written in good faith and seems merely to be using Mrs Sly as an example of the problem it is concerned with. It therefore bears comparison with the articles which escaped liability in the two cases mentioned.

There is the alternative possibility of establishing liability at common law if intention to prejudice proceedings is present, although it should be noted that in the only case in which such liability was established when proceedings were active, the *Hislop* case, the tests under the Act and at common law were satisfied. In any event, a finding that the article was written in good faith under **s 5** would almost certainly preclude a finding that the editor of the paper in question intended to prejudice proceedings (a necessary ingredient of liability at common law).

Section 6(c) of the Act preserves liability for contempt at common law if intention to prejudice the administration of justice can be established. Prejudice to the administration of justice clearly includes prejudice to particular proceedings; therefore, the instant case will fall within **s 6(c)** if the following tests can be satisfied. First, an intention to prejudice the proceedings against D must be established. The test is: did the defendant either wish to prejudice proceedings or foresee that such prejudice was a virtually inevitable consequence of publishing the material in question?

In the instant case, given the lack of any particular involvement that the *Screech* has in the case, it would be hard to show a desire to prejudice D's trial. It would also be difficult to establish that an objective observer would have foreseen that such prejudice would be a virtually inevitable consequence of the publication. Such an observer might consider such a result to be probable (see the argument as to the substantial risk of serious prejudice above), but that is not sufficient.

The argument above tends towards the conclusion that liability cannot be established under either the Act or at common law.

Official Secrecy and Freedom of Information

2

INTRODUCTION

Freedom of information and freedom of expression are very closely linked since some speech is dependent on access to information which is in turn a form of speech. Therefore, what may be termed 'freedom of information' issues could also be treated as aspects of freedom of expression. However, the overlap is not complete: in some circumstances, information may be sought where there is no speaker willing to disclose it. Such a situation would tend to be considered purely as a freedom of information issue (more accurately, as a question of access to information).

The most important value associated with freedom of information is the need for the citizen to understand as fully as possible the working of government, in order to render it accountable. One of the main concerns of the questions in this chapter is therefore the methods employed by governments to ensure that official information cannot fall into the hands of those who might place it in the public domain, and with methods of preventing or deterring persons from publication when such information has been obtained. This chapter also places a strong emphasis on the choices that were made as to the release of information relating to public authorities – not only to central Government – in the **Freedom of Information Act (FOIA) 2000** (in force 2005). Do note that the **Protection of Freedoms Act 2012** made amendments to **s 6** of the **FOIA 2000** with regards to the types of bodies that are under a duty courtesy of the **FOIA 2000**. The intention behind the changes was to clarify the law in this area.

Examiners tend to set general essays, rather than problem questions, in this area; the emphasis is usually on the degree to which a balance is struck between the interest of the individual in acquiring government information and the interest of the State in withholding it. The balance between what may be termed State interests, such as defence or national security, and the individual entitlement to freedom of expression and information is largely struck by the **Official Secrets Act (OSA) 1989** and various common law provisions. However, the interpretation of the **1989 Act** and the application of those provisions are affected by the **Convention** rights as applied under the **Human Rights Act (HRA) 1998**. Where information held by central Government or by other public authorities is not covered by the **OSA 1989**, the citizen may be able to obtain access to it under the **FOIA 2000** which came into force in 2005. The **2000 Act** is a very significant development that is highly likely to feature on exam papers.

It is also worth remembering the 'wikileaks' developments which came to prominence in 2011. The whistle-blowing website is a good example of the difficulties facing official secrets legislation in a digital age and exploring such issues can lead to a helpful critique of the area.

Checklist ✔

Students should be familiar with the following areas:

- key aspects of the **Official Secrets Act 1989**;
- the basic aspects of the **Public Records Act 1958** and very basic, key aspects of the **Data Protection Act 1998**;
- very basic aspects of freedom of information measures in other countries, particularly Canada and the USA;
- the doctrine of breach of confidence as used by the Government;
- the key aspects of the **Freedom of Information Act 2000**; aspects of the early work of the Information Commissioner;
- **Art 10** of the **ECHR**; other relevant rights such as **Art 6**;
- **Art 10** jurisprudence;
- the **Human Rights Act 1998**, especially **ss 3, 4, 6, 12**;
- the decision in *Shayler* (2002).

QUESTION 8

Critically evaluate the means currently available to the Government to prevent disclosure of information. Taking account of relevant developments, including the introduction of the **Freedom of Information Act 2000**, would it be fair to say that the tradition of government secrecy is finally breaking down?

How to Answer this Question

This is clearly quite a general and wide-ranging essay that requires knowledge of a number of different areas. It is concerned with restrictions on access to State information, methods of ensuring that information cannot fall into the hands of those who might place it in the public domain, and with methods of preventing or deterring persons from publication when a leak has occurred. The latter two issues are both aspects of freedom of expression, but the first is given greater prominence here. The question asks you, in essence, to present a critical analysis of the current scheme preventing disclosure of certain State information, and to consider whether the right of access to information introduced in the **2000 Act** is dramatically improving the public's access to information. Since the essay is so wide-ranging, you are not expected to engage in a detailed analysis of the **2000 Act**.

Essentially, the following areas should be considered:

❖ the impact of the **Official Secrets Act 1989** – 'harm tests';

❖ the impact of the **Security Services Act 1989**, the **Intelligence Services Act 1994**, the **Interception of Communications Act 1985** and the **Regulation of Investigatory Powers Act 2000** in terms of creating secrecy (detailed knowledge of these statutes is not needed – but answers should indicate a broad, basic awareness of the relevance of these statutes);

❖ the use of the common law doctrine of breach of confidence as a means of preventing disclosure of State information;

❖ mention very briefly the operation of the **Public Records Acts 1958** and **1967**, as amended;

❖ the key provisions of the **Freedom of Information Act 2000**.

Answer Structure

Official Secrets Act 1989 – what it says and does (and doesn't say and do), with a discussion of some case-law

'Harm tests' and the Official Secrets Act 1989

Relationship between the Official Secrets Act 1989 and the Security Services Act 1989 and the Regulation of Investigatory Powers Act 2000

How the common law doctrine of breach of confidence works and when it can be used for official secrets

s 12 Human Rights Act and its significance

Public Records Acts of 1958 and 1967 and their relevance to this area of law

The Freedom of Information Act 2000 and the impact it has had in this area of law and some of its particular provisions

ANSWER

It has often been said that the UK is more obsessed with keeping government information secret than any other Western democracy. The Official Secrets Act 1989, which decriminalised disclosure of some official information, was heralded as amounting to a move away from obsessive secrecy. However, since it was in no sense a freedom of information measure, it did not allow the release of any official documents into the public domain, although it does mean that if certain information is disclosed outside the categories it covers, the official concerned will not face criminal sanctions. (He/she might, of course, face an action for breach of confidence, as well as disciplinary proceedings.)

The narrowing down of the official information covered by the **1989 Act** was supposed to be achieved by introducing 'harm tests', which took into account the substance of the information. However, there is no test for harm at all in the category of information covered by **s 1(1)** of the **1989 Act**, which prevents members or former members of the security services from disclosing anything at all about the operation of those services (see *Shayler* (2003)).[1] Equally, there is no test for harm under **s 4(3)** of the Act, which covers information obtained by or relating to the issue of a warrant under the **Interception of Communications Act 1985** or the **Security Services Act 1989**.

Thus, the Act was always unlikely to have a liberalising impact on the publication of information allowing the public to scrutinise the workings of government.

The **Official Secrets Act 1989** works in tandem with other measures designed to ensure secrecy. **Sections 1** and **4(3)** work in conjunction with the provisions of the **Security Services Act 1989** to prevent almost all scrutiny of the operation of the security service. In a similar manner, **s 4(3)** of the **Official Secrets Act**, which prevents disclosure of information about telephone tapping, works in tandem with the **Regulation of Investigatory Powers Act 2000**. Under the **2000 Act**, complaints can be made only to a tribunal (set up under the Act), with no possibility of scrutiny by a court.[2]

Developments in the use of the common law doctrine of confidence as a means of preventing disclosure of information provide a further method of ensuring secrecy where information falls outside the categories covered by the **Official Secrets Act**, or where it falls within one of them, but a prosecution is not undertaken. *AG v Guardian Newspapers* (1987), which concerned the publication of material from the book *Spycatcher* by Peter Wright, demonstrated that temporary injunctions could be obtained to prevent disclosure of official information, even where prior publication has ensured that there is little confidentiality left to be protected. However, the House of Lords eventually rejected the claim for permanent injunctions on the basis that the interest in maintaining confidentiality was outweighed by the public interest in knowing of the allegations in *Spycatcher*. Moreover, it was impossible to sustain a restriction based on confidentiality when the worldwide publication of the book meant that the information it contained was clearly in the 'public domain'.

....

1   This background to key issues surrounding the **Official Secrets Act 1989** helps achieve higher marks with the examiner.

2   The awareness of how the **Official Secrets Act 1989** synthesises with other legislation will impress the examiner.

A restraint over obtaining an injunction or damages for breach of confidence is now to be found in **s 12** of the **Human Rights Act (HRA) 1998**. This requires any court considering such relief not to grant any interim injunctions unless it is satisfied that the claimant is likely to be successful at trial. Courts must apply existing statutory and common law rules with a far greater focus upon the public right to know. In this respect, the case of *AG v Times* (2001) is significant. A former MI6 officer wrote a book, *The Big Breach*, about his experiences in MI6 that *The Sunday Times* intended to serialise. There had been a small amount of publication of the material in Russia. The Attorney General sought an injunction to restrain publication. It was found that he had failed to demonstrate why there was a public interest in restricting publication; therefore, no injunction was granted. The requirement to seek clearance should not, it was found, be imposed: the editor had to form his own judgment as to whether the material could be said to be already in the public domain. That position was, the court found, most consonant with the requirements of **Art 10** and **s 12**. This decision suggests that bearing in mind the requirements of the **HRA**, an injunction is unlikely to be granted where even a very small amount of prior publication has already taken place.

The position was affected by the decision of the House of Lords in *Cream Holdings Ltd and Ors v Banerjee* (2004). This decision gives the definitive interpretation of the meaning of **s 12(3) HRA**, which provides, *inter alia*, that no relief affecting the **Convention** right to freedom of expression 'is to be granted so as to restrain publication before trial unless the court is satisfied that the applicant is likely to establish that publication should not be allowed'.[3] The effect of the decision of the House of Lords is that, in nearly all cases – absent the claim of immediate and serious danger to life, limb, or presumably national security – the party seeking the injunction, that is the Government in these kinds of cases, must show not only an arguable case, as previously, but that it is 'more likely than not' that they will succeed at final trial. This approach, assuming it is applied consistently to *Spycatcher*-type cases, should make it significantly harder for future governments to obtain gagging injunctions against the media.

It is clear from the discussion so far that the Government has a range of measures available to it to prevent publication of forms of State information, but that the measures have recently become more liberal. The **1989 Act** is a narrower measure than its predecessor and the action for breach of confidence has a narrower application due to the impact of the **HRA**. However, the narrowing down of the measures available to the State to prevent disclosure of information does not in itself mean that access to official information is available.

Information of historical interest may be obtainable via the UK **Public Records Act 1958**, as amended by the **Public Records Act 1967** and the **Freedom of Information Act 2000**.

3   This very clear exposition of the law in relation to **s 12 HRA** shows the examiner that a good knowledge of the law is present.

However, under the **1958 Act**, public records in the Public Records Office are not available for inspection until the expiration of 30 years, and longer periods can be prescribed for sensitive information. Some information can be withheld for 100 years or for ever, and there is no means of challenging such decisions. For example, at the end of 1987, a great deal of information about a fire in 1957 at the Windscale atomic power station was disclosed, although some items are still held back.[4] Thus, the **1958 Act**, even after amendment, can hardly be viewed as being equivalent to a statutory right of access to current information.

However, for the past decade, there has been a slow but progressive movement towards freedom of information legislation for the UK, culminating in the **Freedom of Information Act 2000**, which came into force in 2005. The Act has a number of important consequences. Primarily, it places a general right of access to information on a statutory basis for the first time, in **s1**. The right allows the public access to information held by a very wide range of public authorities, including local government, the NHS, schools and colleges, and the police. An Information Commissioner has been appointed who supervises the scheme and the public can contact her directly. Public authorities must, on request, indicate whether they hold information required by an individual and, if so, communicate that information to him within 20 working days.

It may be noted that the **2000 Act** is not the only freedom of information measure available, and different bodies may be affected by other measures even though they are not public authorities for the purposes of the **2000 Act**. For example, the Information Commissioner has issued a decision notice that provides that Network Rail is caught by the definition of 'public authority' under the **Environmental Information Regulations 2004**. This decision indicates that a 'public authority' under the Regulations encapsulates a different group of organisations to those caught by the **Freedom of Information Act 2000** and, unlike the Act, includes some private companies such as Network Rail, which had argued previously that as a 'private company' it was not bound by the Regulations.

Under the **2000 Act**, a number of forms of information are exempt, including that relating to security matters or which might affect national security, defence or the economy. The harm-based exemptions under the Act are similar to those indicated in the White Paper: they require the public authority to show that the release of the information requested would or would be likely to cause prejudice to the interest specified in the exemption. However, this test for harm is less restrictive than that proposed under the White Paper. Further, a number of exemptions are class-based, meaning that in order to refuse the request, the authority only has to show that the information falls into the class

---

4   References to, and actually using, practical examples such as this reference to the Windscale atomic power station, help to score high marks with examiners as a high level of understanding is needed in order to be able to use examples.

of information covered by the exemption, not that its release would cause or be likely to cause harm or prejudice.

However, the Act provides a public interest test in relation to some, but not all, of the class exemptions and almost all of the 'harm exemptions'. This requires the authority to release the information unless 'in all the circumstances of the case, the public interest in maintaining the exemption outweighs the public interest in disclosing the information'.

Section 32 provides a particularly controversial class exemption: it covers information *that is only held* by virtue of being contained in a document or record served on a public authority in proceedings, or made by a court or tribunal or party in any proceedings. The public interest test does not apply. The other major class exemption, under **s 35**, has been equally criticised. It amounts to a very broad exemption covering virtually all information relating to the formation of government policy. **Section 36** contains a harm-based exemption that covers almost exactly the same ground.

The imprecise terms used to indicate the exempted information and the introduction of class exemptions may be allowing the Government to exempt from the disclosure provisions much information that is merely embarrassing or damaging to its reputation. Some such information may also be subject to the ministerial veto, where it relates to central Government, which means that it cannot be disclosed even if it is not exempt. **Section 53** of the Act allows a minister to make such a veto. In February 2012 Dominic Grieve, the Attorney General, made a veto in relation to minutes from a Cabinet Sub-Committee discussing devolution issues. However, where the veto is not used, a right to appeal to the Information Tribunal is granted by the Act to complainants and much will depend upon future interpretations of the statute by the Commissioner and the courts. After Dominic Grieve's veto in Februay 2012 the Information Commissioner criticised the use of the veto and called for post-legislative scrutiny of this part of the Act.

It is concluded that the developments described here do suggest that a movement away from the tradition of government secrecy has been occurring over the last three decades, culminating in the **2000 Act** (which played a part in revealing abuses of expenses by MPs, in 2009). Nevertheless, the existence of class exemptions in the Act and of the ministerial veto suggest that some aspects of that tradition are reflected, ironically, in that Act.

QUESTION 9

Douglas Hurd (the then Home Secretary) called the **Official Secrets Act 1989** 'a great liberalising measure'. Do you agree with his view? How far has the **Human Rights Act** been utilised as a means of 'liberalising' aspects of the Act, and what further potential does it have to do so, if any?

How to Answer this Question

This essay clearly demands close analysis of the provisions of the Act; however, the context in which it must be placed should also be considered. The following matters should be discussed:

- ❖ brief mention of **s 2** of the **Official Secrets Act (OSA) 1911** compared with the **1989 Act**;
- ❖ categories of information covered by the **OSA 1989**;
- ❖ harm tests in different categories – lack of a harm test in **s 1(1)**;
- ❖ *R v Shayler* (2001) and the impact of the **HRA**;
- ❖ defences under the **1989 Act** – actual and potential – 'reversed' *mens rea*;
- ❖ *R v Keogh* (2007);
- ❖ other measures creating liability in respect of the disclosure of official information;
- ❖ conclusion: lack of liberalising effect; failure of the **HRA** to bring about liberalisation.

Answer Structure

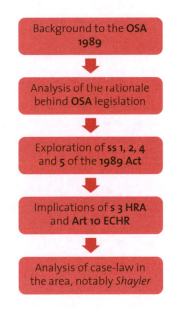

Background to the **OSA 1989**

⬇

Analysis of the rationale behind **OSA** legislation

⬇

Exploration of **ss 1, 2, 4** and **5** of the **1989 Act**

⬇

Implications of **s 3 HRA** and **Art 10 ECHR**

⬇

Analysis of case-law in the area, notably *Shayler*

ANSWER

The **OSA 1989** was brought into being largely in response to the failure of the Government to secure a conviction under **s 2** of the **OSA 1911** in *Ponting* (1985). However, it had been recognised for some time, even before the *Ponting* case, that **s 2** was becoming discredited due to its width: it criminalised the unauthorised disclosure of any official information at all.

Once the decision to reform the area of official secrecy had been made, an opportunity was created for radical change which could have included freedom of information legislation along the lines of the instruments in the US and Canada. However, it was made clear from the outset that the legislation was unconcerned with freedom of information; it did not allow the release of any official documents into the public domain. Thus, any claim that it is a liberalising measure must rest on other aspects of the Act. The aspects which are usually considered in this context include the introduction of tests for harm, the need to establish *mens rea*, the defences available and decriminalisation of the receiver of information. In all these respects, the Act differs from its predecessor. However, the extent to which these differences have brought about any real change, any real liberalisation, is open to question.[5]

This essay will argue that the **1989 Act** was not a liberalising measure in any real sense and, further, that the **HRA** is unlikely to have a significant impact on it in terms of ameliorating its more illiberal aspects, except in relation to reversed burdens.[6]

Clearly, if only to avoid bringing the criminal law into disrepute, a 'harm test' which takes into account the substance of information is to be preferred to the width of **s 2** of the **OSA 1911**, which covered all official information, however trivial. There is no test for harm at all under **s 1(1)**, which is intended to prevent members or former members of the security services disclosing anything at all about the operation of those services. All such members are under a lifelong duty to keep silent, even though their information might reveal serious abuse of power in the security service or some operational weakness. These provisions also apply to anyone who is notified that he or she is subject to the provisions of the sub-section. Equally, there is no test for harm under **s 4(3)**, which covers information obtained by or relating to the issue of a warrant under the **Interception of Communications Act 1985** or the **Security Services Act 1989**.

The harm tests under the **OSA** are further diluted in various ways. Under **s 3(1)(b)**, which covers confidential information obtained abroad, the mere fact that the information is confidential 'may' be sufficient to establish the likelihood that its disclosure would cause harm. Under **s 1(3)**, which criminalises disclosure of information relating to the security services by a Crown servant, as opposed to a member of MI5, it is not necessary to show that disclosure of the actual document in question would be likely to cause harm, merely that the document belongs to a class of documents disclosure of which would be likely to have that effect. Even in categories where it is necessary to show that the actual document in question would be likely to cause harm, such as **s 2(1)** or **s 4(1)**, the task of

....

5   Here, the answer is deconstructing the question and signposting the approach the answer is going to take in relation to the Official Secrets regime. This is an effective way to keep focus and show the examiner you know the area well.

6   Setting out references to what you are going to conclude early on, such as happens here in relation to the **1989 Act**, is a very effective way to improve your structure.

doing so is made easy in two ways: first, it is not necessary to show that any damage actually occurred; and secondly, the tests for harm themselves are very wide. Under s 2(2), for example, a disclosure of information relating to defence will be damaging if it is likely to obstruct seriously the interests of the UK abroad.

The tests for harm are not made any more stringent in instances where a non-Crown servant discloses information. Under s 5, if anyone discloses information which falls into one of the categories covered, the test for harm will be determined by reference to that category.

The Act contains no explicit public interest defence and it follows from the nature of the harm test that one cannot be implied into it; any good flowing from disclosure of the information cannot be considered, merely any harm that might be caused. However, s 3 of the HRA could be used creatively to seek to introduce such a defence, in effect, through the back door, by relying on Art 10. Whether or not this is possible in respect of categories of information covered by a harm test, it appears that it is not possible in respect of ss 1(1) and 4(1). In *Shayler* (2001), the conclusion of the House of Lords that ss 1(1) and 4(1) are not in breach of Art 10 was reached on the basis that Mr Shayler did have an avenue by which he could seek to make the disclosures in question. There were various persons to whom the disclosure could have been made, including those identified in s 12. Also, the House of Lords found a refusal of authorisation would be subject, the Crown accepted in the instant case, to judicial review. The refusal to grant authority would have to comply with Art 10 due to s 6 of the HRA; if it did not, the court in the judicial review proceedings would be expected to say so. The Lords therefore found that the interference with freedom of expression was in proportion to the legitimate aim pursued under Art 10(2) – that of protecting national security.

The Lords found that for the reasons given, the absence of a harm test or 'public interest' defence in ss 1(1) and 4(1) of the 1989 Act did not breach Art 10 of the ECHR. The decision meant that s 3 of the HRA need not be used in relation to ss 1(1) and 4(1). It is probable that the same arguments would apply if, in respect of disclosure of information falling within other categories, the defence sought to introduce a public interest defence, relying on Art 10. The problem with the House of Lords' analysis in *Shayler* is that the avenues available to members or former members of the Security Services to make disclosures are unlikely to be used. It seems highly improbable that such a member would risk the employment detriment that might be likely to arise, especially if he or she then proceeded to seek judicial review of the decision. It is argued that the right to freedom of expression – one of the central rights of the ECHR – is rendered illusory by ss 1(1) and 4(1) of the OSA in relation to allegedly unlawful activities of the Security Services – a matter of great significance in a democracy.[7]

....

7   The law in relation to the 1989 Act and its relationship with the HRA is set out clearly and ends with some excellent analysis of that law.

No express defence of prior publication is provided in the **OSA**; the only means of putting forward such an argument would arise in one of the categories in which it was necessary to prove the likelihood that harm would flow from the disclosure; the prosecution might find it hard to establish such a likelihood where there had been a great deal of prior publication. **Section 6** expressly provides that information which has already been leaked abroad can still cause harm if disclosed in the UK. The test for harm will depend on the category the information falls into. If the information fell within **s 1(3)**, the test for harm might be satisfied even where newspapers all over the world were repeating the information in question, on the basis that although no further harm could be caused by disclosure of the particular document, it nevertheless belonged to a class of documents disclosure of which was likely to cause harm. Thus, the harm tests under the Act are deceptive; the readiness with which they may be satisfied suggests that the Act is unlikely to have a liberalising impact on the publication of official information.

The **1989 Act** includes a requirement of *mens rea* only in two instances – in all the others it creates a reversed *mens rea*: the defence can attempt to prove that the defendant did not know (or have reasonable cause to know) of the nature of the information or that its disclosure would be damaging. However, the **HRA** has been utilised to ensure compatibility with **Art 6(2)**. It was found in *R v Keogh* (2007) in the Court of Appeal that *Attorney General's Reference (No 4 of 2002)* – which had relied on **s 3 HRA** and **Art 6(2)** in the context of the **Terrorism Act 2000** – extends to other offences that impose in effect a reversed burden of proof on the defendant. In *R v Keogh* the Court of Appeal had to consider the **OSA 1989 ss 2(3)** and **3(4)**; the provisions impose a reverse burden according to their natural meaning, namely, that a defendant who was charged under those provisions with making a damaging disclosure has to prove that he had no knowledge or reasonable cause to believe that the disclosure would be damaging. In other words, he has to disprove *mens rea*. It was found that the Act could operate effectively without the imposition of the reverse legal burdens, and that to accord them that meaning would be disproportionate and unjustifiable. If given their natural meaning, those provisions were, it was found, incompatible with **Art 6(2)** of the **ECHR**.

So, following the House of Lords' decision, they should be read down by applying a similar interpretation to that achieved by **s 118** of the **Terrorism Act 2000**, namely, that it was a defence for a defendant to prove a particular matter in that if he adduced evidence which was sufficient to raise an issue with respect to the matter, the court or jury should assume that the defence was satisfied unless the prosecution proved beyond reasonable doubt that it was not.

Under **ss 5** and **6**, the prosecution must prove *mens rea*, in the sense that it must be shown that the disclosure was made in the knowledge that it would be damaging. This is a step in the right direction and a clear improvement on the **1911 Act**; nevertheless, the burden of proof on the prosecution would be very easy to discharge if the information fell within **s 1(3)** or **s 3(1)(b)** due to the nature of the tests for damage included in those sections.

However, where a journalist had disclosed information falling within one of the categories in which a harm test applies, a narrow interpretation of the term 'damaging' could be adopted under s3 of the HRA, relying on Art 10, on the basis that Strasbourg has placed particular stress on the role of the press as a public watchdog. The press, it has been found, has a duty 'to impart information and ideas on matters of public interest' which the public 'has a right to receive' (*Castells v Spain* (1992)). It could be found that where the effect of the disclosure could arguably be to the public benefit in the context in question, or where the journalist had a belief that that would be the case, the burden on the prosecution to prove *mens rea* should be viewed as almost impossible to discharge.

As indicated above, *Shayler* does not suggest that there is a willingness on the part of the judiciary to ameliorate the more illiberal aspects of this Act by use of s3 of the HRA. However, where the words of the statute allow for a gateway to arguments as to the nature of the term 'damaging', it is possible that s3 could be used, as argued above, to reinterpret the term in such a way as to allow for argument as to the intention behind a disclosure to be heard.

QUESTION 10

'Over the last 25 years, there has been a significant movement towards more open government which is largely, but not wholly, attributable to decisions under the European Convention on Human Rights, whether at Strasbourg or under the Human Rights Act.'

▶ Do you agree?

How to Answer this Question

The statement makes a number of separate assertions, each of which must be evaluated.

Essentially, the following issues should be considered:

❖ movements towards openness in government in the 1980s and 1990s – the Official Secrets Act (OSA) 1989, the Security Services Act 1989, the Intelligence Services Act 1994 and the Interception of Communications Act 1985, as well as the influence of the European Convention on Human Rights (ECHR) at Strasbourg in bringing about changes in the area of official secrecy;

❖ features of the Security Services Act 1989, the Intelligence Services Act 1994 and the Regulation of Investigatory Powers Act (RIPA) 2000 – ousting of the jurisdiction of the courts; secrecy as to tribunal decisions;

❖ use of the common law as a means of preventing disclosure of information – common law contempt; breach of confidence; response of the European Court of Human Rights (ECtHR);

❖ the OSA 1989 – 'harm tests'; lack of a public interest defence;

❖   limited influence of the **ECHR** in this context at Strasbourg and under the **HRA**;
❖   the effect of the **Freedom of Information Act 2000**.

Answer Structure

> Background to legislation relevant to 'open government'
>
> ↓
>
> **Official Secrets Act 1989** and **Freedom of Information Act 2000** in particular
>
> ↓
>
> Difficulties and limitations of the various Acts
>
> ↓
>
> Mechanics of the **Official Secrets Act 1989**
>
> ↓
>
> Impact that the **HRA** and the **ECHR** has had on the **OSA** legislation
>
> ↓
>
> *Spycatcher* litigation
>
> ↓
>
> Mechanics of the **Freedom of Information Act 2000**

ANSWER

A general survey of certain recent developments might indeed suggest that a movement towards more open government has been taking place over the last 25 years. Disclosure of a range of information was decriminalised under the **Official Secrets Act (OSA) 1989**; MI6 and GCHQ were placed on a statutory basis by the **Intelligence Services Act 1994**, which also set up a parliamentary committee to oversee the work of the security and intelligence services. The **Freedom of Information Act (FoIA) 2000** (in force 2005) represented a further and very significant step in that direction. A closer look at some of these developments reveals, it will be argued, that they were not invariably imposed due to decisions of the ECtHR, although such decisions have had a significant impact in this context. It will further be argued that, in general, in any event, these changes, apart from the introduction of **FoIA**, have not had a very clear or significant liberalising impact.

The **Interception of Communications Act 1985** came into being after the decision of the ECtHR in the *Malone* (1984) case, but the decision only required the UK Government to introduce legislation to regulate the circumstances in which the power to tap could be used, rather than giving guidance as to what would be acceptable limits on the right to privacy.[8] The limits of the Act (not applying to private telephone systems, for example – see *Halford v UK* (1997)) and massive technological development led to its replacement by the **RIPA**.

The limits to open government found in the **1985 Act** are continued by the **RIPA**, and information about authorised (let alone unauthorised) phone taps remains hard to obtain. Complaints, including allegations of human rights violations, can be made only to a tribunal set up under the Act, with no possibility of scrutiny by a court. Similarly, the **Security Service Act 1989** came into being largely as a response to the finding of the ECtHR that a complaint against MI5 was admissible (*Harman and Hewitt v UK* (1989)). The **Security Service Act** places MI5 on a statutory basis, but prevents almost all effective scrutiny of its operation. Even where a member of the public has a grievance concerning its operation, it will not be possible to use a court action as a means of scrutinising such operation. Complaints, including those involving the **HRA**, can only be made to the tribunal established under **s 65** of the **RIPA**. The proceedings of this tribunal are not open and its decisions are not questionable in any court of law.

This measure was not solely due to the operation of the ECtHR. Its inception was probably also influenced by the challenge to the legality of the tapping of the phones of Campaign for Nuclear Disarmament (CND) members in *Secretary of State for the Home Department ex p Ruddock* (1987), which proved embarrassing to the Government, although it failed. In any event, these statutes are unlikely to open up the workings of internal security to greater scrutiny. They suggest a perception that no breach of the **Convention** will occur so long as a mechanism is in place that is able to consider the claims of aggrieved citizens, however ineffective that mechanism might be.

The two statutes mentioned work in tandem with the **OSA 1989**, which was not brought into being in response to pressure from Europe, but largely due to pressure from other sources. In particular, the failure of the Government to secure a conviction under **s 2** of

8   This explanation of how the *Malone* decision instigated the **1985 Act** impresses the examiner as it shows a keen awareness of the area.

the **OSA 1911** in *Ponting* (1985) probably had a significant effect.[9] It had been recognised for some time even before the *Ponting* case that **s 2** was becoming discredited due to its width. Obviously, the criminal law is brought into disrepute if liability is possible in respect of extremely trivial actions. The **1911 Act** had no test of substance and although obtaining a conviction should therefore have been relatively straightforward, the decisions in *Aitken* (1971) and *Ponting* suggested that the very width of the section was undermining its credibility.

It was made clear from the outset that the **1989 Act** was unconcerned with freedom of information. Thus, one must be cautious in viewing the **OSA 1989** as amounting to a move away from obsessive secrecy; it does not allow the release of any official documents into the public domain, although it does mean that if certain pieces of information are released, the official concerned will not face criminal sanctions. (He or she might, of course, face an action for breach of confidence as well as disciplinary proceedings.)

It is, however, fair to accept that the **1989 Act** covers much less information than its predecessor, due to its introduction of a 'harm test', which takes into account the substance of the information. Clearly, such a test is to be preferred to the width of **s 2** of the **OSA 1911**, which covered all official information, however trivial. However, there is no test for harm at all under **s 1(1)**, which prevents members or former members of the security services disclosing anything at all about the operation of those services. All such members come under a lifelong duty to keep silent, even though their information might reveal serious abuse of power in the security services or some operational weakness. These provisions also apply to anyone who is notified that he or she is subject to the provisions of the subsection. Equally, there is no test for harm under **s 4(3)**, which covers information obtained by, or relating to, the issue of a warrant under the **RIPA** or the **Intelligence Services Act 1994**.

The Act contains no explicit public interest defence, and it follows from the nature of the harm test that one cannot be implied into it: any good flowing from disclosure of the information cannot be considered; merely any harm that might be caused. This was confirmed by the House of Lords in *R v Shayler* (2002) and was said to be compatible with **Art 10** of the **ECHR**. Moreover, no express defence of prior publication is provided. Prior publication can be an issue, however, since the prosecution could find it hard to establish the appropriate type of harm where there had been a great deal of prior publication. Thus, although in likelihood it may be said that some features of the Act suggest a move towards some liberalisation of official secrecy law, it was clearly intended that this move should not be fully carried through. The doctrine of breach of confidence was largely

....

9   This reference to *Ponting* and its impact upon the law helps to provide further evidence to the examiner that you know and understand the area well.

uninfluenced domestically by **Art 10 ECHR**, pre-**HRA**. In relation to publication of the book *Spycatcher* in the USA in 1987, the House of Lords decided (relying on *American Cyanamid Co v Ethicon Ltd* (1975)) to continue the temporary injunctions against the newspapers on the basis that the Attorney General still had an arguable case for permanent injunctions (*AG v Guardian Newspapers Ltd* (1987)). The injunctions continued until, in the hearing of the permanent injunctions, the House of Lords found that it was impossible to sustain a restriction based on confidentiality when the worldwide publication of the book meant that the information it contained was clearly in the 'public domain'.[10]

When the ECtHR considered the case (*The Observer and The Guardian v UK* (1991); *The Sunday Times v UK* (1991)), it found that, given the extent of publication in the USA, the temporary injunctions, although for a legitimate purpose, were disproportionate and a violation of **Art 10**. The injunctions obtained before publication in the USA were not found to breach **Art 10**; therefore, this ruling did little to discourage use of such injunctions in many instances where a disclosure of official information is threatened – although **s 12(3) HRA** has created some liberalisation in this respect.

The *Spycatcher* cases (*AG v Newspaper Publishing plc* (1990), as approved by the House of Lords in *Times Newspapers and Anor v AG* (1991)) had confirmed the principle that once an interlocutory injunction has been obtained restraining one organ of the media from publication of allegedly confidential material, the rest of the media may be in contempt if they publish that material, even if their intention in doing so is to bring alleged iniquity to public attention. In *AG v Punch* (2003), a magazine published articles written by an ex-security services officer in breach of an injunction restraining the officer from publishing. The magazine could only have the *mens rea* for contempt if, by publication, it intended to destroy the purpose of the injunction. The Court of Appeal's view, that the purpose of such an injunction was to prevent damaging confidential material from being published, was rejected by the House of Lords, despite **Art 10** scheduled in the **HRA**, for whom the point of the injunction was to protect the interest of the court as the effective tribunal in which the issue of confidentiality should be determined. This decision makes it easier for the State to prove that the media are in contempt if they publish in breach of a temporary injunction imposed on others.

A much more significant development is the passing of the **FoIA**, which was brought fully into force in 2005. It requires public bodies to publish information and to disclose information on request. The Act is a major step forward in that, under it, access to information is now a statutory right rather than a discretionary privilege depending on the attitude of the Information Commissioner to enforcing it. There are, however, many exceptions, and the success of the Act depends on how these exceptions are interpreted.

....

10 It is important to get key technical and chronological facts of cases right, as this answer demonstrates in relation to *Spycatcher*.

A particularly worrying exception is that, under **s 53**, a government department can substitute its view for that of the Commissioner on whether the public interest does or does not require disclosure of information on a wide range of policy matters involving the department. The findings of the Tribunal in January 2009 regarding the requirement of disclosure of the Cabinet minutes relating to the decision to engage in military action in Iraq, is obviously of great significance due to the importance of the decision. With a further veto under **s 53** by Dominic Grieve in February 2012, in relation to minutes of a Cabinet Sub-Committee that was discussing devolution matters, the existence of **s 53** has called into question again the efficacy of the **FoIA**.[11]

It may be concluded that claims under the **Convention** have led to some breaking down of the tradition of secrecy in government. The failings of the **Security Services Act**, the **RIPA** and the caution of the European Court judgment in the *Spycatcher* case do not, however, support the suggestion that radical change has occurred, or can occur, by this means. This is also true in respect of freedom of information, where the ECtHR has only recently found that **Art 10** provides a right to receive information that others, including the State, wish not to provide (*Matky v Czech Republic* (2006)). British courts adopted that view in *R (Persey) v SSEFRA* (2002), in denying a legal challenge to the Government's refusal to hold a public inquiry into the foot-and-mouth epidemic. The **FoIA** was not introduced as a result of a decision at Strasbourg but rather as a response to a general pressure to come into line with most democracies on this matter. Thus, if greater openness in government has been achieved – a claim that, as indicated, is debatable – it is fair to say that the **ECHR** at Strasbourg or under the **HRA** can claim only a small part of the credit for it.

QUESTION 11

Critically evaluate developments pre- and post-**HRA** in the law of confidence and their likely impact on freedom of information and government secrecy.

How to Answer this Question

This topic might obviously appear as part of a general and wide-ranging essay or, as here, in its own right. It is concerned with the use of prior restraint under the doctrine of breach of confidence as a means of preventing publication of State information and, of course, will involve consideration of the *Spycatcher* case and then of the impact of the **HRA 1998** in this area as indicated in *AG v Times Newspapers* (2001).

Essentially, the following matters should be considered:

❖ breach of confidence – balancing public interest in disclosure of information against the interest in keeping it confidential;

---

11 This incorporation of the Dominic Grieve example illustrates an awareness of contemporary issues, which examiners give credit to.

- ❖ the nature of the public interest defence (*Lion Laboratories v Evans and Express Newspapers* (1985));
- ❖ duty of confidence can bind third parties – use of interim injunctions (*AG v Guardian Newspapers Ltd* (1987));
- ❖ essential aspects of the judgment of the European Court of Human Rights (ECtHR) on the **Art 10** issue (*The Observer and The Guardian v UK* (1991); *The Sunday Times v UK* (1991));
- ❖ the use of common law contempt in conjunction with the law of confidence;
- ❖ **s 12** of the **HRA** and **Art 10** of the **European Convention on Human Rights (ECHR)**;
- ❖ *AG v Times Newspapers* (2001);
- ❖ *AG v Punch* (2003).

Answer Structure

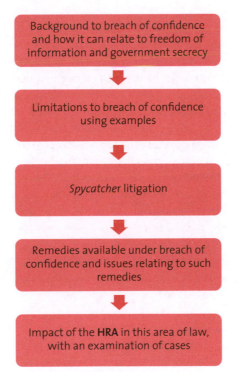

Background to breach of confidence and how it can relate to freedom of information and government secrecy

⬇

Limitations to breach of confidence using examples

⬇

Spycatcher litigation

⬇

Remedies available under breach of confidence and issues relating to such remedies

⬇

Impact of the **HRA** in this area of law, with an examination of cases

ANSWER

Breach of confidence is a civil remedy affording protection against the disclosure or use of information which is not generally known, and which has been entrusted in circumstances imposing an obligation not to disclose it without authorisation from the person who originally imparted it. This area of law developed as a means of protecting secret information belonging to individuals and organisations. However, it can also be used by the Government to prevent disclosure of sensitive information and is, in that sense, a back-up to the other measures available to the Government, including the **Official Secrets Act (OSA) 1989**.[12]

In some respects, it may be more valuable than the criminal sanction provided by the Act. It may attract less publicity than a criminal trial, it offers the possibility of quickly obtaining an interim injunction and no jury will be involved. The possibility of obtaining an interim injunction is very valuable since, in many instances, the other party (usually a newspaper) will not pursue the case to a trial of the permanent injunctions, since the secret will probably no longer be newsworthy by that time. The Government has in the past found it very useful to obtain interim injunctions to suppress information. However, with the advent of the **HRA**, limitations have been placed upon its use of this tool.

In the pre-**HRA** era, some restrictions were apparent: where the Government, as opposed to a private individual, was concerned, the courts did not merely accept that it was in the public interest that the information should be kept confidential. The Government had to show that the public interest in keeping it confidential, due to the harm its disclosure would cause, was not outweighed by the public interest in disclosure. Thus, in *AG v Jonathan Cape* (1976), when the Attorney General invoked the law of confidence to try to stop publication of Richard Crossman's memoirs, on the ground that they concerned Cabinet discussions, the Lord Chief Justice accepted that such public secrets could be restrained, but only on the basis that the balance of the public interest came down in favour of suppression. Since the discussions had taken place ten years previously, it was not possible to show that harm would flow from their disclosure; the public interest in publication therefore prevailed. The nature of the public interest defence – the interest in disclosure – was clarified in *Lion Laboratories v Evans and Express Newspapers* (1985). The Court of Appeal held that the defence extended beyond situations in which there had been serious wrongdoing by the plaintiff. Even where the plaintiff was blameless, publication would be excusable where it was possible to show a serious and legitimate interest in the revelation.[13]

The leading case in this area is the House of Lords' decision in *AG v Guardian Newspapers Ltd (No 2)* (1990), which confirmed that the *Lion Laboratories Ltd v Evans* approach to the public interest defence was the correct one, and also clarified certain other aspects of this area of the law. As will be indicated below, the findings in this case should now be

---

12 It would be easy to go off on a tangent and talk about confidence in general, but it is key, as this answer demonstrates here, for the discussion to be focussed upon the set question, which concerns freedom of information and government secrecy.

13 This is some good concise coverage of the *Lion Laboratories* case. It is important not to spend too long on cases.

considered in the light of the **HRA**. In 1985, the Attorney General commenced proceedings in Australia in an attempt to restrain publication of *Spycatcher* by Peter Wright. The book included allegations of illegal activity engaged in by MI5. In 1986, after *The Guardian* and *The Observer* published reports of the forthcoming hearing which included some *Spycatcher* material, the Attorney General obtained temporary *ex parte* injunctions preventing them from further disclosure of such material. In 1987, the book was published in the US and many copies were brought into the UK. After that point, the House of Lords decided (relying on *American Cyanamid Co v Ethicon Ltd* (1975)) to continue the injunctions against the newspapers on the basis that the Attorney General still had an arguable case for permanent injunctions since publication of the information was an irreversible step. The House of Lords' decision, which gave little weight to freedom of expression, was eventually found to be in breach of **Art 10** of the **ECHR**; the effect of that decision will be considered below.

In the trial of the permanent injunctions (*AG v Guardian (No 2)* (1988)), it was determined that no detriment to national security had been shown that could outweigh the public interest in free speech, given the publication of *Spycatcher* that had already taken place, and therefore continuation of the injunctions was not necessary. Thus, the massive publication of *Spycatcher* seems to have tipped the balance in favour of the newspapers.

In the judgment in the ECtHR on the temporary injunctions granted in the *Spycatcher* case (*The Observer and The Guardian v UK; The Sunday Times v UK*) it was found that the injunctions in force before publication of the book in the US had the aim of preventing publication of material which, according to evidence presented by the Attorney General, might have created a risk of detriment to MI5.[14] The injunctions did not prevent the papers pursuing a campaign for an inquiry into the operation of the security services and, though preventing publication for a long time – over a year – the material in question could not be classified as urgent news. Thus, the interference complained of was proportionate to the ends in view, but proportionality was not established in relation to the injunctions obtained after publication of the book in the US, since their aim was no longer to keep secret information secret; it was to attempt to preserve the reputation of MI5 and to deter others who might be tempted to follow Peter Wright's example. Thus, a breach of **Art 10** was found. It is arguable that this was a very cautious judgment. The court seems to have been readily persuaded by the Attorney General's argument that a widely framed injunction was needed in July 1986, but it is arguable that it was wider than it needed to be to prevent a risk to national security.

Further developments occurred during the *Spycatcher* saga, which allowed breach of confidence a greater potential than it previously possessed to prevent dissemination of

....

14   Good accuracy of case coverage here in relation to the injunctions. Where facts of cases can become detailed, it is important to be accurate as poor accuracy results in lower marks being awarded.

government information. While the temporary injunctions were in force, *The Independent* and two other papers published material covered by them. It was determined in the Court of Appeal (*AG v Newspaper Publishing plc* (1990)) that such publication constituted the *actus reus* of contempt. The case therefore affirmed the principle that once an interlocutory injunction has been obtained restraining one organ of the media from publication of allegedly confidential material, the rest of the media may be in contempt if they publish that material, even if their intention in doing so is to bring alleged iniquity to public attention. Such publication must be accompanied by an intention to prejudice the eventual trial of the permanent injunctions. Thus, the laws of confidence and contempt were allowed to operate together as a significant prior restraint on media freedom, and this principle was upheld by the House of Lords (*Times Newspapers and Another v AG* (1991)).

In *AG v Punch* (2003), the effect of common law contempt in this respect was reaffirmed by the House of Lords, despite the inception of the **HRA**. The Lords found that the purpose the court seeks to achieve by granting the interlocutory injunction is that, pending a decision by the court on the claims in the proceedings, the restrained acts shall not be done. Third parties are in contempt of court if they wilfully interfere with the administration of justice by thwarting the achievement of this purpose in those proceedings. It was found that this would be the case even if in the particular instance, the injunction was drawn in apparently over-wide terms.

Section 12(3) of the **HRA** provides that prior restraint on expression should not be granted except where the court considers that the claimant is more likely than not to establish at trial that publication should not be allowed (*Cream Holdings v Bannerjee* (2004)). Moreover, *ex parte* injunctions cannot be granted under **s12(2)** unless there are compelling reasons why the respondent should not be notified or the applicant has taken all reasonable steps to notify the respondent. All these requirements under the **HRA** must now be taken into account in applying the doctrine of confidence and the rule from *AG v Newspaper Publishing plc* (1990). Current developments suggest that the result is likely to be that the doctrine will undergo quite a radical change from the interpretation afforded to it in the *Spycatcher* litigation.

The case of *AG v Times Newspapers* (2001) is significant. A former MI6 officer wrote a book, *The Big Breach*, about his experiences in MI6, which *The Sunday Times* intended to serialise. There had been a small amount of publication of the material in Russia. The Attorney General sought an injunction to restrain publication.

The key issue concerned the degree of prior publication required before it could be said that the material had lost its quality of confidentiality. The two parties agreed on a formula: that the material had already been published in any other newspaper, magazine or other publication whether within or outside the jurisdiction of the court. The Attorney General, however, contended that the defendants had to demonstrate that this was the case, which meant that they had to obtain clearance from the Attorney General before publishing. The newspaper invoked **Art 10** and also relied on **s 12(4)** of the **HRA**. It was argued that the restriction proposed by the Attorney General would be disproportionate to the aim pursued and therefore could not be justified in a democratic society. The decision in *Bladet-Tromsø v Norway* (1999) was referred to, in which the court said that it is incumbent on the media to impart information and ideas concerning matters of public interest. It was found that the Attorney General had failed to demonstrate why there was a public interest in restricting publication; therefore, no injunction was granted. The requirement to seek clearance should not, it was found, be imposed: the editor had to form his own judgment as to whether the material could be said to be already in the public domain. That position was, the court found, most consonant with the requirements of **Art 10** and **s 12**.

This decision suggests that, bearing in mind the requirements of the **HRA**, an injunction is unlikely to be granted where a small amount of prior publication has already taken place. It does not, however, decide the question of publication where no prior publication has taken place, but the material is of public interest (which could clearly have been said of the Wright material). Following *Bladet-Tromsø v Norway*, it is suggested that an injunction should not be granted where such material is likely, imminently, to come into the public domain, a position consistent with the demands of **s 12(4)**, which refers to such a likelihood. Even where this cannot be said to be the case, it would be consonant with the requirements of **Art 10** and **s 12** to refuse to grant an injunction on the basis of the duty of newspapers to report on such material. The burden would be placed on the State to seek to establish that a countervailing pressing social need was present and that the injunction did not go further than necessary in order to serve the end in view. Thus, although breach of confidence remains a fairly important weapon in the Government's armoury, it is likely to be of more limited effect in the future than seemed probable at the time of the *Spycatcher* litigation. Nevertheless, once an injunction has been granted, it is clear, from *AG v Punch*, that it will – indirectly – affect all of the media.[15]

QUESTION 12

'The **Freedom of Information Act 2000** is a grave disappointment to those who are genuinely committed to the principle of freedom of information.'

▶ **Do you agree?**

How to Answer this Question

This is a very specific essay question that requires a detailed and critical evaluation of the **2000 Act**. It should not be attempted unless the student has quite detailed knowledge

---

15   The question ends with some excellent analysis of the law in relation to freedom of information and government secrecy.

(with references to sections) of this complex Act. In a form similar to that taken here, this question is highly likely to appear on exam papers at the present time.

Essentially, the following matters should be discussed:

- ❖ the general right of access to information under the Act;
- ❖ the exemptions under the Act; implications of the tests for exemptions;
- ❖ the use of and nature of the harm tests;
- ❖ the role of the Information Commissioner and aspects of his/her early work;
- ❖ the enforcement mechanisms in general;
- ❖ concluding evaluation of the Act.

Answer Structure

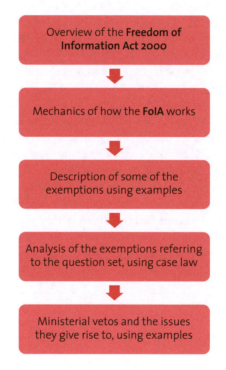

Overview of the **Freedom of Information Act 2000**

Mechanics of how the **FoIA** works

Description of some of the exemptions using examples

Analysis of the exemptions referring to the question set, using case law

Ministerial vetos and the issues they give rise to, using examples

ANSWER

The **Freedom of Information Act 2000** provides a general right of access to the information held by a range of public bodies. The Act covers 'public authorities' and **s 3** sets out the various ways in which a body can be a public authority. Under **s 5**, private organisations may be designated as public authorities insofar as they carry out statutory functions, as may the privatised utilities and private bodies working on contracted-out functions.

Section 1(1) provides that any person making a request for information under the **2000 Act** to a public authority is entitled to be informed of whether it holds information of the description specified in the request, and if it holds the information it must communicate it. From 2005 onwards, when the Act came into force, individuals were able to gain access to information relating to them personally, such as tax and medical records. They also now have the right to obtain information on other, general matters from the departments and bodies covered. As indicated, the Act begins with an apparently broad and generous statement of the rights it confers; it is also generous in its coverage. However, the rights are subject to a wide range of exceptions and exemptions.

The harm-based exemptions under the Act are similar to those indicated in the White Paper: they require the public authority to show that the release of the information requested would (or would be likely to) cause prejudice to the interest specified in the exemption. However, this test for harm is of course less restrictive than that proposed under the White Paper. Further, a number of exemptions are class-based, meaning that in order to refuse the request, the authority only has to show that the information falls into the class of information covered by the exemption, not that its release would cause or be likely to cause harm or prejudice.[16]

However, the Act provides a public interest test in relation to some, but not all, of the class exemptions, and almost all of the 'harm exemptions'. The public authority, having decided that the information is *prima facie* exempt (either because the information falls into the requisite class exemption or because the relevant harm test is satisfied, as the case may be), must still then go on to consider whether it should be released under the public interest test set out in **s 2**. This requires the authority to release the information unless 'in all the circumstances of the case, the public interest in maintaining the exemption outweighs the public interest in disclosing the information'.

The discussion in this essay cannot cover all of the freedom of information class exemptions, but will consider some of the more controversial ones. **Section 23(1)** covers information supplied by, or which relates to, the intelligence and security services. The bodies mentioned in this exemption are not themselves covered by the Act at all. This exemption therefore applies to information that is held by *another public authority*, but which has been supplied by one of these bodies. Because it is a class exemption, it applies to information that has no conceivable security implications, such as evidence of a massive overspend on MI5 or MI6's headquarters. Bearing in mind the complete exclusion of the security and intelligence services from the Act, the use of this class exemption, unaccompanied by a harm test and not subject to the public interest test, means that sensitive matters of great political

---

16 Sometimes large amounts of description are needed, such as happens here in relation to the FOIA. Where this happens be as concise as possible, as this answer demonstrates.

significance will remain undisclosed, even if their disclosure would ultimately benefit those services or national security. **Section 32** covers information *that is only held* by virtue of being contained in a document or record served on a public authority in proceedings, or made by a court or tribunal or party in any proceedings, or contained in a document lodged with or created by a person conducting an inquiry or arbitration, for the purposes of the inquiry or arbitration. The public interest test does not apply.

Certain class exemptions are subject to the public interest test. In relation to these exemptions, in practice, while the Information Commissioner always has the last word on whether the information falls into the class in question, he/she will not always be able to enforce a finding that it should nevertheless be released on public interest grounds if the information is held by certain governmental bodies, since the ministerial veto may be used (see below). **Section 30(1)** provides a sweeping exemption, covering all information, whenever obtained, which relates to investigations that may lead to criminal proceedings. It represents a specific rejection of the recommendation of the Macpherson Report that there should be no class exemption for information relating to police investigations. It overlaps with the law enforcement exemption of **s 31**, which does include a harm test. There are certain aspects of information relating to investigations that would appear to require disclosure in order to be in accord with the principle of openness enshrined in the Act. For example, a citizen might suspect that his telephone had been tapped without authorisation or that he had been unlawfully placed under surveillance by other means.[17] Under the Act, no satisfactory method of discovering information relating to such a possibility will exist. It is therefore unfortunate that telephone tapping and electronic surveillance were not subjected to a substantial harm or even a simple harm test.

The **s 30(1)** exemption extends beyond protecting the police and the Crown Prosecution Service (CPS). Other bodies are also protected: it covers all information obtained by safety agencies investigating accidents. It covers routine inspections as well as specific investigations, since both can lead to criminal prosecution. It is particularly hard to understand the need for such a sweeping class exemption when **s 31** specifically exempts information that could prejudice the prevention or detection of crime, or legal proceedings brought by a public authority arising from various forms of investigation. That exemption ensures that no information is released that could damage law enforcement and crime detection.

The other major class exemption in this category, under **s 35**, has been equally criticised. It amounts to a very broad exemption covering virtually all information relating to the formation of government policy. **Section 36** contains a harm-based exemption that covers almost exactly the same ground. Since it covers all information the release of

---

17   Good use of an example in relation to telephone tapping to help illustrate how the law works.

which might cause damage to the working of government – and is framed in very broad terms – it appears to be unnecessary to have a sweeping class exemption covering the same ground. Moreover, this exemption is not restricted to Civil Service advice; it also covers the background information used in preparing policy, including the underlying facts and their analysis.

While information in this category under the Act is subject to a public interest test, if the Commissioner orders disclosure on public interest grounds, the ministerial veto is usually available to override her. However, the Commissioner has issued important guidance on this provision that all but changes it into a 'harm-based' test. There must be some clear, specific and credible evidence that the formulation or development of policy would be materially altered for the worse by the threat of disclosure under the Act.

The Information Commissioner has issued a series of guidance notes on the interpretation and operation of the Act, one of which deals with the 'prejudice' test. As to the meaning of prejudice, the Commissioner indicates that the term is to be interpreted, in general terms as meaning that the prejudice need not be substantial, but the Commissioner expects that it be more than trivial. The phrase 'likely to prejudice' has been considered by the courts in the case of *R (on the application of Alan Lord) v The Secretary of State for the Home Department* (2003). Although this case concerns the **Data Protection Act 1998**, the Commissioner regards this interpretation as persuasive. Following this judgment the probability of prejudice occurring need not be 'more likely than not', but there should certainly be substantially more than a remote possibility.

The enforcement review mechanism under the Act is clearly crucial, but it is also open to criticism in certain key respects. The rights granted under the Act are enforceable by the Data Protection Commissioner, now known as the Information Commissioner. **Section 50** provides that any person can apply to the Commissioner for a decision as to whether a request for information made by the complainant to a public authority has been dealt with in accordance with the Act. In response, the Commissioner has the power to serve a 'decision notice' on the authority, stating what it must do to satisfy the Act. The Commissioner may ultimately force a recalcitrant authority to act by serving upon it an 'enforcement notice' (**s 52(1)**) requiring it to take the steps specified in the notice. If a public authority fails to comply with a decision, enforcement or information notice, the Commissioner can notify the High Court, which (**s 52(2)**) can deal with the authority as if it had committed a contempt of court. The Commissioner's decisions are themselves subject to appeal to the Information Tribunal, and this power of appeal is exercisable upon the broadest possible grounds. The Act provides that either party may appeal to the Tribunal against a decision notice and a public authority against an enforcement or information notice (**s 57(2)** and **(3)**) either on the basis that the notice is 'not in accordance with the law', or 'to the extent that the notice involved an exercise of discretion by the Commissioner, that he ought to have exercised his discretion differently' (**s 58(1)**). The Tribunal is also empowered to review any finding of fact on which the notice was based.

There is a further appeal from the Tribunal to the High Court, but on a 'point of law' only (**s 59**). The **Convention** rights under the **Human Rights Act 1998** could be invoked at this point.

Enforcement can be affected by the ministerial veto, which is another highly controversial aspect of the Act. The veto can be exercised if two conditions are satisfied under **s 53(1)**: first, the notice that the veto will operate to quash must have been served on a Government department, the Welsh Assembly or 'any public authority designated for the purposes of this section by an order made by the Secretary of State'; second, the notice must order the release of information that is *prima facie* exempt but which the Commissioner has decided should nevertheless be released under the public interest test in **s 2**. Such a veto clearly dilutes the basic freedom of information principle that a body independent from Government should enforce the rights to information.

In January 2009 the Information Tribunal decided that disclosure was required under the Act of the Cabinet minutes relating to the decision to engage in military action in Iraq. Since information of this nature is covered by an exemption under **s 35** which is subject to a public interest test, the Tribunal had to engage in a careful balancing exercise, weighing up the public interest in disclosure against the interest in maintaining confidentiality. The Tribunal found that this was an exceptional case due to the strong public interest in knowing what was said as Ministers discussed the decision to approve the invasion. But once the Tribunal had decided in the 2009 Iraq War Cabinet minutes decision in favour of disclosure, however, the Ministerial veto was used by Jack Straw, the Justice Secretary, to override the decision – the first time the veto had been used. The veto was also used by the Attorney General, Dominic Grieve, in February 2012. The Information Commissioner had given a notice requiring disclosure of Cabinet Sub-Committee meeting minutes that discussed devolution matters. This decision notice was subsequently vetoed by the Attorney General.[18]

In conclusion, it is suggested that the Act is indeed disappointing. It creates so many restrictions on the basic right of access that, depending upon its interpretation, much information of any conceivable interest can still be withheld. Nevertheless, the Act does represent a turning point in British democracy since, for the first time in its history, the decision to release many classes of information has been removed from Government and from other public authorities and placed in the hands of an independent agency, the Information Commissioner. Most importantly, for the first time, a statutory 'right' to information, enforceable if necessary through the courts, has been established.

---

18   Good use of the Jack Straw and Dominic Grieve examples to illustrate how the law works.

Aim Higher ★

The issue of exemptions could be considered further and it could be pointed out that the Act, through amendments to the **Public Records Act 1958**, provides that some of the exemptions will cease to apply after a certain number of years, although these limitations are hardly generous.

Common Pitfalls ✗

Students sometimes fail to discuss specific sections of the Act and make the discussion too general; it is essential to focus closely on specific exceptions where the information can be withheld.

Freedom of Assembly and Association

3

INTRODUCTION

Freedom of assembly is a subject which almost invariably appears on examination papers in civil liberties and human rights courses, often, but not always, in the form of a problem question. The concern in such questions is with the conflict between the need on the one hand to maintain public order and, on the other, to protect freedom of assembly. Whether problem questions or essays are set, the concern in either case will be with those provisions of the criminal law most applicable in the context of demonstrations, marches or meetings. The common law power to prevent a breach of the peace is still extensively used. Students should be aware of recent decisions on this power. The **Public Order Act 1986** is still the most significant statute, but it is also particularly important to bear in mind the public order provisions of the **Criminal Justice and Public Order Act 1994**. The **Serious and Organised Crime Act 2005 ss 132–138** could be mentioned in a general question about freedom of assembly or in a specific question relating to demonstrations in the vicinity of Parliament. The **Criminal Justice and Police Act 2001** could be mentioned in relation to harassing behaviour directed at persons in dwellings. The **Racial and Religious Hatred Act 2006** adds **Part 3A** to the **Public Order Act**, and would be relevant if issues of hate speech arise in a question. The relevance of any particular provision obviously depends on the wording of the question; there are a very large number of public order provisions and questions are unlikely to cover all of them. Police powers (covered in Chapter 5), may also be relevant. If freedom of association features on the course, it tends to be considered in an essay question which also covers freedom of assembly, but it sometimes arises as an independent essay topic.

Problem questions sometimes call on the student to discuss *any* issues which may arise, as opposed to considering criminal liability only, in which case any question of tortious liability incurred by members of an assembly or by police officers may arise, as well as questions of criminal liability. The possibility of judicial review of police decisions may also occur.

At the present time, the **Human Rights Act 1998** is of course especially important and is relevant in all questions on public protest and assembly. Examiners will expect some discussion of its relevance and impact as found in the post-**HRA** cases. **Articles 10** and **11** of the **European Convention on Human Rights**, which provide guarantees of freedom of expression and of association and peaceful assembly respectively, were received into UK law once the **Human Rights Act 1998** came fully into force in 2000. (Note that **Art 10** protects 'expression', not merely 'speech', thus covering many forms of expressive activity, including forms of public protest.) Therefore, **Arts 10** and **11** and other **Convention** articles relevant in this area are directly applicable in UK courts, and are taken into account in interpreting and applying common law and statutory provisions affecting public protest. **Section 3(1)** of the **HRA** requires: 'So far as it is possible to do so, primary and subordinate legislation must be read and given effect in a way which is compatible with the **Convention** rights.' **Section 3(2)(b)** reads: 'this section does not affect the validity, continuing operation or enforcement of any incompatible primary legislation'. **Section 3(1)** goes well beyond the pre-**HRA** obligation to resolve ambiguity in statutes by reference to the **Convention**. All statutes affecting freedom of assembly and public protest therefore have to be interpreted so as to be in harmony with the **Convention**, if that is at all possible.

Under **s 6**, **Convention** guarantees are binding only against public authorities; these are defined as bodies which have a partly public function. In the context of public protest, this will normally mean that if the police, local authorities or other public bodies use powers deriving from any legal source in order to prevent or limit peaceful public protest, the protesters can bring an action against them under **s 7(1)(a)** of the **HRA** relying on **Art 11**, probably combined with **Art 10**. Under **s 7(1)(b)**, if the protesters are prosecuted or sued, they can rely on those Arts and can seek reinterpretation of the legal provision involved under **s 3 HRA**. Depending on the interpretation afforded to those Arts, including the exceptions to them, the protesters might be successful unless a statutory provision absolutely unambiguously supported the limitation or banning of the protest. Where a statute limiting/affecting public protest is applied, the court is likely to rely on **ss 3** and **6** of the **HRA**; where a common law provision creating such a limitation is relevant, the court will rely on **s 6** alone. (For further discussion, see Chapter 9.)

Policing protests have continued to be in the news throughout 2011 and 2012. In particular, the police tactic of 'kettling' and detaining protestors in cordons has come under intense scrutiny in domestic courts (*R on the app of Hannah McClure and Joshua Moos) v The Commissioner of Police of the Metropolis* (2012)) and in Strasbourg (*Austin v UK* (2012)). The police tactic of kettling has been ruled lawful by the Court of Appeal and holding protestors and bystanders in a cordon for several hours to prevent and deal with a breach of the peace raises no **Article 5** issues according to the House of Lords (*Austin v Commissioner of Police of the Metropolis* (2009)) and Strasbourg (*Austin v UK* (2012)). Whilst the questions in this chapter do not address these issues directly students should familiarise themselves with them as they may crop up in exams in the future.

Checklist ✔

Students should have general knowledge of the proscription provisions of the Terrorism Act 2000, as amended, the background to the Public Order Act 1986, as amended, and the public order provisions of the Criminal Justice and Public Order Act 1994 and – in relation to questions relating to demonstrations in the vicinity of Parliament or general questions about the current range of public order provisions – of the Serious and Organised Crime Act 2005; in particular, they should be familiar with the following areas:

- the freedom of assembly, association and public protest jurisprudence under **Arts 10** and **11** of the **European Convention on Human Rights**;

- provisions affecting association under the **Terrorism Act 2000**;

- **s 2** of the **Public Order Act 1936**;

- the **Human Rights Act 1998**, especially **ss 3** and **6**;

- the notice requirements under **s 11** of the **Public Order Act (POA) 1986**;

- the conditions which can be imposed under **ss 12** and **14** of the **POA 1986**, as amended, on processions and assemblies;

- the banning power under **ss 13** and **14A** of the **POA 1986**;

- liability under **ss 1, 2, 3, 4, 4A** and **5** of the **POA 1986**;

- liability for assault on, or obstruction of, a police officer under **s 89** of the **Police Act 1996**;

- the common law power to prevent a breach of the peace; the House of Lords' decision in *Laporte* (2006); the House of Lords' decision in *Austin v Commissioner of Police of the Metropolis* (2009); Strasbourg's decision in *Austin v UK* (2012);

- public nuisance;

- the obstruction of the highway under **s 137** of the **Highways Act 1980**;

- the public order provisions of **Part V** and **s 154** of the **Criminal Justice and Public Order Act 1994**;

- **ss 132–138** of the **Serious and Organised Crime Act 2005** (only relevant if a question relates to demonstrations in the vicinity of Parliament);

- the **Criminal Justice and Police Act 2001** (only relevant in relation to harassing behaviour directed at persons in dwellings);

- the **Racial and Religious Hatred Act 2006** (only relevant if a question mentions hate speech).

QUESTION 13

How far does UK law afford recognition to freedom of association?

How to Answer this Question

A fairly common and quite straightforward essay question. It requires a sound knowledge of the key provisions in the area and of the influence of Art 11 of the European Convention on Human Rights (ECHR).

Essentially, the following matters should be considered:

- ❖ lack of legal recognition of freedom of association;
- ❖ s 2 of the POA 1936;
- ❖ Pt II of the Terrorism Act 2000;
- ❖ *AG's Reference (No 4 of 2002)*;
- ❖ Art 11 of the ECHR;
- ❖ *Council of Civil Service Unions v Minister for the Civil Service* (1984).

Answer Structure

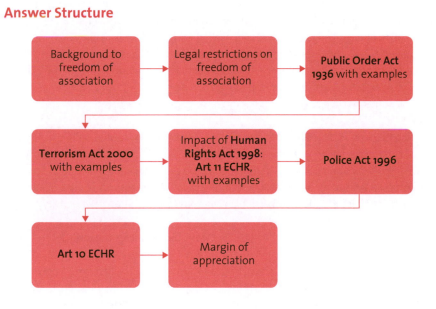

Background to freedom of association → Legal restrictions on freedom of association → Public Order Act 1936 with examples

Terrorism Act 2000 with examples ← Impact of Human Rights Act 1998: Art 11 ECHR, with examples → Police Act 1996

Art 10 ECHR → Margin of appreciation

ANSWER

In general, there are no restrictions under UK law on the freedom to join or form groups which do not constitute conspiracies, although, equally, there is little likelihood of legal redress if a person is excluded from a group or prevented from joining one. However, in two areas, freedom of association is subject to constraints.

A number of specific statutory provisions place limits on the freedom to join or support groups associated with the use of violence for political ends. The most general restriction arises under **s 2** of the **Public Order Act 1936**, which prohibits the formation of military or quasi-military organisations. Few prosecutions have been brought under this provision. The last successful one was in *Jordan and Tyndall* (1963). The defendants were both members of a fascist group called Spearhead. They engaged in various activities, which included practising foot drill and storing sodium chloride, with the probable aim of using it to make bombs.

Under **s 2(1)(a)**, a group organised, trained or equipped in order to allow it to usurp the function of the army or police would fall within this prohibition against quasi-military groups, thus possibly catching vigilante groups, such as the Guardian Angels (a group organised with the object of preventing crime on underground railways).

By far the most important restrictions on political association relate to the proscription powers in **Pt II** of the **Terrorism Act 2000**, as amended in 2006 (extending powers originally found in the **Prevention of Terrorism Act 1989**). The Secretary of State has a power to proscribe groups that he or she identifies as being 'concerned in terrorism'. This is a wide power. 'Concerned in' is a loose phrase: an organisation need not engage in terrorism itself; it is enough if it promotes or encourages it. Also, the term 'terrorism' is widely defined. It involves intimidating threats or actions aimed at political, religious or ideological ends and, though the types of threat include the use of serious violence against persons, they can also include non-violent means such as computer hacking.

Proscribed groups are listed in **Sched 2** to the Act. Proscription was at one time largely limited to paramilitary groups connected to the politics of Northern Ireland, but the list is now dominated by international terrorist groups including Al-Qaeda.[1] **Part II** of the **2000 Act** then goes on to create a range of offences defined in respect of proscribed organisations; these include membership and various forms of supportive activity.

The decision to proscribe is subject to judicial review, but only once the remedy considered below has been exhausted (*R (Kurdistan Workers Party) v Secretary of State for the Home Department* (2002)). The **2000 Act** introduced for the first time a right of appeal against the Secretary of State's refusal to 'deproscribe' an organisation. Under **s 5** of the Act, appeals go to a specially constituted Proscribed Organisations Appeal Commission (POAC) and from thence on a point of law to the Court of Appeal. There is therefore now some judicial control over this area, in which the courts have in the past shown reluctance to become involved. Control over the very broad proscription power was exercised in *R (Home Secretary) v Lord Alton of Liverpool* (2008), in which the Court of

---

1   The examiner will be impressed with this background knowledge of proscription.

Appeal found that an organisation that is taking no step to acquire the capacity to carry out terrorist acts cannot be said to be concerned in terrorism merely because its leaders have a contingent intention to resort to terrorism in future.

Under the **HRA**, decisions to proscribe and not to de-proscribe an organisation are subject to **Art 11** of the **ECHR** in **Sched 1**. The POAC, for instance, needs to take this provision, along with all the other scheduled articles, into account. A ban is an interference with the freedom in **Art 11(1)** and so the issue is whether the ban can be upheld under the provisions of **Art 11(2)**. The interests of national security, the prevention of crime and protecting the rights of others are purposes that such a ban is likely to serve. There may be issues about whether the width of the definition of 'terrorism' allows the proscription provisions in the Act to meet the 'prescribed by law' test in **Art 11(2)**; though, in line with *Brogan v UK* (1989),[2] the Court of Human Rights may find that the test is satisfied in so far as, in any particular case, terrorism is used to describe activities which can be identified with some precision and which are offences.

The key question may relate to the proportionality of any ban – broadly speaking, whether it can be said to be necessary in the sense of serving a pressing social need in a way which minimises the consequential impact on individual rights. Cases involving both freedom of association and of expression (**Art 10**) show the Court upholding these freedoms most strongly in the context of political speech. *United Communist Party of Turkey v Turkey* (1998) is an example of a case in which the Court stressed the importance of political pluralism, freedom of political association and expression, in an effective democracy. Such issues should be taken into account by the POAC as it determines the proportionality of any refusal to de-proscribe.

Under **s 11(1)** of the **Terrorism Act 2000**, it is an offence to belong to a proscribed organisation, requiring the accused to disprove involvement in the organisation at the time in question. In *AG's Reference (No 4 of 2002)*, Lord Bingham, giving the opinion of the House, found that a person who had not engaged in any blameworthy conduct could come within **s 11(1)** and that the presumption of innocence was infringed by requiring him or her to disprove involvement in the organisation at the time in question. He said that there was a real risk that a person who was innocent of any blameworthy or properly criminal conduct, but who was unable to establish a defence under **s 11(2)**, might fall within **s 11(1)**, thereby resulting in a clear breach of the presumption of innocence and an unfair conviction. He found that, bearing in mind the difficulties a defendant would have in proving the matters contained in **s 11(2)**, and the serious consequences for the defendant in failing to do so, the imposition of a legal burden upon the defendant was not a proportionate and justifiable legislative response to the threat of terrorism. Further, it was found that while security considerations always carried weight, they did not

2   This use of *Brogan* demonstrates a good way of adding in, and using, authority in your answer.

absolve Member States from their duty to ensure that basic standards of fairness were observed; and that since **s 11(2)** impermissibly infringed the presumption of innocence, it was appropriate, pursuant to **s 3** of the **1998 Act**, to read down **s 11(2)** so as to impose on the defendant an evidential burden only, even though that was not Parliament's intention when enacting the subsection.

Thus the Lords found that **s 11(2)** imposes an evidential burden only. A majority of the House of Lords relied on **s 3** to read the word 'prove' as though it meant 'adduce sufficient evidence to raise an issue in the case'. Thus the Lords ameliorated the difficulty facing defendants in proving their innocence in relation to **s 11** and created a compatibility with **Art 6(2)** that was not previously present.[3] The decision has implications for a number of the offences in the **Terrorism Act 2000** and **2006**, as discussed below.

But it is not a defence to prove that the defendant did not know that the organisation was proscribed or that it was engaged in activities covered by **s 1(1)** and **3** of the Act. This was reaffirmed in *R v Hundal (Avtar Singh)* (2004) and *R v Dhaliwal (Kesar Singh)* (2004).

Under **s 13** of the **Terrorism Act 2000**, it is an offence to wear any item which arouses a reasonable apprehension that a person is a member or supporter of a proscribed organisation. This provision is obviously aimed at preventing such organisations arousing public support. A previous version of this offence was invoked in *DPP v Whelan* (1975) against leaders of a provisional Sinn Fein protest march against internment in Northern Ireland, all of whom wore black berets, while some wore dark glasses, dark clothing and carried Irish flags. It was found that, first, something must be 'worn' as apparel and, secondly, that it must be a uniform. Something might amount to a uniform if it was worn by a number of persons in order to signify their association with each other or it was commonly used by a certain organisation. By this means, the third requirement that the uniform shall signal the wearer's association with a particular political organisation can also be satisfied. Alternatively, it may be satisfied by consideration of the occasion on which the uniform was worn without the need to refer to the past history of the organisation. The justification for retention of these provisions is doubtful as they clearly overlap with those under **s 1** of the **POA 1936**.

On the issue of whether an employee may join the union of his choice, the ECtHR has again emphasised that States have a wide margin of appreciation over the practices that are permitted, so long as the essence of the right to freedom of association is preserved and some element of real choice is maintained for the applicant. So long as there is no stark choice between continuing employment or union membership, detrimental arrangements, such as requiring a person to work at a different depot,

3   This analysis of how the **HRA** has impacted the area demonstrates good understanding of how the law works.

which are consequences of the applicant's choice of union, are unlikely to violate **Art 11** (see *Sibson v UK* (1993)).

The ECtHR has emphasised the wide margin of appreciation enjoyed by States over the regulation of union membership given the basic right of freedom of association (see *Gustafsson v Sweden* (1996) and *AB Kurt Kellermann v Sweden* (2003)).[4]

Certain bodies, such as the army under Queen's Regulations, the police under **s 64** of the **Police Act 1996**, and certain public officials, have traditionally been debarred from union membership, but this group was enlarged when civil servants working at GCHQ were de-unionised. In the GCHQ case (*Council of Civil Service Unions v Minister for the Civil Service* (1984)), the House of Lords held that previous practice had created a legitimate expectation of prior consultation before altering the terms of service. However, they refused a remedy, on the grounds that the Government had acted in the interests of national security and this outweighed the duty to act fairly. The decision was challenged at Strasbourg as a breach of **Arts 11** and **13**. However, the Commission of Human Rights found against the union primarily on the basis of the second sentence of **Art 11(2)**, which permits 'lawful restrictions on the exercise of freedom of association by members of the administration of the State'.

Article 11 has been similarly unhelpful to the thousands of civil servants, local government officers, police officers and other officials who are banned by their terms of employment or by statute from various forms of political activity, mainly taking an active role in political parties or becoming a member of legislative assemblies and local councils. Such restrictions on freedom of association and political freedom are said to be justified in order to maintain the impartiality of the public service and the proper functioning in the public interest of elected legislative assemblies. They have been widely criticised as wide-ranging and disproportionate restrictions on political freedom, which include far too many officials than is necessary. In *Ahmed v UK* (1999), however, the ECtHR accepted the legitimacy and proportionality of the statutory ban imposed on certain types of local government officers and found there was no violation of **Art 11**.

In conclusion, it is clear that the extent to which the UK 'affords recognition' to freedom of association has been subject to major change. Most importantly, as we have seen, the courts and other relevant public bodies must now approach the matter in terms of the rights to freedom of association and expression found in **Arts 10** and **11** of **Sched 1** to the **HRA 1998**. Prior to the Act, in a case such as *McEldowney v Forde* (1971), the basic question was whether the minister, in banning the Republican Clubs, had adopted a policy which was within the range of actions that were reasonably available to him. Under the Act, where there has been a restriction of such a freedom, there is now a clear burden on

---

4   The examiner will give credit to this awareness of wider contextual issues, such as the role the margin of appreciation has played in this area.

the State to satisfy the court that the restriction is justified in terms of it having a proper legal basis, being for a legitimate purpose and, on its individual facts, being a proportionate restriction. This should mean that the judicial (and quasi-judicial, applying such a term to the POAC) scrutiny should be much more intense and more capable of being grounded in the independent, rights-aware judgment of the court than before. This applies to the trade union issues as much as to the anti-terrorism issues. Regarding the latter, however, there is evidence (for example, in the detention without trial case, *A v Secretary of State for the Home Department* (2002)) that the courts are showing considerable deference to the State on the question of the extent of a threat to national security and this may, perhaps, show itself in proscription cases too. Similarly, the trade union cases mentioned and also political restriction cases such as *Ahmed v UK* (1999) demonstrate that, compatibly with the ECHR, States enjoy a wide margin of appreciation in respect of freedom of association.

QUESTION 14

A demonstration is taking place in Outfield city-centre. Its residents are demonstrating against proposals for a high-speed rail-line to be introduced to the city. Harriet and James and about 20 of their friends are taking place in the demonstration as they believe building the new train line will significantly harm much of the countryside next to Outfield. They hold placards and banners that read *'Say No To High Speed Rail!'*

Harvey and Darcey and about 15 of their friends would like to see the new rail-line introduced to the city as they regularly commute and it would reduce their travelling time. They also have placards and banners and theirs say *'High Speed Rail For Outfield!'*

Harriet and her friends notice Harvey and his group of friends and they take a disliking to their messages. They approach Harvey's group and start shouting at them telling them they are 'a bunch of yuppies' and that they should 'move out of Outfield and get lost'. Harvey and Darcey laugh in the faces of Harriet and James and tell them to 'grow up and see the bigger picture'.

Harriet and James were incensed by this and they lunge at Harvey and Darcey and try to hit them with their placards. A scuffle then breaks out between the four of them.

This really angers Harriet's friends and they start to throw stones and other items at Harvey's friends. This angers Harvey and his friends in turn and they grab Harriet's group's placards and banners and rip them up. A scuffle then breaks out between the two large groups and they start fighting.

Some of the other demonstrators are scared by what is happening so they notify the police who were waiting nearby.

▶ **Comment upon any public order statutory offences that may be relevant to the above scenario.**

How to Answer this Question

This is a classic style problem question relating to public order offences. Whilst some questions can raise numerous issues that need to be identified and covered, some questions, like this one, are more specific and focussed. Questions like this, which are more focussed, therefore require more depth in the answer than questions which cover many issues. The particular focus of this question are the serious offences of riot and violent disorder. With numerous instances in contemporary times of demonstrations becoming violent, these offences are particularly relevant at this time.

The key areas that need to be discussed in the answer are:

- ❖ public order offences of riot (**s1 POA 1986**) and its various constituent elements;
- ❖ public order offence of violent disorder (**s2 POA 1986**) and its various constituent elements.

Applying the Law

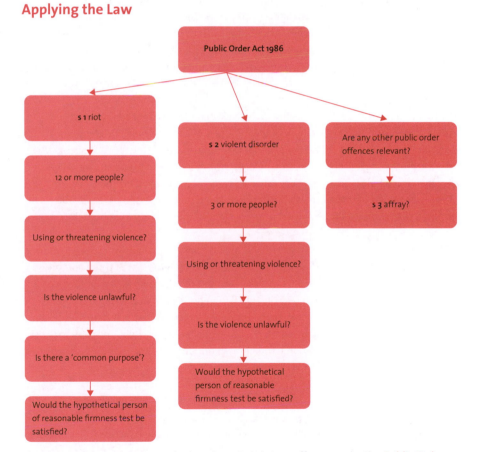

*This diagram shows how to apply the relevant statutory offences under the **Public Order Act 1986** to the given scenario.*

ANSWER

The given scenario raises some public order offence issues. The question specifically asks for comment upon statutory offences and the relevant public order statutory offences are set out in the **Public Order Act 1986 (POA)**. **Sections 1–5** of the **POA** contain public order offences. Some of these offences, such as riot (**s 1 POA**) have their roots in very old common law offences which were first put on a statutory footing by the **Public Order Act 1936**, which in turn was largely replaced by the **POA** (although some provisions of the **1936 Act** still remain in place).[5]

Harriet and her friends and Harvey and his friends are all present at a demonstration and they have placards and banners that contain non-contentious phrases. There are therefore no public order issues raised by these facts. It is important to remember that courtesy of the **Human Rights Act 1998** (**HRA**) individuals have positive rights to freedom of association and assembly and freedom of expression as set out in **Arts 10** and **11** of the **European Convention on Human Rights** respectively. The police, as a public authority, are under a positive legal duty, courtesy of **s 6** of the **HRA** to make sure they do not act incompatibly with people's **Convention** rights. The impact of this is that the police must not act in such a way as to impede people's **Convention** rights without such actions being justified.

The first issue that needs to be dealt with is the initial incident involving Harriet, James, Harvey and Darcey. **Section 2** of the **POA** sets out the offence of violent disorder.[6] According to **s 2(1)** violent disorder takes place where three or more people who are present together use or threaten unlawful violence and their conduct taken together as a whole is such as would cause a person of reasonable firmness present at the scene to fear for their safety. **Section 2(3)** states that no person of reasonable firmness needs to actually be present at the scene though; this is a hypothetical person.

As there are four people involved at this stage, the first requirement of three or more people who are present together is satisfied. The next requirement is that unlawful violence must be used or threatened. **Section 8 POA** defines what is mean by 'violence'. It says that it includes violent conduct towards people. When Harriet and James lunge at Harvey and Darcey and try and hit them with their placards, this will be enough to satisfy the requirement of violence. A scuffle then breaks out between the four of them which is further evidence of violence.[7]

---

5   This brief background to the Public Order Acts helps to provide some context.
6   When you have lots of detail to get through, get straight to the point, as this passage does in relation to violent disorder.
7   This application of the law about what is 'violence' to the given facts is concise and accurate, which is what you want to try and achieve with your application of the law.

Another element is that the violence must be unlawful. Whilst this may appear strange: violence can be lawful, for example if it used in self-defence. Harriet and James instigate the attack upon Harvey and Darcey so they cannot argue that they are acting in self-defence. Harvey and James may, perhaps, be able to argue that they were acting in self-defence as Harriet and James attacked them. In the absence of more detailed information about the conduct of Harvey and James, it cannot be stated with certainty that they were or they were not acting in self-defence. As it is stated that a scuffle took place between them all it appears that it is more likely that they were voluntarily fighting and as such they would be engaging in unlawful violence. The significance of this issue is that if they could be seen to be acting in self-defence, then the offence of violent disorder cannot be satisfied as there needs to be at least three people using or threatening unlawful violence.

If Harvey and Darcey could not be said to be acting in self-defence and they were engaging in unlawful violence, then the next requirement that needs to be satisfied is that a person of reasonable firmness present at the scene must fear for their safety (s 2(1)). Section 2(3) states this person need not actually be present at the scene. Although this requirement may appear strange upon first glance, this is a key requirement for the offence. This is the legal test which sets out the threshold for unacceptable behaviour. As no actual victim is required this offence is against society, and this test says that if behaviour meets the required threshold then society does not accept this type of behaviour and it amounts to an offence. In the given scenario it is safe to say that this test has been satisfied as we do have a number of people who were present who did fear for their safety and notified the police, so there is evidence that this test is satisfied. The question does arise though whether these people were persons of reasonable firmness. There is nothing to indicate that they were not and it appears reasonable for people to fear for their safety by the actions of the people involved.

In addition to the above requirements there is also a mens rea element that has to be satisfied for violent disorder to be committed. The mens rea for violent disorder (and indeed all of the other statutory offences in the POA) is set out in s 6. Section 6(2) states that a person is only guilty of violent disorder if they intend to use or threaten violence or they are aware that their conduct may be violent or threaten violence. There do not appear to be any indicators that this requirement is not satisfied in the given scenario. They all appear to be voluntarily participating in violent conduct so the *mens rea* element will be satisfied.

After exploring all of the elements of the offence of violent disorder it appears that Harriet, James, Harvey and Darcey will all be guilty of committing violent disorder. Violent disorder is an either way offence which carries a maximum penalty of 5 years imprisonment on indictment, so the four of them are guilty of committing a very serious offence.[8]

The next issue raised by the given scenario is when a scuffle breaks out between Harriet's group and Harvey's group. A fight takes which leaves members of the public scared. **Section 1 POA** sets out the offence of riot and states that the offence is made out when 12 or more people use or threaten unlawful violence for a common purpose and their conduct is such as would cause a person of reasonable firmness who was present at the scene to fear for their safety, but such a person does not actually have to be present.

We are told that Harriet's group numbers about 20 people and Harvey's group numbers about 15, so there are sufficient people for the purposes of riot as only 12 are needed. The next requirement is that they must be using or threatening unlawful violence, and the requirements are the same as discussed above for violent disorder. **Section 8** specifically includes as violence throwing a missile towards a person that is capable of causing injury, regardless whether or not it actually hits its intended target. Harriet's group threw stones and other items at Harvey's group and ultimately they start fighting. This behaviour is sufficient to class as violent conduct within the definition given in **s 8**. There does not appear to be any arguments that either group was acting lawfully in self-defence, as Harvey's friends retaliate by grabbing placards and ripping banners which then leads to a fight, so the violence here will be unlawful.

The next requirement for riot is that the unlawful violence must be used for a 'common purpose'. Common purpose is not defined in the **POA** so we need to look to case-law to help understand what his means. In *R v Jefferson & others* (1994) the court stated that a tacit agreement prior to the activity in question is not needed for a common purpose to be established. Common purpose can be inferred from conduct and it need not be an unlawful purpose in itself, all that is required is that the purpose is then carried out in an unlawful manner. In the given scenario Harriet and Harvey's groups are both present at the same demonstration and participating in it. This may be enough to establish a common purpose. There is a further issue however. As there are two opposing sides here, Harriet's group and Harvey's group, the question arises whether they can possibly be acting together for a common purpose if they are opposed to each other. However, as there are more than 12 people in each group, this question is rendered redundant as each group itself could be said to be acting for a common purpose.

---

8   Always try and come to conclusions after you have applied the law, like this confident conclusion about whether an offence under **s 2** has been committed.

The above requirements are not sufficient for riot to be committed. There is also the requirement for a hypothetical person of reasonable firmness present at the scene to fear for their safety. This is the same test as was discussed above in relation to violent disorder. It is safe to say that this test has been satisfied for the same reasons as was discussed above; there were a number of people who were present who did fear for their safety and notified the police.

For riot to be established there is one further consideration that needs to be explored. As with violent disorder, there is also a *mens rea* or mental requirement needed as well. The *mens rea* for riot is set out in **s 6(1)** which states that a person is only guilty of riot if they intend to use violence or they are aware that their conduct may be violent. There do not appear to be any difficulties in concluding that this requirement is satisfied in the given scenario. Both groups appear to be consensually participating in violent conduct so this *mens rea* element will be satisfied.

Having explored the relevant constituent elements of riot it appear that both Harriet's group and Harvey's group will be guilty of committing riot. Riot is a very serious offence which is an indictable only offence which carries a maximum penalty of 10 years imprisonment.

There are also four other offences set out in the **POA** in **ss 3, 4, 4A** and **5**. These offences set reduce in severity as they proceed. Less serious behaviour and fewer requirements are needed for the offences than riot and violent disorder. For example with **s 3** (affray), only one person needs to be using or threatening unlawful violence towards another (so this time a specific victim is required). The requirement for a hypothetical person of reasonable firmness is the same as with riot and violent disorder, and the mens rea is the same as that for violent disorder. Given the large number of people involved in this incident though it is unlikely and unsuitable for all the people involved to be individually charged with affray. Riot and violent disorder are specifically designed for such incidents with large numbers of people so they are the most suitable and relevant offences and the other offences in the POA need not be discussed further.

QUESTION 15

Citizens of Southton are very concerned about plans to build a nuclear power station on the outskirts of the town. On Saturday morning, Brenda, a citizen of Southton, holds a meeting in Southton Town Hall in order to discuss the matter, which is attended by 100 Southton residents. The meeting becomes heated and Brenda suggests that they should all march at once to the town square (half a mile away at the head of the main road through the town, which leads to the shopping centre) in order to gain more publicity for their cause. The group sets off, Brenda leading.

As the group moves down the main road and nears the town square, two police officers, Elaine and George, approach Brenda and tell her that she must disperse part of the group because it is holding up traffic and may cause other pedestrians to move off the pavement into the road. Brenda does not comply with the request. The procession arrives at the town square and Brenda begins to address the meeting. George again asks Brenda to disperse half the group and, further, to re-site the meeting on the outskirts of the town. She refuses, and George then informs her that he is arresting her for failing to comply with his orders.

Seeing the arrest of Brenda, the group becomes angry. One of the demonstrators, Roger, shouts and swears at the shoppers who are attempting to push past. He waves his fists threateningly at them and calls on other members of the group not to allow them to pass. Elaine and George move to arrest Roger.

▌ Consider the criminal liability (if any) incurred by Brenda and Roger. Did George have a power under the breach of the peace doctrine to re-site the meeting on the outskirts?

How to Answer this Question

This question concentrates on criminal liability incurred by members of the assembly; and the question of breach of the peace in relation to George's powers must also be considered. Therefore, other possible issues, such as the lawfulness of any of the arrests, need not be considered. This question raises a large number of issues which typically appear on exam papers.

The essential matters to be discussed are:

- ❖ notice requirements under **s 11** of the **Public Order Act (POA) 1986**;
- ❖ 'triggers' under **ss 12** and **14** of the Act;
- ❖ conditions which can be imposed under **ss 12** and **14** on processions and assemblies;
- ❖ liability which may arise under **ss 5** and **4** as amended;
- ❖ obstruction of the highway under **s 137** of the **Highways Act 1980**;
- ❖ the breach of the peace doctrine;
- ❖ *R (on the application of Laporte) v CC of Gloucester Constabulary* (2006);
- ❖ relevance of **Arts 10** and **11** of the **European Convention on Human Rights (ECHR)** as incorporated into UK law under the **HRA 1998**;
- ❖ relevant Strasbourg jurisprudence.

Applying the Law

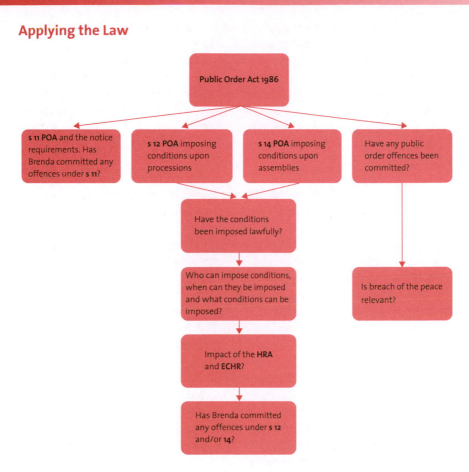

This diagram shows how to apply the **Public Order Act 1986** requirements to Brenda's situation.

ANSWER -

Liability in this case arises mainly under the **POA 1986** (hereinafter 'the Act'), but common law provisions will also be relevant. The possible criminal liability incurred by Brenda and Roger will be considered in turn. The effect of **Arts 10 and 11** of the **ECHR**, as incorporated into UK law under the **HRA**, will be taken into account at relevant points.

Under **s 11** of the Act, advance notice of a procession must be given if it falls within one of three categories. The march from the town hall falls within **s 11(1)(a)**, as it is intended to demonstrate opposition to the building of the power station. As no notice of the march was given, Brenda may have committed an offence under **s 11(7)(a)** of the Act, as she is the organiser of the march. However, the notice requirement does not apply under **s 11(1)** if it was not reasonably practicable to give any advance notice.[9] It can be argued that the word 'any' should not be interpreted so strictly as to exclude spontaneous processions where a few minutes was available to give notice, because to do so would defeat the intention behind including the provision. If it were not so interpreted, it might be argued that s 11 breaches the guarantee of freedom of expression or freedom of assembly under Art 10 or 11 of the Convention since it fails to exempt spontaneous marches from liability – even including peaceful ones. Under s 3 of the HRA, s 11 should be interpreted in so far as possible in accordance with Art 10 or 11. Following this argument, arguably liability will not arise under s 11.[10]

Brenda may further incur liability under s 12(4) of the Act, as she was the organiser of a public procession, but failed to comply with the condition imposed by Elaine to disperse part of the group. Elaine can impose conditions on the procession only if one of the four 'triggers' under s 12(1) is present. The third of these, that the police officer in question must reasonably believe that 'serious disruption to the life of the community' may be caused by the procession, may arguably arise. The group of 100 citizens was marching down the main street of the town; Elaine's fear that traffic may be obstructed or passers-by forced into the road may found a reasonable apprehension that the life of the community will be disrupted, and it is arguable that such disruption may be termed serious. On this argument, Elaine is entitled to impose conditions on the march.[11]

The condition imposed must relate to the disruption apprehended. This may be said of the requirement to disperse half the group; Brenda will therefore incur liability under s 12(4), unless she can show that the failure arose due to circumstances outside her control. Although the powers of an organiser to disperse members of a march are limited, it is clear that Brenda made no effort at all to fulfil the condition. It is therefore argued that she has committed an offence under s 12(4).

Brenda may further incur liability under s 14(4) of the Act, as she was the organiser of a public assembly, but failed to comply with the condition imposed by the most senior police officer present at the scene (who can be a constable) to re-site the assembly and disperse part of the group. It should be noted that as the group was in a public place and comprised more than two persons, it constituted a public assembly under s 16 of the Act. George can impose conditions on the assembly only if one of four 'triggers' under s 14(1) is present (the possible relevance of breach of the peace is considered below). These are identical to those arising under s 12(1) and the third of these will again be considered as the easiest to satisfy in the circumstances.

....

9 This concise application of s 11 POA to the facts is good as there are many issues that need to be discussed, so you cannot spend too long on small matters here.

10 This application of the HRA and the Art 11 ECHR takes the answer to a higher level.

11 This passage about when conditions can be imposed illustrates well how to apply law to given facts.

It is argued that, at the point of imposing the condition, the behaviour of the assembly did not fulfil the terms of the 'trigger', although it may have done so at a later stage. Unlike the march, there is no evidence that, at this stage, the assembly held up traffic. In the case of *Reid* (1987), it was determined that the 'triggers' should be strictly interpreted: the words used should not be diluted. In the instant case, a group of 100 citizens were gathered on the street in the morning on a Saturday; although it could be argued that such a circumstance might cause some disruption in the community (in terms of blockage of the pavement), it is less clear that a reasonable person would expect the disruption to be serious. Such a strict interpretation would appear to accord with the demand that the guarantee of peaceful assembly under **Art 11** should only suffer interference where that can be justified as necessary in a democratic society – a demand that has been strictly interpreted (see *Ezelin v France* (1991)).

However, in *R (Brehony) v Chief Constable of Greater Manchester* (2005) a regular demonstration had occurred outside a Marks and Spencer's store. The Chief Constable had issued a notice under **s 14** requiring the demonstration to move to a different location due to the disruption it would be likely to cause to shoppers over the Christmas period, when the number of shoppers was likely to treble in number. The demonstrators sought judicial review of this decision; the judge refused the application on the basis that, in **Arts 10** and **11** terms, the restraint was proportionate to the aim pursued, that of maintaining public order. This decision confirms that 'serious disruption to the life of the community' can mean mere anticipated inconvenience to shoppers. On this argument, the police may have had a power to impose conditions on the assembly and the condition imposed is one allowed for under **s 14** – to limit the number of persons in the assembly (see *DPP v Jones* (2002)). Liability may therefore arise under **s 14(4)** unless Brenda could successfully argue that the failure to comply with the condition imposed arose due to circumstances beyond her control. On this argument, George appears to have had a power to impose conditions on the assembly; liability therefore arises under **s 14(4)**.

Brenda may also have incurred liability under **s 137** of the **Highways Act 1980**, which provides that a person will be guilty of an offence if he 'without lawful authority or excuse in any way wilfully obstructs the free passage of the highway'. In *Hirst and Agu v Chief Constable of West Yorkshire* (1986) it was said that courts should have regard to the freedom to demonstrate. On that basis, the purpose of an assembly as a means of legitimate protest may suggest that it can amount to a reasonable user of the highway. Some support for this approach is to be found in the House of Lords' decision in *DPP v Jones* (1999), where two members of the majority specifically held that there is a right of peaceful assembly on the public highway, so long as the assembly is peaceful and provided it does not obstruct the public's primary right of passage. The interpretation in *Hirst* appears to be in accord with the demand that peaceful protest should only be interfered with where that is necessary to serve a legitimate aim under **Arts 10** and **11** of the **ECHR**. The police and courts must abide by that demand under **s 6** of the **HRA**. The level of obstruction caused by Brenda's procession may well, therefore, be the crucial factor in deciding on her liability.

Roger may also incur liability under **s14(6)** as inciting others to commit the offence under **s14(5)** of taking part in a public assembly and knowingly failing to comply with the condition imposed. However, this point cannot be settled, as it is unclear from the facts whether or not other members of the group were aware of the condition imposed. Moreover, he may incur liability under **s14(6)** as an organiser, in that he calls on other members of the group to impede shoppers. He may be said to have taken on the role of organiser at this point. However, these points cannot be settled, as it is unclear from the facts whether or not Roger was aware of the condition imposed.

Roger may further incur liability under **s5(1)** of the Act in respect of his behaviour towards the shoppers. In order to show this, his behaviour must amount to 'threatening, abusive or insulting words or behaviour or disorderly behaviour' which takes place in the hearing or sight of a person likely to be caused harassment, alarm or distress thereby.[12] The three terms used must be given their ordinary meaning (*Brutus v Cozens* (1973)). Had Roger confined himself to abuse, it could be argued that his behaviour would be likely merely to irritate the shoppers. However, his use of threatening gestures might be likely to cause the stronger emotion connoted by the concept of harassment. Moreover, Roger appears to satisfy the *mens rea* requirement under **s6(4)**; it appears probable that he is aware or intends that his words or behaviour are threatening, although possibly not abusive or insulting.

However, a defence under **s5(3)(c)** is available to Roger if it can be argued that his behaviour was reasonable. An argument for giving a wide interpretation to the term 'reasonable' can be supported on the basis that in so far as possible **s5** should be interpreted in accordance with **Arts 10** and **11** of the **ECHR**. As already noted, a statute should be interpreted in conformity with the **ECHR** if at all possible (**s3** of the **HRA 1998**). **Article 10** was used in *Percy v DPP* (2002) under **s6** of the **HRA** to argue that liability should not arise under **s5** in respect of an entirely peaceful protest. However, it may be argued that Roger is not acting in an entirely peaceful manner. Thus, even if the term 'reasonable' is widely interpreted, it is arguable that it would not appear wide enough to encompass the behaviour in question which, it seems, went beyond persuasion and became coercion. It is submitted that this defence would fail. It appears then that Roger may incur liability under **s5**.

Roger's behaviour may also support an argument that he has committed an offence under **s4**, which is couched in the same terms as **s5**, except for the omission of 'disorderly behaviour' and with the added need to show that somebody was likely to apprehend the use of immediate violence by Roger or another, or that he intended to arouse such an apprehension. Following the ruling in *Horseferry Road Metropolitan Stipendiary Magistrate ex p Siadatan* (1991), 'violence' in this context must mean

··

12   This exploration of **s5 POA** is good as it does not merely copy out the section of the Act itself; rather, it summarises the key relevant points.

immediate and unlawful violence. This was confirmed in *Winn v DPP* (1992). It is concluded that Roger's behaviour does not satisfy this strict test, although it may fall within **s 4A** (inserted by **s 154** of the **Criminal Justice and Public Order Act 1994**), which creates liability for intentionally causing harassment, alarm or distress.

It is necessary finally to consider whether George could have relied on the breach of the peace doctrine in seeking to re-site the assembly. In *Howell* (1981), in which it was determined that a breach of the peace will arise if an act is done or threatened to be done which either: harms a person or *in his presence* his property or is likely to cause such harm or which puts a person in fear of such harm. *Laporte* (2006) must be taken into account.

The key argument following *Laporte* is that subject to **Arts 10(2)** and **11(2)** of the **ECHR**, the protesters have a right to attend the lawful assembly in the town square. The conduct of the police, in seeking to re-site the assembly to a place at which it would have little or no impact may be viewed as interference by a public authority (**s 6 HRA**) with the claimant's exercise of her rights under **Arts 10** and **11**. It could be argued that the interference (a) was not prescribed by law, because it was not warranted under domestic law, and (b) could not have been seen as necessary in a democratic society, because it was premature; accordingly it was disproportionate. It can be argued, following *Laporte* that there is nothing in domestic authority to support the proposition that action short of arrest (dispersal to another site) may be taken when a breach of the peace is not so imminent as would be necessary to justify an arrest. Here, members of the procession had not been violent or threatened violence before that point. It can also be argued that the proposed action would have been premature because there was no disorder before this point. It would therefore have been disproportionate to restrict the exercise of the rights under **Arts 10** and **11** of the protesters because some of them might, at some time in the future, breach the peace.

QUESTION 16

Clare is a member of the City Youth Club. She and 40 other teenagers attend the youth club on Friday evening and are told that it has to close down that night due to sudden drastic cuts in funding imposed by the council. All of the teenagers immediately walk out of the club in protest and assemble on the pavement outside. While they are angrily discussing the closure of the club, Edwin and Fred, two police officers in uniform, approach the group.

Clare begins to address the group, telling them that they must remain peaceful in order to air their grievances more effectively. Edwin tells her that she must disperse part of the group if she wants to hold a meeting. She ask some of the teenagers to leave, but takes no action when they make no attempt to do so. The meeting continues and becomes more heated. Clare then suggests that they should march through the town.

The group sets off, Clare leading. Traffic is held up for ten minutes as the group enters the town. Edwin asks Clare to disperse half the group of marchers. Clare asks two of the teenagers to leave, but takes no further action when they fail to comply with her request. Edwin then says that she will have to give him the names and addresses of the members of the group. She refuses, and Edwin then informs Clare that he is arresting her for failing to comply with his orders.

▶ Consider the criminal liability, if any, incurred by Clare. Take account of the **Human Rights Act** where relevant.

How to Answer this Question

This is a fairly typical problem question confined to quite a narrow compass, dealing with issues that arise mainly, but not entirely, under the **Public Order Act (POA) 1986** in respect of marches and assemblies. It also requires an awareness of the provisions of **Arts 10** and **11** as interpreted at Strasbourg, and of their possible impact on UK law under the **Human Rights Act (HRA) 1998**. If any of the statutory provisions considered leave open any room at all for a different interpretation (not only on the grounds of ambiguity), they should be interpreted in harmony with **Arts 10 and 11** of the **European Convention on Human Rights (ECHR)**.

It is very important to note that the answer is confined to the question of possible criminal liability incurred by Clare. Possible tortious liability incurred by Clare or the police officers is therefore irrelevant, as is the possibility that Clare could seek to challenge the police decisions by way of judicial review. Breach of the peace is not technically a criminal offence, so it is also irrelevant. The demands of **Arts 10** and **11** as received into UK law under the **HRA** will be relevant at a number of points.

The essential matters to be discussed are:

- ❖ introduction – mention the need to consider the **HRA** and the demands of **Arts 10** and **11** of the **ECHR**;
- ❖ notice requirements under **s 11** of the **POA**; take account of **s 3** of the **HRA**;
- ❖ 'triggers' under **ss 12** and **14** of the **POA**; take account of **s 3** of the **HRA**;
- ❖ conditions that can be imposed under **ss 12** and **14** of the **POA** on processions and assemblies;
- ❖ liability that may arise under **ss 12** and **14**;
- ❖ obstruction of the highway under **s 137** of the **Highways Act 1980**; take account of **s 3** of the **HRA**;
- ❖ conclusions – dependent on interpretation of statutory provisions based on the demands of **Arts 10** and **11** as received into UK law under the **HRA**.

Applying the Law

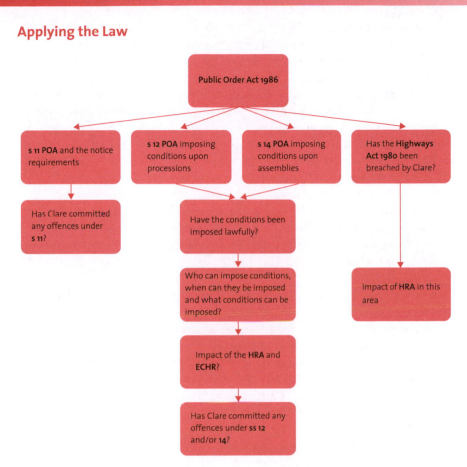

This diagram shows how to apply the **Public Order Act 1986** requirements to Clare's situation.

ANSWER

Liability in this case arises mainly, but not exclusively, under the **Public Order Act (POA) 1986**. Since the question demands consideration of possible restrictions on protest and assembly, the requirements of **Arts 10 and 11** as received into UK law under the **Human Rights Act (HRA) 1998** must be taken into account.

Under **s 11** of the **POA**, advance notice of a procession must be given if it falls within one of three categories. This march falls within **s 11(1)(a)**, as it is intended to demonstrate opposition to the action of the local authority in closing the youth club. As no notice of the march was given, Clare may have committed an offence under **s 11(7)(a)** of the **POA** as she is the organiser of the march. However, the notice requirement does not apply under **s 11(1)** if it was not reasonably practicable to give any advance notice. This provision was intended to exempt spontaneous demonstrations such as this one from the notice requirements, but is defective due to the use of the word 'any'. This word would suggest that a phone call made five minutes before the march sets off would fulfil the requirements, thereby exempting very few marches.[13] Although the march sets off suddenly, it is possible that Clare had time to make such a phone call; on a strict interpretation of **s 11**, she is therefore in breach of the notice requirements, as it was reasonably practicable for her to fulfil them. However, it can be argued that notice was informally and impliedly given to the police officers already on the scene, or alternatively that the term 'reasonably practicable' could be interpreted, under **s 3** of the **HRA**, so as to exempt spontaneous processions from liability even where a few minutes were available to give notice, because to fail to do so would be out of harmony with **Art 11**, which protects freedom of peaceful assembly (*Ezelin v France* (1991)), since peaceful spontaneous marches could incur liability. The word 'written' could be read into **s 11** relying on **s 3** (*see Ghaidan v Mendoza* (2004)) and clearly there was insufficient time to give written notice. Thus, assuming that either argument was accepted by the court, liability would not arise under **s 11**.

Clare may attract liability under **s 14(4)** of the **POA**, as she was the organiser of a public assembly, but failed to comply with the condition imposed by the most senior police officer present at the scene (Edwin) to disperse part of the group (where the officers are of equal rank, this condition will be fulfilled when one of them issues an order). It should be noted that as the group was in a public place and comprised more than two persons, it constituted a public assembly under **s 16** of the **POA**, as amended. Edwin can impose conditions on the assembly only if one of four 'triggers' under **s 14(1)** is present. The third of these, and arguably the easiest to satisfy, provides that the police officer in question must reasonably believe that 'serious disruption to the life of the community' may be caused by the assembly. In the case of *Reid* (1987), it was determined that the 'triggers' should be strictly interpreted: the words used should not be diluted. It would appear to be in accordance with **Art 11**, and indeed **Art 10** (see *Steel v UK* (1998)) to adopt such an interpretation under **s 3** of the **HRA**, since otherwise an interference with assemblies outside the legitimate aims of **para 2 of Arts 10 and 11** might be enabled to occur. However, in *R (Brehony) v Chief Constable of Greater Manchester* (2005), a regular demonstration had occurred outside a branch of Marks and Spencer, protesting about the firm's support for the Government of Israel. The Chief Constable had issued a notice under **s 14** requiring the demonstration to move to a different location due to the disruption that it would be likely to cause to shoppers over the Christmas period. The judge refused the application for judicial review on the basis that, in **Art 10** and **11** terms, the restraint was proportionate to the aim pursued, that of maintaining public order. This decision confirms that 'serious disruption to the life of the community' can mean mere

13   This interpretation of **s 11 POA** with the use of an example shows an ability to use the law, which will impress the examiner.

anticipated inconvenience to shoppers. On this argument, Edwin may have had a power to impose conditions on the assembly and the condition imposed is one allowed for under s14 – to limit the number of persons in the assembly (see *DPP v Jones* (2002)). Liability may therefore arise under s14(4) unless Clare could successfully argue that the failure to comply with the condition imposed arose due to circumstances beyond her control.

Will Clare incur liability under s12(4) of the POA, as she was the organiser of a public procession, but failed to comply with the conditions imposed by Edwin to provide the names and addresses of the group or to disperse part of it? Edwin can impose conditions on the procession only if one of the four 'triggers' under s12(1) is present. The triggers are identical to those under s14(1). The third of these may possibly arise, following *Brehony*. The group of teenagers was marching through the town; in such circumstances, it may be more readily argued that serious disruption to the life of the community may reasonably be apprehended. Such disruption could be argued for either on the basis that passers-by may be jostled by the group, especially if it has grown more excitable, or on the basis that traffic may be seriously disrupted. The fact that traffic has already been held up for ten minutes may support a reasonable belief that such disruption may occur.[14] Serious obstruction of the traffic might arguably amount to some disruption of the life of the community. Both possibilities taken together could found a reasonable apprehension that the life of the community will be seriously disrupted. However, courts are required under both ss6 and 3 of the HRA to determine that the nature of the risk anticipated is one that would constitute one of the legitimate aims for limiting the primary rights under Arts 11 and 10. The vague and ambiguous phrase, 'serious disruption to the life of the community', could be reinterpreted under s3 of the HRA by reference to Arts 11(2) and 10(2) of the ECHR.[15] The grounds for imposing the conditions would have to be justified, either on the basis of protecting 'the rights of others' or because the 'serious disruption' feared amounted to 'disorder' for the purposes of those second paragraphs. Following *Brehony*, it seems probable that a court would be satisfied that serious disruption could reasonably be apprehended, and that in asserting a power to impose conditions the police did not breach Arts 10 or 11. However, the discretion as to the imposition of the conditions in s12 could be viewed narrowly (either under Art 10 or 11 or on ordinary principles of statutory construction). It could be argued that the restrictions are necessary in order to protect the rights of others. However, arguably, they are disproportionate to that aim, bearing in mind the importance of freedom of assembly (*Ezelin*). In particular, a requirement to provide names and addresses appears to be disproportionate to the aim in view, since it is unclear that it could serve that aim. In order to avoid breaching Arts 10 and 11, a court

---

14   This application of s14 POA demonstrates how to successfully apply law to facts without it taking up too much time and space.

15   This brief analysis shows the examiner that you are thinking about the law in context.

that took this view could adopt a strict interpretation of **s 12**, possibly finding either that the behaviour in question is not serious enough and/or that the condition could not be viewed as 'necessary'.

On the other hand, a court could rely on *Christians Against Racism and Fascism v UK* (1980), in which a ban on a peaceful assembly was not found to breach **Art 11**. *A fortiori*, a mere imposition of conditions might be found to be proportionate within the terms of **Art 11(2)**. Following this argument, and bearing *Brehony* in mind, Edwin would be entitled to impose conditions on the march. The conditions imposed would have to relate to the disruption apprehended; this may be said of the requirement to disperse half the group, but not of the order that Clare should disclose the names and addresses of the group. Thus, liability may arise only in respect of the failure to comply with the former condition. Clare made some attempt to comply with it but did not succeed; she would, therefore, following this argument, incur liability under **s 12(4)** unless she can show that the failure arose due to circumstances outside her control. Although the powers of an organiser to disperse members of a march are limited, it may be argued that in approaching only two members of the group, Clare made in any event a token effort only; it is therefore arguable that she has committed an offence under **s 12(4)**.

Clare may further have incurred liability under **s 137** of the **Highways Act 1980**, which provides that a person will be guilty of an offence if he 'without lawful authority or excuse in any way wilfully obstructs the free passage of the highway'. In *Arrowsmith v Jenkins* (1963), it was held that minor obstruction of traffic can lead to liability under the **Highways Act**. However, the question of the purpose of the obstruction was given greater prominence in *Hirst and Agu v Chief Constable of West Yorkshire* (1986): it was said that courts should have regard to the freedom to demonstrate.

This approach was to an extent confirmed by *DPP v Jones* (1999), where the House of Lords recognised that a demonstration need not be treated as an improper use of the highway where it does not cause obstruction to other users. Such an approach is, of course, given added weight by the need for the courts to give appropriate weight, by virtue of **s 3** of the **HRA**, to the rights of freedom of expression and assembly in **Arts 10** and **11** of the **ECHR**.[16] One possibility would be to interpret the uncertain term 'excuse' in order to seek to ensure harmony between **s 137** of the **Highways Act** and **Arts 10** and **11** under **s 3** of the **HRA**, since otherwise **s 137** would allow interferences with peaceful, albeit obstructive, assemblies, arguably contrary to the findings of the European Court of Human Rights in *Steel* and in *Ezelin*. On this basis, the brevity of the obstruction and its purpose as part of a legitimate protest, suggest that the march amounted to a

---

16   This application of the **HRA** to this area of law improves the quality of the answer by showing additional awareness and understanding of the law.

reasonable use of the highway. The stronger argument seems to be that liability under the **Highways Act** for inciting the group to obstruct the highway will not be established.

Thus, in conclusion, Clare is most likely to attract liability under **ss 14(4)** and **12(4)** of the **POA**.

QUESTION 17

Section 3 of the **Human Rights Act (HRA) 1998** requires that statutes should be interpreted, if possible, so as to accord with the demands of the **European Convention on Human Rights (ECHR)**. Is it fair to say that the restraints on assemblies in **ss 11–14A** of the **Public Order Act (POA) 1986**, as amended, create a balance between the public interest in freedom of assembly and in the need to maintain order that is in harmony with **Arts 10** and **11** of the **ECHR**, and that therefore no reinterpretation of those provisions under **s 3** is necessary?

How to Answer this Question

The **Public Order Act (POA) 1986** remains the central statute in this area, but its amendment by the **Criminal Justice and Public Order Act (CJPOA) 1994** created a significant new area of liability. The general public order scheme now created by the two statutes is very likely to appear on examination papers. This essay question requires a sound knowledge of certain key **POA** provisions that are particularly relevant to public assembly and protest. **Section 16 POA** was amended by the **Anti-Social Behaviour Act 2003** so that an assembly is now a meeting of two or more persons in a public place. It also requires an awareness of the provisions of **Arts 10** and **11** as interpreted at Strasbourg, and of their potential impact on this area of UK law under the **Human Rights Act (HRA) 1998**. It is suggested that a distinction should initially be drawn between prior and subsequent restraints contained in the **POA** as amended. The provisions in question operate to a significant extent as prior restraints.

Essentially, the following matters should be considered:

- ❖ the value of freedom of assembly;
- ❖ the provisions of **Arts 10** and **11** as interpreted by Strasbourg;
- ❖ Strasbourg free expression and protest cases;
- ❖ the provisions aimed specifically at processions and assemblies under **ss 11, 12, 13, 14, 14A, 14B** and **14C** of the **1986 Act** (as amended by the **1994 Act**);
- ❖ the need for further protection of assembly by reinterpretation of the provisions under **s 3** in accordance with the demands of **Arts 10** and **11** as received into UK law under the **HRA**;
- ❖ conclusions.

Answer Structure

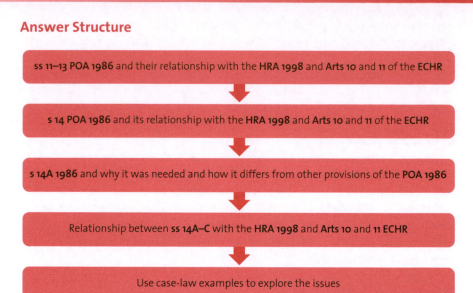

ss 11–13 POA 1986 and their relationship with the HRA 1998 and Arts 10 and 11 of the ECHR

s 14 POA 1986 and its relationship with the HRA 1998 and Arts 10 and 11 of the ECHR

s 14A 1986 and why it was needed and how it differs from other provisions of the POA 1986

Relationship between ss 14A–C with the HRA 1998 and Arts 10 and 11 ECHR

Use case-law examples to explore the issues

ANSWER

The restraints available under **ss 11–14A** of the **Public Order Act (POA) 1986** as amended by the **Criminal Justice and Public Order Act (CJPOA) 1994**, affect demonstrations, marches and meetings. **Articles 10** and **11** of the **ECHR**, afforded further effect in domestic law under the **Human Rights Act (HRA) 1998**, seek to avoid suppression of protest in providing guarantees of freedom of expression and of peaceful assembly, subject to exceptions under **Arts 10(2)** and **11(2)**, which allow restraints on protests and demonstrations to be justified only if they are prescribed by law, have a legitimate aim, and are 'necessary in a democratic society'. The European Court of Human Rights has found that the right to organise public meetings is 'fundamental' (*Rassemblement Jurassien Unite Jurassienne v Switzerland* (1979)).[17] All forms of protest that can be viewed as the expression of an opinion fall within **Art 10**, according to the findings of the Court in *Steel v UK* (1998). In *Ezelin v France* (1991), the Court found that **Art 11** had been violated: it found that the freedom to take part in a peaceful assembly is of such importance that it cannot be restricted in any way, so long as the person concerned (whose freedom of assembly has suffered interference through arrest, etc.) does not himself/herself commit any reprehensible act. Domestically, where protest is in question, there seems to be a preparedness, evident from the decision in *DPP v Percy* (2001) and

---

17   References to these ECtHR decisions demonstrates excellent knowledge of the area to the examiner.

Laporte (2007), to accept that **Arts 10** and **11** apply, even if the protest in general includes offensive or disorderly elements.

This essay will ask whether the UK controls under **ss 11–14C** of the **POA** as amended are in harmony with **Arts 10** and **11**, taking into account the above Strasbourg jurisprudence. **Sections 12** and **13 POA** are underpinned by **s 11**, which provides that the organisers of a march (not a meeting) must give advance notice of it to the police. The notice must specify the date, time and proposed route of the procession and give the name and address of the person proposing to organise it. Under **s 11(7)**, the organisers may be guilty of an offence if the notice requirement has not been satisfied or if the march deviates from the date, time or route specified. Clearly, **s 11** may have some deterrence value to organisers; such persons obviously bear a heavy responsibility in ensuring that any deviation does not occur. It can be argued that the word 'any' should not be interpreted so strictly as to exclude spontaneous processions where a few minutes were available to give notice, because to do so would defeat the intention behind including the provision. If read in combination with the requirements as to giving notice by hand or in writing, it should be interpreted to mean 'any written notice' under **s 3** of the **HRA**. If it were not so interpreted, it might be argued that **s 11** breaches the guarantees of freedom of assembly under **Art 11** and of expression under **Art 10**, since it could lead to the criminalisation of the organisers of a peaceful spontaneous march. Such an interpretation would seem to be in accordance with the findings in *Ezelin v France*.

The power to impose conditions on public assemblies under **s 14** and on processions under **s 12** can be exercised in one of four situations: the senior police officer in question must reasonably believe that serious public disorder, serious damage to property or serious disruption to the life of the community may be caused by the procession. The fourth 'trigger' condition, arising under **ss 12** and **14(1)(b)**, requires that the senior police officer must reasonably believe that the purpose of the assembly is 'the intimidation of others with a view to compelling them not to do an act they have a right to do or to do an act they have a right not to do'. 'Serious disruption to the life of the community' is a very wide phrase and clearly offers the police wide scope for interpretation. In *R (Brehony) v Chief Constable of Greater Manchester* (2005), a regular demonstration had occurred outside a branch of Marks and Spencer, protesting about the firm's support for the Government of Israel; a counter-demonstration had also occurred, supporting the Government. The Chief Constable had issued a notice under **s 14** requiring the demonstration to move to a different location due to the disruption that it would be likely to cause to shoppers over the Christmas period. The judge refused the application for judicial review on the basis that, in terms of **Arts 10** and **11**, the restraint was proportionate to the aim pursued, that of maintaining public order. This decision confirms that 'serious disruption to the life of the community' can mean mere anticipated inconvenience to shoppers. It might be possible to rely on **s 3 HRA** and **Art 11** to curb the width of the term.

The conditions which may be imposed under **s 14** are much more limited in scope than those that can be imposed under **s 12**, presumably because it was thought that marches presented more of a threat to public order than meetings.[18]

Under **s 13**, a ban must be imposed on a march if it is thought that it may result in serious public disorder. This power is open to criticism, in that once a banning order has been imposed, it prevents all marches in the area that it covers for its duration. Thus, a projected march likely to be of an entirely peaceful character would be caught by a ban aimed at a violent march. It is arguable that **s 3 HRA** could be relied on to limit the banning power to the particular marches giving rise to fear of serious public disorder.

Originally, the **1986 Act** contained no power to ban assemblies, possibly because it was thought that such a power would be too draconian, but provision to allow for such bans was inserted into it by **s 70** of the **CJPOA**. The banning power, arising under **s 14A**, provides that a chief officer of police may apply for a banning order if he reasonably believes that an assembly is likely to be trespassory and may result in serious disruption to the life of the community or damage to certain types of building and structure. If an order is made, it will subsist for four days and operate within a radius of five miles around the area in question. The meaning and ambit of **s 14A** were considered in *Jones and Lloyd v DPP* (1997), which concerned an assembly on the road leading to Stonehenge, at a time when a **s 14A** order was in force. The key finding of the House of Lords was that since *the particular assembly in question* had been found by the tribunal in fact to be a reasonable user of the highway, it was therefore not trespassory and so not caught by the **s 14A** order. The Lords' conclusion was that the demands of this 'right' to assemble are satisfied, provided merely that an assembly on the highway is not invariably tortious. This interpretation did little, it is suggested, to ensure that **s 14A** is compatible with **Arts 10** and **11**, since it allows interferences with peaceful assemblies.

In general, it is argued that **ss 12–14A** appear to be out of accord with the demands of **Arts 10** and **11** of the **ECHR**. Under all of those provisions, it is possible that those organising or taking part in protests and demonstrations can be subject to criminal penalties and hence to an interference with their **Arts 10** and **11** rights, even though they themselves were behaving wholly peacefully. Thus, the effects of **ss 12–14A** appear to be contrary to the statement of principle set out in *Ezelin*, above, since the arrest and conviction of demonstrators under them cannot be seen to be directly serving one of the legitimate aims of preventing public disorder or ensuring public safety under **para 2** of **Arts 10** and **11**. But there is a consistent line of case law from the European Commission on Human Rights that indicates that bans – and therefore *a fortiori* the imposition of

....

18   This brief analysis of **ss 12** and **14** by comparing them shows the examiner that you can actively think about the law.

conditions – on assemblies and marches are in principle compatible with Art 11, even where they criminalise wholly peaceful protests (*Pendragon v UK* (1998); *Chappell v UK* (1987)) or prevent what would have been peaceful demonstrations from taking place at all (*Christians Against Racism and Fascism v UK* (1980)).[19]

Under s 14A, attention could focus upon scrutiny of the risk of 'serious disruption to the life of the community' in granting the original ban. This method could also be used to bring ss 12 and 14 into line with the Convention. A court could consider whether the nature of the risk anticipated is one that would constitute one of the legitimate aims for limiting the primary rights under Arts 10 and 11. This vague and ambiguous phrase could be reinterpreted under s 3 of the HRA by reference to Arts 10(2) and 11(2) of the Convention. The ban or conditions would have to be found to be necessary and proportionate to the legitimate aim applicable. Thus, s 3 has the potential to be used to limit and structure the tests allowing for the use of these curbs on protests. However, the decision in *Brehony* does not encourage the idea that the judiciary would be eager to take this course. *R (on the application of Gillan) v Commissioner of Metropolitan Police* (2006) also encourages a pessimistic view: the House of Lords found that, assuming that Art 10 was applicable in an instance in which a protester had been stopped and searched – arguably an interference that had occurred in order to impede him in joining the protest – the exception for the prevention of crime under para 2 was satisfied, without engaging in any proportionality analysis.

Section 13 could be reinterpreted under s 3 in order to achieve compatibility with Arts 10 and 11 in various ways. For example, it could be argued that a power to seek an order to ban all marches could be interpreted as a power to ban all marches espousing a particular message, using s 3 of the HRA creatively, as the House of Lords did in *R v A* (2001) and *Ghaidan v Mendoza* (2004). It is concluded that the far-reaching nature of the public order scheme under discussion argues strongly for establishing further protection for freedom of assembly under the HRA, by reinterpretation of a number of the provisions under s 3. The scheme is to an extent pursuing legitimate aims – the prevention of disorder and crime – under Arts 10 and 11, but insofar as certain of its provisions allow for interference with peaceful assemblies, it appears, as indicated, that in certain respects it goes further than is necessary in a democratic society. However, ironically, the very fact that the scheme employs imprecise phrases such as 'serious', possibly in an attempt to afford maximum discretion to the police, works against it in favour of freedom of protest, since it could render the task of reinterpretation under s 3 of the HRA relatively straightforward. However, these possible reinterpretations of these provisions have not yet been undertaken under the HRA.[20]

....

19 This analysis of the law adds depth to the answer.

20 This detailed analysis of the HRA's impact shows the examiner that you truly understand this area of law.

Aim Higher ★

In relation to **s 14A** there are strong grounds to justify a development of the ruling from *DPP v Jones*, taking account of **s 3 HRA** and **Art 11**; a court could find that if an assembly is peaceful and non-obstructive, it must always be termed reasonable and therefore non-trespassory, and so outside the terms of any **s 14A** order in force.

Common Pitfalls ✗

Students must focus on **s 3 HRA** and clear possible changes that could be created to the statutory provisions relying on **Arts 10, 11**, or **5 ECHR**, not on general criticisms of the provisions.

QUESTION 18

The Asian community in Northton become increasingly concerned about apparent racism in Northton City Council employment practices. A number of council workers have recently been made redundant; a disproportionate number of them are Asians. A group of 40 Asians decides to hold a demonstration outside the Civic Centre on the lawns and courtyard in front of it. On the appointed day, they assemble, nominate Ali and Rashid as their leaders, and shout at workers going into the Centre, telling them not to go in but to join the demonstration. When the workers do not respond, some of the Asians, including Ali, become angrier; they shout and wave their fists threateningly at some of the workers, but make no attempt to impede them physically. Some of the workers appear to be intimidated.

One of the Asians, Sharma, tries to persuade workers not to enter the Civic Centre and to support the anti-racism protest, but eventually becomes involved in a heated argument with a group of white workers. He continues more angrily to attempt to persuade them not to enter; they threaten to beat him up if the Asian group continues with its efforts.

Three police officers arrive on the scene. One of them, John, arrests Sharma, stating that this is for breach of the peace, since the group of white workers is about to become violent. Sharma tries to leave, pushing John aside in the process; John seizes Sharma's arm. Belinda, one of the police officers, orders Ali to disperse half of the group; when he makes no effort to comply, she says that she is arresting him for failing to comply with the order. She also orders Rashid to leave the area. He fails to do so.

▶ **Discuss.**

How to Answer this Question

This question is partly concerned with liability that may arise in respect of assemblies under the **Public Order Act (POA) 1986**, as amended, and under **ss 68** and **69** of the

Criminal Justice and Public Order Act (CJPOA) 1994. The common law power to prevent a breach of the peace is significant in the question. The statutory provisions considered should be interpreted in harmony with **Arts 10** and **11** of the **European Convention on Human Rights (ECHR)** (and any other relevant Articles) under **s 3** of the **Human Rights Act (HRA) 1998**; the common law doctrine of breach of the peace must be interpreted and applied in accordance with the duty of the court under **s 6** of the **HRA**. It should be borne in mind that the problem concerns an assembly only, and not a march. Further, the assembly is not taking place on the highway. Therefore, liability particularly associated with marches and with assemblies on the highway will not arise. Note that a broad, wide-ranging discussion is called for due to the use of the word 'discuss'.

Essentially, the following matters should be discussed:

- ❖ introduction – a mention of the need to consider the **HRA**; demands of **Arts 10** and **11** as received into UK law under the **HRA**;
- ❖ 'triggers' under **s 14** of the Act;
- ❖ conditions that may be imposed under **s 14**; take account of **s 3** of the **HRA**;
- ❖ liability under **ss 4, 4A** and **5** of the **POA**; take account of **s 3** of the **HRA**;
- ❖ liability under **ss 68** and **69** of the **CJPOA**; take account of **s 3** of the **HRA**;
- ❖ arrest for breach of the peace; **s 6** of the **HRA**; liability under **s 89(1)** of the **Police Act 1996**;
- ❖ conclusions.

Applying the Law

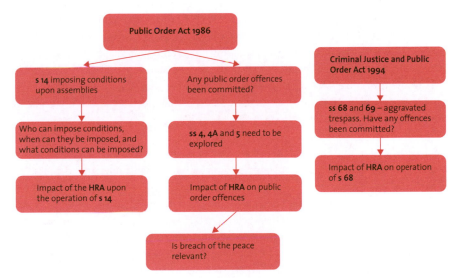

This diagram shows how to apply the ***Public Order Act 1986*** *requirements to Ali and Rashid's situation.*

ANSWER

Liability in this case may arise mainly, but not exclusively, under the **Public Order Act (POA) 1986**, as amended. Since the question demands consideration of possible restrictions on protest and assembly, the requirements of **Arts 10** and **11** as received into UK law under the **Human Rights Act (HRA) 1998** must be taken into account. **Article 14**, which provides protection from discrimination in the context of another right, will also be considered briefly.

Ali may attract liability under **s 14(4)** of the **POA**, as he was the organiser of a public assembly, but failed to comply with the condition imposed by the most senior police officer present at the scene (where the officers are of equal rank, this condition will be fulfilled when one of them issues an order) to disperse half of the group. It should be noted that as the group was in a public place and comprised more than two persons, it constituted a public assembly under **s 16** of the **POA**, as amended. Belinda can impose conditions on the assembly only if one of four 'triggers' under **s 14(1)** is present. The fourth 'trigger', arising under **s 14(1)(b)**, requires that the senior police officer present must reasonably believe that the purpose of the assembly is 'the intimidation of others with a view to compelling them not to do an act they have a right to do or to do an act they have a right not to do'.[21]

The fourth 'trigger' seems to be most clearly indicated. In the case of *Reid* (1987), it was determined that the triggers should be strictly interpreted: the words used should not be diluted. In *Reid*, the defendants shouted, raised their arms and waved their fingers; it was determined that such behaviour might cause discomfort but not intimidation and that the two concepts could not be equated. In *News Group Newspapers Ltd v SOGAT 82* (1986), it was held that mere abuse and shouting did not amount to a threat of violence. In the instant case, it could be argued that the Asians' behaviour in merely shouting at the Civic Centre workers could not amount to intimidation, but that in making threatening gestures with their fists, it crossed the boundary between discomfort and intimidation.

However, the imposition of conditions, the arrest of Ali and (potentially) the imposition of criminal liability under **s 14** create interferences with the rights under **Arts 10** and **11** of assembly and expression (*Steel v UK* (1998)). Therefore, it must be asked whether the demands of **s 14** as applied in this instance are in accordance with those rights. In *Ezelin v France* (1991), the Court found that the freedom to take part in a peaceful assembly is of such importance that it cannot be restricted in any way, so long as the person concerned does not himself commit any reprehensible act. It may be argued that the intimidation of others is reprehensible and that therefore the tests under **Art 11(2)**

---

21   This express application of **s 14 POA** shows how to apply the law well but whilst doing so quickly.

(and **Art 10(2)**) are satisfied by the application of **s 14** in this instance, taking account of **s 6 HRA**. The lenient stance taken towards the application of the third trigger in *R (Brehony) v Chief Constable of Greater Manchester* (2005) indicates that this stance would probably also be taken here. On that basis, it appears that Belinda had the power to impose a condition on the assembly. Thus, Ali's arrest appears to be justified under **s 14(7)** and he may be likely to incur liability under **s 14(4)**. Other members of the Asian group who were aware of the condition may commit the offence under **s 14(5)**.

Ali, Rashid, and possibly other members of the Asian group may also incur liability under **s 68** of the **Criminal Justice and Public Order Act (CJPOA) 1994**. The section requires, first, that the defendant has trespassed. This seems to be satisfied, since Ali, Rashid and the other protestors appear to have exceeded the terms of an implied licence to be in the courtyard, and the courtyard is not excluded from **s 68** since it is arguably 'land in the open air' – it is clearly not part of the highway (**s 68(5)(a)**). Second, it must be shown that the defendant intended to disrupt or obstruct a lawful activity or to intimidate persons so as to deter them from that activity. This last requirement may also be satisfied by the Asians' behaviour in shouting at the workers entering the Civic Centre. The broad view of **s 68** taken in *Winder* (1996) indicates that a court would not scrutinise the application of **s 68** to the facts too closely.[22] Rashid (and possibly other Asians aware of John's order that members of the assembly should disperse) may also commit the offence under **s 69** of failing to leave land after a direction to do so is given, founded on a reasonable belief that the offence under **s 68** is being committed. Belinda tells Rashid to leave the land and he refuses to do so.

However, these possibilities of liability under **ss 68** and **69** must be considered in relation to the **HRA**. The European Court of Human Rights made a clear finding in *Steel* (1998), confirmed in *Hashman* (2000), that protest that takes the form of physical obstruction nevertheless falls within the protection of **Art 10** – and presumably **Art 11**. It seems clear from the findings in *Steel* as to the first and second applicants, and from the Commission decision in *G v Federal Republic of Germany* (1980), that where a protester is engaged in obstructive, albeit non-violent activity, arrest and imprisonment are in principle justifiable under the **Convention**. It is arguable therefore that the imposition of liability in this instance is compatible with the duty of the court under **s 6** of the **HRA**. On this basis, liability under **s 69** would also be established since it is dependent on establishing a reasonable belief that the offence under **s 68** has been committed.

It could also be argued that in shouting and waving their fists at the Civic Centre workers, Ali and the other demonstrators may incur liability under **s 5** of the **POA**. Their behaviour must amount to 'threatening, abusive or insulting words or behaviour or disorderly

---

22   This use of the *Winder* case demonstrates how to use cases without spending too long on them.

behaviour', which takes place 'in the hearing or sight of a person likely to be caused harassment, alarm or distress thereby'. The word 'likely' imports an objective test into the section: it is necessary to show that a person was present at the scene, but not that he actually experienced the feelings in question. The demonstrators shout and gesture aggressively; this behaviour may clearly be termed disorderly or even threatening, and it is arguable, given the width of the concept of harassment, that it would be likely to cause feelings of harassment, although probably not of alarm, to the workers. It appears then that the demonstrators may incur liability under **s 5**, subject to the argument below as to the *mens rea* requirement under **s 6(4)**. On the same argument, liability under **s 4A** of the **POA** may be established, assuming that they *intended* to cause harassment and did cause it. It should be noted however that in *Dehal v DPP* (2005) it was found that **s 4** should be interpreted restrictively when applied to public protest due to the impact of the **HRA**, and **Arts 10** and **11**.

However, it is necessary to consider whether **ss 4A** and **5**, interpreted as covering the behaviour in question, are compatible with **Arts 10** and **11** under **s 3** of the **HRA** (see *Percy v DPP* (2001)). Compatibility may be achieved by affording a broad interpretation to the defence of reasonableness in both sections (**ss 5(3)(c)** and **4A(3)(b)**). However, in the context under discussion, the demonstrators appear to have intended to intimidate others, rather than to make points that others could find offensive. It is arguable that the instant behaviour would fall outside the meaning of 'reasonable', even bearing in mind the requirements of **Arts 10** and **11**.[23]

Under **s 6(4)**, it must be established in respect of **s 5** that the defendant intended his words, etc., to be threatening, abusive or insulting or was aware that they might be. Under **s 4A**, intent to cause harassment alone is needed. In *DPP v Clarke* (1992), it was found that to establish liability under **s 5**, it is insufficient to show only that the defendant intended to or was aware that he might cause harassment, alarm or distress; it must also be shown that he intended his conduct to be threatening, abusive or insulting or was aware that it might be. It therefore places a significant curb on the ability of **s 5** (and to an extent, impliedly of **s 4A**) to interfere with **Art 10** and **Art 11** rights. Persons participating in forceful demonstrations may sometimes be able to show that behaviour that could be termed disorderly and which might be capable of causing harassment to others was intended only to make a point, and that they had not realised that others might find it threatening, abusive or insulting. This does not appear to be the case here, since the threats appear to be used not in order to make a point forcefully, but to intimidate.

---

23 This application of the **POA** offences to the Articles of the **ECHR** heightens the quality of the answer by adding an extra layer.

Sharma may have committed a breach of the peace or his behaviour might have given rise to a reasonable belief that a breach of the peace was threatened; breach of the peace is not in itself a criminal offence, but it would justify the arrest of Sharma by John.[24] If the arrest was lawful, Sharma's action in pushing John away would be an assault on an officer in the execution of his duty, an offence under **s 89(1)** of the **Police Act 1996**. In *Howell* (1981), the court said that a breach of the peace will arise if a positive act is done or is threatened to be done that harms a person or, in his presence, his property, or is likely to cause such harm, or which puts a person in fear of such harm. In *Nicol v DPP* (1996), it was found that a natural consequence of lawful conduct could be violence in another only where the defendant rather than the other person could be said to be acting unreasonably and, further, that unless rights had been infringed, it would not be reasonable for those others to react violently. However, in *Redmond-Bate v DPP* (1999), it was found that, taking **Art 10** into account, the court should ask where the threat was coming from; the person causing the threat should be arrested. The threat would appear to be coming from the white workers. Therefore, it may be argued that the police breached their duty under **s 6** of the **HRA** in arresting Sharma, since they did not comply with **Art 10** (and arguably **Art 14** – the right to non-discrimination, which arises in the context of another right). Further, the court's findings in *Steel v UK* (1998) may be taken to suggest that the power to prevent a breach of the peace may infringe **Arts 5, 10** and **11** when used against an entirely peaceful protestor. The decision in *Laporte* (2006) would support this argument. In the instant case, Sharma may have remained peaceful, albeit 'heated' and angry. On this interpretation, therefore, which would accord with the court's duty to shape the common law in accordance with the **ECHR** under **s 6** of the **HRA**, Sharma should not have been arrested; therefore, he has not committed the offence under **s 89(1)** of the **Police Act 1996**. He could sue John in tort for assault if the arrest is found to be unlawful. Following this argument, it is therefore possible that if the protestors who did use intimidatory tactics had been arrested for breach of the peace, their arrests would not have breached **Art 10**.

---

24 Credit will be given for this examination of the common law, as many students forget about the common law and focus only on statutory provisions.

Privacy

4

INTRODUCTION

Examiners tend to set general essays in this area, rather than problem questions, although the latter do arise from time to time. The emphasis is often on the degree to which a balance is struck between the interest of the State and other bodies in intruding on the individual, or in obtaining and publishing personal information, and the interest of the individual in maintaining personal privacy and the privacy of personal information. These two areas of privacy can be broken down into bodily and sexual privacy, the privacy of the home, access to personal information and the protection of personal information.

Questions are often asked which concern the balance struck between privacy and freedom of expression. There have been various government proposals for reform, including the introduction of a tort of privacy. A recent re-examination of this area by the Joint Select Committee on Privacy and Injunctions resulted in a conclusion that a separate tort was still not needed (2012). The main reason for this is the debate about the extent to which the **Human Rights Act (HRA) 1998** has led to the courts developing a common law right to privacy. This in turn raises difficult issues about the impact of the **HRA** such as whether the Act creates 'horizontal' protection for human rights. The protection of privacy interests is an issue which has been the subject of a number of high profile cases involving celebrities and the media. Another important topic concerns the needs of national security and crime control which clearly conflict with privacy in a range of ways arising from the provisions of a certain group of statutes: the **Security Services Act 1989**, the **Intelligence Services Act 1994**, the **Police Act 1997**, the **Regulation of Investigatory Powers Act (RIPA) 2000** (which replaced the substantive provisions of the **Interception of Communications Act 1985**) and the **Serious Organised Crime and Policing Act (SOCAP) 2006**. Essay questions may ask you to consider the conflict between those public interest needs and the individual's interest in maintaining personal privacy and the privacy of the home. The **HRA** will also be relevant to discussions of this area.

A further issue that is relevant to this chapter, and to freedom of expression issues as well, is how the press is regulated. At the time of writing this chapter the Leveson Inquiry into the culture, practice and ethics of the press is still underway. It was established in July 2011 as a result of the phone-hacking scandal which involved large swathes of the press. Its aim is to make recommendations about the future of press regulation to ensure freedom of the press whilst maintaining the highest standards of ethics and professional standards. Students of this area will want to keep a keen eye on developments in this area and the conclusions of the inquiry and how they are put into practice in particular.

Checklist ✔

Students should be familiar with the following areas:

- breach of confidence;
- defamation and malicious falsehood;
- trespass and nuisance;
- proposals for a tort of invasion of privacy;
- the developing role of the **HRA 1998** and, in particular, **Art 8** of **Sched 1**;
- the **Data Protection Act 1998** and the **Freedom of Information Act 2000**;
- the **Official Secrets Act 1989**, the **Security Services Act 1989**, the **Intelligence Services Act 1994**, **Pt 3** of the **Police Act 1997**, the **RIPA 2000**, **Pt 2** of **SOCAP**, **Pts 3** and **11** of the **Anti-Terrorism, Crime and Security Act 2001**, and the **Prevention of Terrorism Act 2005**.

QUESTION 19

'The law of confidence has developed so far that it can now confidently be said that it provides adequate protection from media intrusion into personal information; therefore, a statutory tort of invasion of privacy is not needed.'

▶ To what extent do you agree with the above statement?

How to Answer this Question

This is a fairly demanding essay question, which requires familiarity with the law of confidence and the rapidly developing domestic decisions post- **HRA**. The statement made in the title can be analysed as follows. First, does confidence provide adequate protection for personal information? Secondly, assuming that it does, is it better, in terms of preserving the balance between privacy rights and media freedom, to protect such information through the doctrine of confidence or through a new tort? Remember to limit your answer to the context of media intrusion. Essentially, the following points should be considered:

- ❖ development of doctrine of confidence – relationship between the parties may be informal;
- ❖ obligation of confidentiality may be imposed on third parties;

❖   the public interest defence;
❖   ambit of the proposed tort;
❖   comparison between the proposed tort and breach of confidence: impact on media freedom;
❖   **Arts 8** and **10** of the **European Convention on Human Rights (ECHR)** and the impact of the **HRA 1998**.

Answer Structure

Brief overview of privacy law position (or rather the lack thereof) in the UK

Background and overview of Breach of Confidence

Examination of case law to track developments in Breach of Confidence

Impact the **HRA** has had in the development of privacy law in the UK

Examination of post-**HRA** case law in the area, including ECtHR cases

Discussion of contemporary developments and issues

ANSWER

No tort of invasion of privacy exists in the UK as in the US to control the activity of the media in obtaining information regarding an individual's private life and then publishing the details, possibly in exaggerated, lurid terms. Certain legal controls arising from the law of confidence do exist, although they have not traditionally been aimed directly at the invasion of privacy, they can be used against the media when private information is published. It will be argued that this control is still fairly limited in scope but it is sufficiently well developed to undermine the argument for a privacy law.[1]

Breach of confidence will be established, according to Lord Greene MR in *Salt-man Engineering Co Ltd v Campbell Engineering Co Ltd* (1963), if information which has a quality of confidence about it, as it is not in the public domain, is transmitted in circumstances importing an obligation of confidence, and there is then unauthorised use of that information, usually, but not necessarily, involving detriment to the complainant. As *Duke of Argyll v Duchess of Argyll* (1965) demonstrated, these ingredients may arise when confidential information is imparted in a relationship of trust not of a contractual nature and, therefore, personal information is clearly covered. However, that ruling suggests that breach of confidence is relevant only where a formal relationship can be identified.

In *Stephens v Avery* (1988), however, which concerned information communicated within a close friendship, it was not found necessary to identify a formal relationship between the parties at the time when the information was communicated, thus suggesting that the confidential nature of the information was the important factor. *Stephens v Avery* also demonstrated that a newspaper which was not a party to the original relationship, but

---

1   This brief overview of privacy law and indication of the approach the answer will take serves as a very good introduction.

was directly involved, in that it had been approached by one of the parties, could have obligations associated with a relationship of trust imposed upon it. *AG v Guardian Newspaper Ltd* (1987) (the *Spycatcher* case) took this stage further, in making it clear that if an editor of a newspaper is not directly approached, but has merely acquired the information, he or she can be held to be under the same duty of confidence if he or she is aware that the information is confidential. Breach of confidence has been the basis of an action against the press in a number of cases. In *A v B plc* (2002), for example, a Premier League footballer failed to prevent the publication of a 'kiss and tell' story, and in *Theakston v MGN* (2002) a television presenter failed to prevent publication of a story about his using a prostitute (but interestingly did prevent publication of associated photographs). In the leading case of *Campbell v Mirror Group Newspapers* (2004), the House of Lords upheld a distinction between the fact of drug-taking – which was not confidential – and the treatment for the drug problem – which was. In *Douglas v Hello!* (2003) damages were awarded against *Hello!* magazine for the unauthorised publication of photographs of the wedding of Michael Douglas and Catherine Zeta-Jones. Outside the celebrity world, breach of confidence was relied on, in *Venables v News Group Newspapers* (2001), to impose an injunction preventing the publication of the new identities of two men convicted when they were children of murdering a toddler.[2]

Though these cases were not brought directly under the **HRA**, the Act, and in particular the right to private life under **Art 8**, has influenced the development of the common law by widening the protection available under the pre-existing cause of action. An overarching right of privacy was expressly denied by the House of Lords in *Wainwright v Home Office* (2003). In *Campbell v MGN* Lord Nicholls, while agreeing there was no separate tort of privacy, highlighted the extent of the metamorphosis of the law of confidentiality by saying that the essence of the tort is better expressed now as 'misuse of private information'.

The question of the public interest in the context of media disclosures about the lives of celebrities was considered by the Court of Appeal in *A v B plc*. A married Premier League footballer sought to prevent a Sunday newspaper from publishing accounts by two women of their brief adulterous relationships with him. In discharging the High Court's injunction, the Court laid down guidelines for such cases. In particular, the Court stressed that press freedom was, in itself, a matter of public interest and that privacy claims were easy to make. It followed from this that an approach which allowed restraints on the press unless a significant public interest in the story could be shown was wrong. It is legitimate for the press to publish stories the public are interested in. The proper approach was that it was the restraints on the press that needed specific justification in terms of the strength of the arguments for confidence and privacy. Public figures, for

....

2   The chronological examination of all the confidence cases mentioned thus far demonstrates an excellent way to structure the answer.

example, had to accept a greater degree of media interference than ordinary persons and confidentiality about transient relationships was likely to be weaker than about married or long-term relationships. In other cases, such as *Woodward v Hutchins* (1977), the courts have refused injunctions where the claimants had used the media to promote a particular image of themselves and then tried to prevent the publication of stories which countered that image. *Campbell v Frisbee* (2002), for example, involved a story about Naomi Campbell's relationship with a film star, which was published, possibly in breach of confidence. The Court of Appeal held that it was arguable that a remedy should be refused in so far as the story was true and showed the claimant in a less favourable light than through the image she had been promoting of herself.

These cases must now be seen in light of the House of Lords' decision in *Campbell v MGN*, in which the majority did not lay as much stress on the general need for a free press. They were of the view that the media's privileged position under **Art 10** of the **ECHR** was subject to them acting in good faith and in accordance with the ethics of journalism.

Of potentially even more significance is the decision of the European Court of Human Rights in *Von Hannover v Germany* (2005) which concerned the failure of the German courts to prevent publication of photographs of Princess Caroline of Monaco in various public places. The European Court held that this amounted to a violation of her **Art 8** right to respect for privacy. Although she was a person about whom there was a lot of public interest, she had no official functions and had not sought to put aspects of her private life in the public domain. The court thought that even public figures had a legitimate expectation that their privacy would be respected. This applied even in public places, as there was a zone of interaction with others even in public that falls within the scope of private life. Crucially, the photographs did not fall within the sphere of any political or public debate.[3] The case was followed by the Court of Appeal in *McKennitt v Ash* (2006) in preventing publication of aspects of an unauthorised biography. The Court suggested that *Von Hannover* pushed the boundaries of expectations of privacy and meant that the more media-friendly statements in *A v B plc* were of less significance now.

Mosley v News Group Newspapers Ltd (2008) was another important case where breach of confidence was successfully used in relation to the publication of a story and images, this time involving sexual encounters. The court stated that there was a reasonable expectation that sexual matters between consenting adults on private property would remain private and that there was no public interest in publishing the story, therefore there were no **Art 10** interests to outweigh the claimant's **Art 8** rights.

---

3   This exposition of the *Von Hannover* case shows that it is good to spend more time on key cases when it serves your purposes well.

In deciding whether to grant an injunction, a court must, of course, give full weight to freedom of expression as provided for under **Sched 1, Art 10** of the **HRA**. An injunction will be compatible with **Art 10** if it is lawful and proportionate and aimed at protecting the rights of others, such as the right to confidentiality. **Section 12** of the **HRA** goes further and requires the courts to have particular regard to the importance of freedom of the press when deciding whether to make an order restricting expression. Since the balancing of **Art 8** by **Art 10** is inherent in **Convention** jurisprudence anyway, it seems clear that **s 12** adds little. **Section 12** also requires the courts to have regard to any Code of Practice. The Press Complaints Commission's Code is accepted as a relevant provision. This, of course, just leads the debate back to the public interest question since, regarding privacy, the Code permits a public interest justification.

Even if there are gaps in the protection offered to privacy by the common law doctrine of confidence, it does not necessarily follow that a statutory tort should be created to address this. This was the view of the Joint Select Committee on Privacy and Injunctions which concluded in a report in 2012 that the law on privacy should not be put on a statutory footing. They concluded that due to the continually developing nature of the area it would not be wise to attempt to crystalise it in statutory form; flexibility was needed.[4] Possible gaps might be best filled by context specific statutory provisions rather than a general tort. On the one hand, a tort might provide greater certainty than is provided by the uncontrolled and perhaps unpredictable development of confidence. In identifying the particular grounds of the public interest defence, a tort might also provide clearer protection for freedom of speech, though, on the other hand, the more flexible common law approach might, in fact, be more sensitive to the demands of the media.

In conclusion, it is suggested that the continuing development of breach of confidence is preferable to the introduction of a new tort. In terms of protection of privacy, breach of confidence, especially when linked to data protection, has now developed to the point where personal information will be protected in a wide range of situations. There will, of course, be gaps, but it is suggested these are better dealt with by specific reform and regulation and do not need a new tort. The important point is that the reasonableness of any privacy claim must be capable of being weighed against the public interest, including press freedom, in disclosure, and that process is central to breach of confidence. The **HRA** now provides both substantive rights and the background to the development of the law. **Article 8** provides a basic right to privacy which the courts, even when dealing with private law, must follow; and at the same time the courts must balance **Art 8** with freedom of expression under **Art 10**. Breach of

---

4   This reference to the Joint Select Committee's report is a good demonstration of how to incorporate relevant wider reading to your answer to help enrich it.

confidence cases decided under the influence of the **Convention** suggest that media freedom is recognised but that there are limits. Such developments, it is suggested, make a new tort unnecessary. There are now no serious calls for a statutory privacy tort as the courts have used the **HRA** to significantly fill the gaps in pre-existing law.

QUESTION 20

How far, if at all, does the law protect bodily and sexual privacy? Is reform in this area needed?

How to Answer this Question

A fairly tricky essay question since, unlike access to personal information, there is no obvious and coherent body of law which is relevant. It is probably a good idea to begin by considering what is meant by bodily and sexual privacy. You should then analyse the various strands of law that protect these interests, including recent reforms, before assessing whether further change is necessary. Note the key focus of the question is on *bodily* and *sexual privacy*. Thus take care not to focus too much on material of broader significance such as legislation on gender identity and civil partnerships.

Essentially, the following areas should be considered:

❖ possible ambit of bodily and sexual privacy;
❖ bodily privacy and crime control: police powers in this area;
❖ corporal punishment;
❖ bodily privacy in the medical context: *Pretty v United Kingdom* (2002);
❖ personal autonomy as to the expression of sexuality – legal restraints;
❖ **Art 8, Sched 1** of the **HRA 1998** and relevant European Court of Human Rights (ECtHR) decisions – *Laskey* (1997), *Lustig-Prean* (1999), *ADT* (2000);
❖ the **Sexual Offences Act 2003**.

Answer Structure

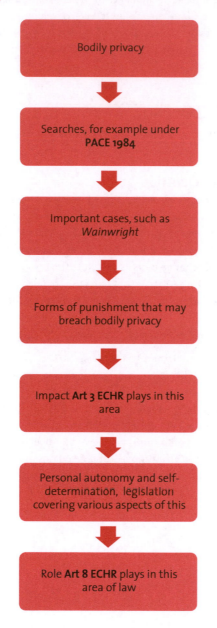

Bodily privacy

Searches, for example under **PACE 1984**

Important cases, such as *Wainwright*

Forms of punishment that may breach bodily privacy

Impact **Art 3 ECHR** plays in this area

Personal autonomy and self-determination, legislation covering various aspects of this

Role **Art 8 ECHR** plays in this area of law

ANSWER

Bodily and sexual privacy may be seen as encompassing two main interests. First, individuals have an interest in preventing actual physical intrusions on the body. This interest consists of a negative right to be 'left alone' in a physical sense, but may also encompass a positive claim on the State to ensure that bodily integrity is not infringed. However, the main concern here is with the extent to which the State allows such infringement. Secondly, an individual has an interest in retaining autonomy as regards freedom of choice in decisions as to the disposal or control of his or her own body. Usually, the individual is, in effect, asking the State to leave him or her alone to make such decisions in order to preserve autonomy. In some instances, however, the individual will be requiring the assistance of the authorities in ensuring that he or she is able to exercise autonomy. Thus, personal privacy at its simplest level may be defined as the freedom from physical intrusion, but, arguably, the concept may be expanded to encompass individual autonomy, thereby allowing a variety of interests to be considered under this head.[5]

The law determines that, in certain circumstances, bodily privacy may give way to other interests. Thus, **s 55** of the **Police and Criminal Evidence Act (PACE) 1984** (Code C Annex A) allows intimate and strip searches, but recognises that the violation they represent may occur only in well-defined circumstances. Intimate searches may occur only if there is reasonable suspicion that Class A drugs or implements which might be used for self-harm or to harm others may be found and there are other safeguards regarding the conduct of the search.

The question as to how far clothing must be removed on instruction of State officials has been considered in *Lindley v Rutter* (1980), where a general order to remove the bras of all female detainees in the police station was challenged. It was found that such treatment constituted an affront to human dignity and therefore could not be standard practice, but needed a clearer justification which could be derived only from the specific circumstances

5   This explanation of the terms bodily and sexual privacy serves as a very useful starting point and gives a clear focus to the answer.

of the arrestee. In *Wainwright v Home Office* (2003), the House of Lords accepted that the voluntary strip search of a prisoner's visitor, which was done in a humiliating and unseemly manner, was a breach of the prison's regulations. However, the House would not create a remedy by recognising a general right of privacy. Under the **HRA**, intimate searches, strip searches and other matters such as the taking of bodily samples clearly engage **Art 8(1)** and so will require justification in terms of legal basis, purpose and proportionality under **Art 8(2)**. In *Wainwright*, it was suggested that any remedy under the Act would require the violation of privacy to be intentional rather than simply negligent. However, in *Wainwright v United Kingdom* (2006), the European Court ruled that the manner of the searches, irrespective of intent, and the lack of safeguards violated **Art 8**.[6]

Certain forms of punishment may be seen as an unjustified intrusion onto bodily integrity. Corporal punishment was outlawed in state schools after the decision of the ECtHR in *Campbell and Cosans v UK* (1982), and the ban was extended to private schools by the **Schools Standards and Framework Act 1998**. In *R (Williamson) v Secretary of State for Education* (2005), where a group of Christian parents and teachers challenged the ban applying to private schools, the House of Lords decided that the statutory ban was necessary in a democratic society for the protection of the rights and freedoms of others. The legislation was intended to protect children against the distress, pain and other harmful effects of physical violence. In *Costello-Roberts v UK* (1993), the ECtHR found that the UK had a positive duty that schools, of whatever kind, should only use punishments that were compatible not only with **Art 3** of the **ECHR** (which requires a sufficient level of severity) but also with **Art 8**. The latter, in certain circumstances, might afford a broader protection to physical integrity than that afforded by **Art 3** (see *Wainwright* above). In *A v UK* (1999), the ECtHR showed itself willing to interfere in family life in order to protect the rights of a child. A nine-year-old boy had been repeatedly beaten with a cane by his stepfather. The stepfather was acquitted of assault, having relied on the defence of reasonable chastisement. The ECtHR held that, by leaving the question of reasonableness to a jury and thus failing to protect the boy from ill-treatment, the UK was in breach of **Art 3**. To this extent, the **ECHR** will protect bodily integrity, and this raises the possibility of the English courts further developing this area under the **HRA**.

Section 58 of the **Children Act 2004** prevents the use of the parental chastisement defence in any assault charge amounting to wounding or actual or grievous bodily harm and child cruelty offences. This was criticised by some as a missed opportunity to completely prohibit violence against children but probably does enough to bring UK law into line with the **ECHR**.[7]

....

6   This exploration of *Wainright*, and how it received different treatment in UK courts and the ECtHR shows a good way to explore cases.

7   This description and comment on the **2004 Act** and the **ECHR** will be well received by the examiner as it shows knowledge and ownership of the law.

Personal autonomy connotes an interest not in preventing physical intrusion by others, but in the extent to which the law allows an individual a degree of control over his or her own body. Recognition of the need to allow such self-determination has become more prominent this century. Thus, abortion and suicide are no longer crimes under the **Abortion Act 1967** and the **Suicide Act 1961**. However, limits as to self-determination are represented by the **Prohibition of Female Circumcision Act 1985** and the **Surrogacy Act 1985** (although it should be noted that surrogacy is only curbed by the Act, not outlawed: it only prevents commercial surrogacy arrangements). Such measures may suggest that the twentieth century placed greater value on bodily self-determination: the presumption is that, in this matter, the individual should apply his or her own moral standards, except when this allows something particularly abhorrent in British society to occur, such as female circumcision. Then, the law will impose the wider social standard on the particular individual.

The question of the ambit of self-determination has arisen most frequently in the context of medical treatment.

Recent decisions of the courts indicate a greater willingness to accept adult patient autonomy. There are a number of cases in which the right of patients to refuse treatment has been upheld even though doctors believe the treatment is in the patient's best interests. For example, refusal of a Caesarean birth (*St George's Healthcare NHS Trust v S* (1998)) or refusal of amputation of a gangrenous leg (*Re C (Adult: Refusal of Medical Treatment) (1994)*). The leading authority is *Re B (Consent to Treatment: Capacity) (2002)*, in which the Court of Appeal upheld the right of a mentally alert but seriously ill woman to choose to have her life support machine turned off and, consequently, to die. In relation to assisted suicide *R (Pretty) v DPP (2002)* maintained that a homicide charge could still be brought irrespective of consent. The ECtHR held that there is no right to die inherent in **Art 2** of the **ECHR** although, on the issue of dignity in death, **Art 8** could be engaged (*Pretty v UK (2002)*). This was followed by the House of Lords in *R (Purdy) v DPP* (2010) in holding that the requirement in **Art 8** for accessibility and foreseeability required the DPP to issue offence-specific guidelines to delineate the circumstances when a prosecution was likely to be brought for assisted suicide.

Self-determination as regards the body in areas relating to sexuality may be regarded as a related interest, because it raises questions as to the extent to which individuals have the power of choice in relation to the expression of sexuality. Until recently, the criminal law continued to prohibit or restrict certain forms of sexual activity even though they were undertaken by consenting adults and did not involve harm to others. The tendency of the law is now clearly set against prohibiting harmless conduct by consenting adults, and this principle is embodied in the **Sexual Offences Act 2003**.[8]

8   This background knowledge to the **2003 Act** provides context and shows the examiner you have good knowledge of the area.

Prior to this, crimes such as buggery or gross indecency between men (**s13** of the **Sexual Offences Act 1956**), were decriminalised by the **Sexual Offences (Amendment) Act 1967**, so long as they were undertaken in private. Indeed, the outright criminalisation of male homosexual acts involves an interference with private life, under **Art 8(1)** of the **ECHR**, which a State would find hard to justify under **Art 8(2)**, even though States have a wide margin of appreciation on moral matters. In *Dudgeon v UK* (1981), the continuation of the threat of prosecution for private homosexual acts in Northern Ireland (to which the **1967 Act** did not apply) was held to be disproportionate: it involved a grave interference with the applicant's private life despite, and on the other hand, little evidence of damage to morals.

The **1967 Act** set the age of consent at 21 and this was finally reduced to 16 by the **Sexual Offences (Amendment) Act 2000**, thus ending decades of discrimination between heterosexuals and homosexuals on the issue. Legal discrimination remained, particularly because the narrow conception of privacy in the **1967 Act** meant that the criminal law could still be applied if, for example, there were more than two people present even in a private dwelling. Such discrimination may well be an unjustified intrusion into the right to private life in **Art 8** of the **ECHR**, as was held in *ADT v UK* (2000).

The **Sexual Offences Act 2003** introduced comprehensive reform. The Act redefined and created a whole new range of sexual offences; it included the abolition of the offences of buggery and indecency for both men and women. In general terms, the new offences were defined to deal with non-consensual (therefore harmful) sexual acts or to criminalise sexual acts involving children, or which breached a relationship of trust or other exploitation. A guiding principle was that sexual offences should not be gender-specific. In so far as these reforms mean that the law on sexual behaviour is no longer based on moral disapproval and removes residues of discrimination based on gender and sexual orientation, it is to be welcomed as a necessary reform.

Some types of sado-masochistic behaviour are held to be unlawful whether or not the participants consent to it. The level of behaviour which will be unlawful despite consent is of a surprisingly minor nature; in *Donovan* (1934), it was defined as 'any hurt or injury calculated to interfere with health or comfort . . . it need not be permanent, but must be more than merely transient or trifling'. However, such interference may be justified as in the public interest, thus exempting blows given in the course of friendly athletic contests which, following the ruling in *Coney* (1882), are seen as being for 'good reason'.

In *Brown* (1993), a group of sado-masochistic homosexuals had regularly, over 10 years, willingly participated in acts of violence against each other for the sexual pleasure engendered in the giving and receiving of pain. It was found that the inflicting of injuries amounting to actual bodily harm could not fall within the category of 'good reason' and therefore, despite the consent of all the participants, the defendants were convicted of actual bodily harm under the **Offences Against the Person Act 1861**. In *Laskey, Jaggard and*

Brown v UK (1997), the ECtHR unanimously found that there had been no violation of **Art 8**, since it was within the State's competence to regard the convictions as necessary for the protection of health within **Art 8(2)**.

It is concluded that, until recently, the law had failed to give proper protection to bodily and sexual privacy. There is no question, however, that, in terms of the law, the situation is being transformed and, in most areas, autonomy, non-discrimination and equality is now recognised as the policy of the law.

QUESTION 21

Consider the extent to which UK law maintains a reasonable balance between respect for privacy of the home and the State's need to fight crime and maintain internal security.

How to Answer this Question

This is clearly quite a general and wide-ranging essay which requires knowledge of a number of different areas. It is limited by the reference to 'home' so that you do not need to consider invasions of personal privacy such as bodily searches or the taking of samples. The following areas should be considered:

- ❖ the **Security Services Act 1989**, the **Intelligence Services Act 1994**, the **Police Act 1997**, the **Regulation of Investigatory Powers Act (RIPA) 2000** – safeguards against unreasonable intrusion;
- ❖ the influence of the European Court of Human Rights (ECtHR) in this area;
- ❖ **ss 17** and **18** of **PACE 1984** – safeguards in respect of the search and seizure power;
- ❖ Code of Practice B made under **PACE** (revised March 2011);
- ❖ comparison between powers of the security services to enter premises and those of police officers.

Answer Structure

```
┌─────────────────────────────┐
│ Intrusion types, such as direct │
│   and covertly intrusive    │
└─────────────────────────────┘
              ↓
┌─────────────────────────────┐
│     Covert surveillance     │
└─────────────────────────────┘
              ↓
┌─────────────────────────────┐
│ Legislation that is relevant to │
│   area of covert surveillance │
└─────────────────────────────┘
              ↓
┌─────────────────────────────┐
│   Role Art 8 ECHR plays in  │
│ relation to the law in this area │
└─────────────────────────────┘
              ↓
┌─────────────────────────────┐
│      Direct intrusions      │
└─────────────────────────────┘
              ↓
┌─────────────────────────────┐
│  Statutory powers to enter  │
│ property, such as under PACE │
└─────────────────────────────┘
```

Aim Higher ★

Exam markers often provide feedback along the lines of 'more depth required'. What does this mean and how can you achieve it? Essentially, you need to try show that you do not just know the basic law but that you have scratched beneath the surface and are aware of the underlying issues or complexities. Clearly within a standard exam question it is not feasible to do this throughout but try to show that you can articulate some of the subtleties of the law. See for example the section in the answer below relating to scrutiny of interception of communications under **RIPA**. This seeks to outline the limitations of the scrutiny process while at the same time building an argument about the dangers of arbitrariness inherent in such a scheme.

ANSWER

Before addressing this question, it is necessary to consider what is meant by 'respect for privacy of the home'. Interference with this right does not merely connote physical intrusion, but could clearly occur in a number of ways. Apart from entry to property, search and seizure, it could include the use of long-range surveillance devices, telephone tapping and the planting of surveillance devices on property. It would seem to include any form of violation of the privacy of the home. The concern here is with intrusion by or on behalf of the State, with the aim of preventing crime or promoting internal security. Such aims are clearly legitimate; the question is whether the safeguards against unreasonable intrusion are adequate.[9]

The first point to be made is that the citizen may not even be aware that intrusion is taking place. This is particularly true of telephone tapping and the use of surveillance devices. Public awareness of the use of such devices is severely curtailed by the operation of the **Official Secrets Act 1989**, the **Security Services Act 1989** and the **RIPA 2000**. In addition to preventing information as to the operation of the security services reaching the public domain, these statutes provide very wide grounds for interference.

The ECtHR in, for example, *Klass v Germany* (1979) has accepted that surveillance for national security purposes may be compatible with **Art 8**. Non-national security cases such as *Malone v UK* (1984) and *Kopp v Switzerland* (1999) confirm that surveillance must be regulated by law and the circumstances in which it is likely to be used be made reasonably foreseeable, and that there must be appropriate protection built into the regulatory scheme, albeit such protection is bound to reflect the secrecy of the process.[10]

In Britain, the Home Secretary may issue warrants for the interception of communications by the security services under wide powers found in **s 5** of the **RIPA 2000**. The purposes for which warrants may be issued include that the warrant is necessary 'in the interests of national security' and 'for the purpose of safeguarding the economic wellbeing of the UK'. An important restriction on the Home Secretary's powers, in line with **ECHR** requirements under **Art 8(2)**, is that an interception warrant 'shall not' be issued unless the Home Secretary believes that the conduct it authorises 'is proportionate to what is sought to be achieved'.

Public scrutiny is weak. Complaints can be made only to a tribunal set up under the Act with no possibility of scrutiny by a court. Whether the tribunal meets the requirements of independence and impartiality required by **Art 6** is unclear. Tribunal decisions are not published and, although an annual report giving some information on the number of intercept warrants issued must be made available, it is first subject to censorship by the Prime Minister. In any case, there is a statutory bar to disclosure in court of information indicating that warranted telephone interceptions had been made (**ss 17** and **18** of the

....

9   This explanation of 'respect for privacy in the home' is an excellent way to start as it defines the terms that will be explored from the outset to give the answer clarity and focus.
10   These references to ECtHR cases show a good way of incorporating authority into your answer.

RIPA 2000), and the danger of unaccountable State actions seriously affecting the liberty and private lives of citizens is real.

If the security services wish to enter or interfere with property, the Secretary of State can issue a warrant under s 5 of the Intelligence Services Act 1994. The warrant can be issued so long as the Secretary of State thinks it is 'necessary' for 'assisting' the various secret services in the discharge of their functions. The safeguards are internal and hard to challenge: the Secretary of State must be satisfied that the issue of a warrant is 'proportionate' to what is to be achieved, that this could not be achieved by other means and that there are adequate procedures to prevent improper disclosure of information gained.[11] The functions of the Security Service are widely defined in s 1 of the 1989 Act and include 'the protection of national security and, in particular, its protection from . . . actions intended to overthrow or undermine parliamentary democracy by political, industrial or violent means'.

Warrants for the interception of communications under s 5 of the RIPA 2000 can be issued to the police or the Serious Organised Crime Agency (SOCA) for purposes including the detection of serious crime. The Security Service also has jurisdiction regarding serious crime. In a surveillance context and generally, the increasing involvement of security services in the traditional police function (against organised crime and terrorism, for example) is a matter for concern because of the far weaker legal regulation that applies to the security services.

For general purposes, the police may only enter premises in certain carefully defined circumstances and must follow a procedure, once there, designed to allow the citizen a reasonable chance of making a complaint if he or she wishes to do so. The basis of the procedure is in PACE and these powers are subject to more detailed requirements found in Code of Practice B.

First, the power to enter premises conferred by ss 17, 18 and 32 of PACE can be exercised either where an officer wants to arrest a person suspected of an indictable offence, or where a person has been so arrested and the intention is to search the person's premises or to search the area where s/he was immediately prior to arrest. Searching of premises other than under ss 17, 18 and 32 can only occur if a search warrant is issued by a magistrate. A warrant will only be issued if there are reasonable grounds for believing that an indictable offence has been committed and where the material is likely to be of substantial value to the investigation of the offence (s 8 PACE). The warrant must identify the articles to be sought, although once the officer is on the premises, other articles may be seized under s 19 if they appear to relate to any other offence. Part 2 of the

---

11   This analysis of the Secretary of State's powers demonstrates a good way to incorporate analysis into your answer as you go along.

Criminal Justice and Police Act 2001 further extends the situations in which material may be seized and retained by the police. A warrant normally authorises entry to premises on one occasion unless the warrant specifies that multiple entry is permitted in order to secure the purposes of the warrant. In such situations the authorisation of an Inspector not involved in the investigation is required for any subsequent entry. Important privacy issues can arise in respect of various types of confidential material and information. Police may not search for legally privileged material and other forms of confidential material, including journalistic material, cannot be searched for but require a disclosure order made by a judge usually on the basis of a hearing. A disclosure order can be refused on public interest grounds. These restrictions do not apply to warrants obtained by the security services, discussed above. The **Criminal Justice and Police Act 2001** allows police to remove documents in order to see whether they come within one of the forbidden or restricted categories.

Under para 6.7 of Code B, the subjects of all searches, consensual or otherwise, must receive information about the search in the form of a Notice of Powers and Rights and, under para 6.8, where a search has taken place but the occupier is absent, the Notice should be endorsed with the name of the officer and the date and time.

These provisions suggest some determination to strike a reasonable balance between the perceived need to confer on the police a general power to search property and the need to protect the citizen. If the powers are exceeded, an action for trespass will lie. However, it may be argued that, although the provisions governing the power to enter premises show a respect for privacy, the provisions governing seizure, particularly **s 19** of **PACE** and **Pt 2** of the **Criminal Justice and Police Act**, come too close to allowing a general ransacking of the premises once a lawful entry has been effected.[12]

The **Police Act 1997** put bugging and surveillance (other than searches) on a statutory footing for the first time. A warrant in respect of private premises can only be granted if the independent Commissioner has been consulted first. Complaints are to the surveillance tribunal, discussed above, and the same problems of lack of judicial oversight apply, but the Act does not prevent unauthorised surveillance being admitted as evidence in a later trial and, hence, has attracted much negative criticism.

The **RIPA 2000** has extended the **Police Act** approach to 'directed' and 'intrusive' surveillance by the police and the security services. An example of directed surveillance would be where a 'bugging' device is placed in the hallway of a block of flats, thus providing information of a lesser quality than if the device was inside one of the flats. Intrusive surveillance would occur, for example, where a bugging device is placed in a car

---

12 This is very good analysis of the search powers and shows the level of depth that can be achieved in a short space.

parked near a private house, thus providing information of the same quality as if the device was inside the house. The difference between the two types of surveillance is also indicated by the level of authority required to authorise it. As far as the police are concerned, for example, directed surveillance must generally be authorised by a Superintendent; intrusive surveillance, on the other hand, must generally be authorised by the Chief Constable. Moreover, unless the case is urgent, approval for intrusive surveillance must generally be obtained in advance from an independent Surveillance Commissioner. It has been argued that this 'twin-track' approach to the different types of surveillance is unsatisfactory and, in particular, that the scheme for directed surveillance demonstrates little respect for individual privacy.

Although it is to be welcomed that the statutory controls over surveillance now encompass both the police and the security services, it is not clear that the balance between personal privacy and the needs of internal security has been struck in the right place. There may well be challenges to the operation of these powers under the **HRA** and the desire to forestall such challenges clearly explains much of the legislation, particularly the extensive references to the need for proportionality. Nevertheless, the conclusion must be that the balance, particularly regarding national security, is still in favour of the police and security services as opposed to the privacy of the individual.

QUESTION 22

Newtown United football team has reached the European Champions League final in Belgium. The team's hotel and training camp is a former castle overlooking a quaint town near the French border. The team has a state-of-the-art training and treatment centre near the hotel. After a few days of intensive training, the manager, Eric Svensson, decides that the players need a break from it all to recover so arranges a day off, during which he intends them to relax and recuperate.

The star midfielder, Doug Beckford decides to visit Paradise Beach, a dramatic coastal spot in the south of the country. The beach is owned by the Paradise Country Club and has signs around it saying, 'Private – Club Patrons Only'. Doug decides to top up on his suntan by lying in the sun without any clothes on. However, a group of journalists from the *Daily Moon* newspaper hire a speedboat and take photographs of his bare bottom with a long-lens camera. The next day the photographs are published in the *Daily Moon* with the headline, 'Naked Cheek – is this how Doug prepares for the big game?'

Doug is also disturbed by a proposed 'special feature' in *Just Super!* magazine which will contain lots of pictures of Doug, his wife and their children shopping, eating at restaurants, driving, playing in the park and various other everyday activities back home. Although he has previously done a lot of publicity work in glossy magazines showing his family and home life, he is getting increasingly frustrated with paparazzi photographers invading his life and he wants to stop it.

Meanwhile, Mike Bassett, the centre forward, goes to a lap-dancing bar in the town centre. He is given free cocktails and invited to the VIP lounge for a 'personal dance' by Heidi, the top dancer in the club. Mike ends up going back to Heidi's hotel and has a night of passion with her. The next day he is contacted by *Sport Daily* who say they intend to run a story headed, 'Mike scored with me!' from Heidi telling about their affair, together with photographs taken from a hidden camera in her room. It turns out that *Sport Daily* had paid Heidi in advance to seduce Mike and had set up the camera in her hotel room. Mike is due to marry his long-time girlfriend this summer and is anxious that she should not find out about what happened.

Although apparently cool and collected on the outside, unknown to the players and the public, Eric Svensson is very stressed by his job as the Newtown manager. As a consequence, he has developed a drink problem over the past few months. He seeks counselling through Alcoholics Anonymous. Due to the stress of the lead-up to the cup final, Eric has felt tempted to drink and has therefore attended a number of Alcoholics Anonymous sessions. The *Newtown Inquirer* newspaper had an undercover journalist pose as an alcoholic so as to gain access to the meetings and recorded the counselling sessions, including Eric's confessions of temptation and the pressures of his work. The *Newtown Inquirer* plans to run a front page spread headed, 'Eric in Booze Shock', detailing his drink problem and urging the Newtown Club hierarchy to urgently put the assistant coach in charge of the team, 'in the vital interests of the Club and the City'.

◗ **Advise Doug, Mike and Eric as to whether the law of confidence might protect their privacy interests in the above situations.**

How to Answer this Question

This is an example of a problem question in relation to the law of confidence and protection of privacy. Such questions do crop up from time to time and require detailed application of the case law to the factual scenario presented. In this case there is a need for discussion of the situation with three potential claimants. The question is narrowed by the explicit reference to the law of confidence so there is no need to consider other potential remedies such as the Press Complaints Commission, defamation, harassment etc. Essentially the following areas should be covered:

- ❖ the test for breach of confidence where privacy interests are at stake;
- ❖ reasonable expectation of privacy;
- ❖ whether publishers know or ought to know of the expectation of privacy;
- ❖ balancing **Art 8** and **Art 10** rights;
- ❖ publication in the public interest;
- ❖ the use of 'super-injunctions';
- ❖ relevance of the Press Complaints Commission code of conduct;
- ❖ relevance of prior disclosure of private material;
- ❖ distinction between text and photographs;
- ❖ therapeutic information.

Applying the Law

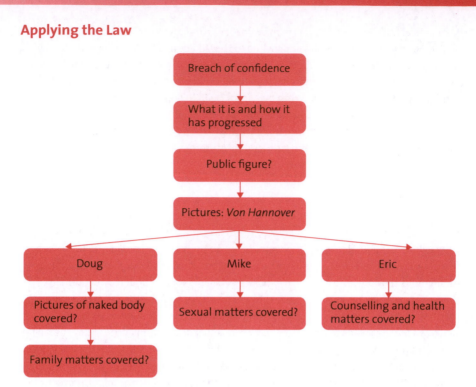

This diagram shows how to apply the common law doctrine of Breach of Confidence to the circumstances of Doug, Mike and Eric.

Common Pitfalls ✗

When you encounter a problem question the examiner is seeking to test not only your legal knowledge but also your problem solving and fact management skills. Unfortunately, some students when addressing problem questions feel the need to show that they are aware of the policy issues or controversies by entering into critical analysis of the law. You should generally reserve any critical commentary for essay questions and focus instead on identification of causes of action, application to the facts etc. so as to suggest potential solutions to the problem posed.

ANSWER

Traditionally the approach towards breach of confidence has involved applying the three stage test as stated in *Coco v Clark* (1969): Does the information have a 'quality of confidence'? Is it received in confidence? And is there unauthorised use of the information? However, as will be seen, the law has moved on significantly since the passing of the **Human Rights Act 1998** so that now following *Campbell v MGM* (2004) the key issues are: Is there an interest of a private nature? Does the claimant have a reasonable expectation of privacy? And does/ought the defendant to know the information is private? In addition, whenever the press is concerned, as it is here, the court will need to address the balance between privacy interests on the one hand and free expression interests on the other.[13]

It seems fairly clear that Doug, Mike and Eric could have interests of a private nature to protect. The invasion regarding Doug consists of pictures of his naked body. This appears to be deserving of protection. He did not consent to the taking of the photos. In addition, he was on a private beach and on his day off and so might reasonably expect not to be photographed. Furthermore, his complaints about the paparazzi photographs of him and his family in restaurants etc. potentially deserves protection. According to *Von Hannover v Germany* (2005) the fact that the photographs were taken in a public place does not necessarily mean that privacy interests cannot exist. Indeed photographs of a similar nature to those Doug takes issue with were at stake in the *Von Hannover* case and the European Court had no hesitation in ruling that they were private in nature. It is not the location that is conclusive but the activity. Family activities of the kind described do seem by their nature to be private.[14] A further consideration for a court though, would be the extent to which Doug can reasonably expect protection of his private life in light of his status as a public figure and his previous publication of his private life. In *A v B plc* (2003) the Court of Appeal emphasised that all public figures can expect less privacy than ordinary members of the public. In particular, where a person has previously courted public attention they have less ground to object to later intrusion.

Mike is also a public figure but we do not know the extent to which, if at all, he has previously courted attention. For him the invasion is pictures and information about a sexual act. On the face of it this is clearly deserving of protection as a private matter. However, it is a transitory relationship and therefore, according to *Theakston v MGN* (2002), it appears not as deserving of protection as sex within marriage or other stable relationship. The question of whether he could reasonably expect the relationship to remain private might be affected by the fact it started off in a public place, the lap-dancing bar and finished off in a hotel. In *A v B plc* the Court of Appeal said an extra marital affair carried out in similar semi-public surroundings was 'at the outer limits of relationships which may require the protection of the law'. *Theakston v MGN* is also a case that draws an interesting distinction between the facts of a story and accompanying photographs. Theakston was photographed in a brothel with a prostitute. The judge held that although the story was

---

13   This brief overview of key aspects of the law of confidence provides a good starting point and sets the scene well.

14   This application of the *Von Hannover* case demonstrates very well how to use and apply law to the given facts of a problem.

not confidential, he did have a reasonable expectation that intimate photographs would not be published – Theakston had never put such material in the public domain himself and had not consented to their being taken. In light of this, it seems Mike will also be protected by the law of confidence. Mike would also need to be advised about obtaining a 'super-injunction'. Super-injunctions are so named because they prevent not only the publication of information that is held to be confidential but the very fact an injunction even exists (see *LNS v Persons Unknown* (2010) (John Terry case)).

Eric seems to have an even stronger argument for protection of his privacy. Although he is a public figure, he is in a therapeutic environment seeking help with his illness (alcoholism) and can surely expect that his disclosures will remain secret. The whole point about Alcoholics Anonymous is that it is anonymous and confidential to the group. It also arguably involves quasi-medical information and should be treated in a similar way not only by the therapist but also, impliedly, by the other people present. *Campbell v MGN* is clear authority for the proposition that such information should be protected by the law of confidence.

Moving onto the question of whether the journalists knew or ought to have known about the expectation of privacy it is clear that at its broadest this is an objective assessment for the court to make. In view of the measures they took (hiring a boat and using long lens photography) it seems clear that the photographers for the *Daily Moon* knew Doug was having private time on a private beach. They must also have known he would not consent to the photographs being taken. In respect of the photographs of him and his family it is less clear cut, particularly given that he has consented to similar types of photographs in the past.[15] In Mike's case, *Sport Daily* planned in advance the sting operation. Their covert involvement is likely to mean a court would have little difficulty in finding that they ought to have known this would be a private situation, at least insofar as Mike was concerned. The *Newtown Inquirer* would no doubt have known that Eric's disclosures at the alcohol support and counselling meetings were intended to be and were reasonably expected to be a private matter.

The first two issues – the existence of private interests and reasonable knowledge of this on the part of the press – seem fairly easy to establish. The claims are therefore likely to come down to justification. In *A v B plc* and in *Campbell* the Court established that rather than create a separate privacy tort the **HRA 1998** had acted as the catalyst for absorbing the **Convention** rights into the existing equitable tort of breach of confidence. Ultimately then these disputes will require the court to balance the claimants' **Art 8** rights against the **Art 10** right of the press. The court will have to decide on the facts of each case whether preventing or punishing publication would be a proportionate interference with press freedom of expression in light of the privacy rights of the claimants.

....

15   This acceptance that the law is difficult to apply, but having a go at doing so will be given credit by the examiner as the law very often has grey areas. Acceptance of this without panicking shows good understanding of the area.

In respect of Doug, his previous exploitation of his private life will be relevant in deciding whether the current intrusion is permissible. There is also likely to be intense interest among sections the public about his performance and activities in the Champions League final. Although the paper did not trespass on land it did resort to long lens photography to take intimate pictures of him on private land. This is prohibited by the Press Complaints Commission code of conduct unless it is in the public interest. The relevance of the Code is that in **s12(4)** of the **HRA** the court should take into account any relevant industry code. Brooke LJ in *Douglas v Hello!* (2001) did say that a newspaper which flouted the code was likely to have its claim to free expression trumped by considerations of privacy. The newspaper has obviously taken a particular angle on the story suggesting that there may be something improper about Doug lying on a beach rather than, say, training. It is arguably in the public interest that the public should know how top players prepare for a key European cup final, but whether this would justify the photographs showing his naked body is less clear.

The proposed pictures of Doug and his family in *Just Super!* cause real difficulties. In *Campbell* the House of Lords implicitly accepted that being photographed in public was inevitable. However, in *Von Hannover* Princess Caroline of Monaco claimed that the German courts failed to protect her **Art 8** privacy rights by refusing some injunctions against the tabloid press taking photographs of her shopping, eating, riding etc. The European Court found that the intrusion into her private life was not justified in the public interest. Even public figures had a legitimate expectation that their privacy would be respected. Applying this to Doug's case is not straightforward. The photographs do seem to be of a similar nature to those dealt with in *Von Hannover*. Of more significance might be the fact that he has previously willingly placed such material in the public domain so it will be very difficult for him now to argue that he should be able to stop future intrusions.

As regards Mike, the paper could argue that it is justified in the public interest to publish the story to expose Mike's infidelity, particularly when he is about to marry his girlfriend. This could be covered by the PCC Code public interest exception of preventing the public being misled.[16] Even in the absence of such a factor, it is arguably in the public interest to expose immoral behaviour by role models. The behaviour might be said to be the willingness to frequent lap-dancing bars, the willingness to exploit women in the sex industry, or simply the willingness to have a one-night-stand outside the context of a 'loving relationship'. Whether this is in fact the paper's motive is perhaps questionable, particularly given the way the story is presented ('Mike scored with me!'). It appears there was no agreement that the information about the affair would remain confidential. As in *A v B plc*, Heidi's freedom of expression is a countervailing interest to be considered – she

----

16   This reference to the PCC code will be given credit by the examiner as it shows wider understanding of the area and how it is regulated.

clearly *does* want the relationship to be made public. However, she is effectively an employee of the paper, who went with the intention of deceiving Mike to get the story. Her free expression is thus probably not as important as someone who had a 'normal' relationship with Mike and then wanted to disclose it. The fact that the story arises in quasi-public places (lap-dancing bar and hotel) might be said to add to the justification for the invasion, although clearly the sexual acts took place in a private room.

On the other hand, the paper may have real difficulty in justifying the subterfuge and payments made to Heidi (both in breach of the PCC code unless in the public interest). In effect the paper has employed a prostitute to entrap Mike. It is hard to see how exposing an affair created at the behest of the paper itself could be said to be in the public interest. Even if the story may be published, the *Theakston* case provides support to enable Mike to prevent the publication of the photographs.

With Eric, the public interest in revealing his drink problem may be thought to be quite high. He is responsible for the whole Newtown team who are through to the final of a prestigious cup competition. There is a clear link between the stresses of that job and his problems with alcohol. If there is a risk of his performance being affected it is arguably very important that this fact is exposed and pressure put on the club management to remove him. This is clearly the angle that the paper has taken in its story. Again, subterfuge has been used to obtain the story so in terms of the PCC Code, the public interest would have to be engaged to justify this step. Arguably, the public and the club are being misled by Eric's apparently calm exterior given his problems. In this case the *Newtown Inquirer* may be able to go further than in the *Campbell* case and publish details of the counselling at Alcoholics Anonymous. Unlike Naomi Campbell's situation, Eric's condition and therapy has an ongoing impact on the performance of the football team and so is more clearly central to the importance of the story.

QUESTION 23

Assume that you are an adviser to the Parliamentary Joint Committee on Human Rights. The Committee is investigating the UK's compliance with its Human Rights obligations. You have been asked to research whether the UK requires a new privacy law in order to comply with its obligations under the European Convention on Human Rights. Present the findings of your research.

How to Answer this Question

This is a slightly more inventive way of presenting a reasonably straightforward essay question, which requires consideration of the current law of privacy and of means of developing it to ensure that there are no gaps in its protection of the right to privacy. Since the essay is so wide ranging, it will be necessary to be selective in the coverage of topics; otherwise, it will be too superficial. Since protection of personal information is seen as a key privacy issue at present, the coverage below has largely concentrated on that area.

Essentially, the following areas should be considered:

- ❖ breach of confidence;
- ❖ defamation and malicious falsehood;
- ❖ trespass and nuisance;
- ❖ development of existing remedies;
- ❖ possible incompatibility with the **European Convention on Human Rights (ECHR)**;
- ❖ proposals for a new tort of invasion of privacy;
- ❖ controversial legislation such as the **Regulation of Investigatory Powers Act (RIPA) 2000**.

Answer Structure

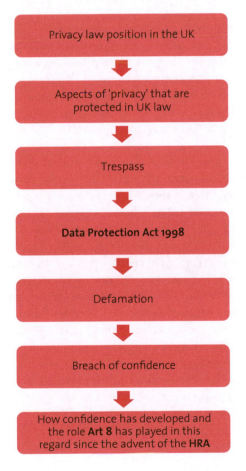

Privacy law position in the UK

⬇

Aspects of 'privacy' that are protected in UK law

⬇

Trespass

⬇

Data Protection Act 1998

⬇

Defamation

⬇

Breach of confidence

⬇

How confidence has developed and the role **Art 8** has played in this regard since the advent of the **HRA**

Common Pitfalls ✗

When you are analysing English law in the context of civil liberty issues be careful to check whether any of the cases you refer to have subsequently resulted in a decision of the European Court of Human Rights. Failure to do so will make your answer incomplete. Where you do refer to European Court cases be careful not to suggest that the domestic decision was 'overturned' or 'upheld' by the Strasbourg court. Remember that the **European Convention** does not provide an appeal route from domestic decisions but rather a distinct, international law remedy. The Strasbourg decision is likely to be highly persuasive for later domestic cases by virtue of **s 2 HRA** but it is not binding.

ANSWER

Since the **ECHR** has been incorporated into UK law, a right to respect for private and family life has for the first time become part of domestic law due to **Art 8**. It should be noted that this is not, strictly speaking, a right to privacy, but merely a right to 'respect', which is a lesser measure. Further, UK law by no means ignores privacy rights, but rather has a piecemeal and complicated way of protecting them. Thus, in order to decide whether and how reform is necessary, the present law must first be considered and then compared with relevant European Court of Human Rights (ECtHR) case law.[17]

Privacy may be said to encompass two broad interests, which may be termed control over intrusions and control over personal information. At present, UK law recognises no general rights to privacy, although there is some evidence that judges consider breach of privacy to be a wrong which should be remedied. However, the House of Lords, confirming cases such as *Kaye v Robertson* (1991), made clear in *Wainwright v Secretary of State for the Home Department* (2003) that English law covers specific and distinct interests without an overarching law of privacy. *Wainwright* is a revealing case. Two people visiting a prison were, prior to the **HRA** coming into effect, subject to strip searches which represented a gross invasion of their privacy. An action for damages against the prison authorities failed because, in the absence of an intention by prison officers to harm, the search could not be brought within the definition of the tort of trespass to the person. The European Court in *Wainwright v UK* (2006) ruled that there had indeed been a violation of **Art 8** (but not **Art 3**) by the searches. The intrusive nature of the searches and the lack of safeguards took the conduct outside of the justification in **Art 8(2)** despite the lack of any intention to humiliate. The lack of an effective remedy in domestic law gave rise to a violation of **Art 13**. Of course if the same conduct occurred

---

17 This brief overview of **Art 8** sets the scene well and provides a clear starting point for the answer.

now the **HRA** could be used and a direct action for breach of **Art 8** might succeed. Thus the **HRA** has filled some, but not all, of the 'gaps' in the protection of privacy.

Limited protection from such intrusion is afforded by actions for the torts of trespass or nuisance. Trespass is defined as entering onto land in the possession of another without lawful justification. It is confined to instances in which there is some physical entry; neither prying with binoculars nor electronic eavesdropping from outside the target's land is covered. *Bernstein v Skyviews* (1978) illustrates another limit to the ability of trespass to protect privacy. The defendants flew over the plaintiff's land in order to take photographs of it. It was held that either the claimant had no rights of possession over the air space or, alternatively, **s 40** of the **Civil Aviation Act 1942** exempted reasonable flights from liability. The court was not prepared to find that the taking of one photograph was unreasonable and a remedy could not be based solely on invasion of privacy as, of course, there is no such tort.[18] The tort of nuisance involves disturbing a person in the enjoyment of his or her land to an extent that the law regards as unreasonable. *Dicta* in *Bernstein* favoured the possibility that grossly invasive, embarrassing surveillance would amount to a nuisance and in *Khorasandjian v Bush* (1993), the Court of Appeal held that harassment could amount to nuisance. However, the House of Lords in *Hunter v Canary Wharf* (1997) restricted the range of plaintiffs in nuisance cases to those with a proprietary interest in the land affected. 'Harassing' behaviour of the kind which occurred in *Bush* is now easiest dealt with under the terms of **s 1** of the **Protection from Harassment Act 1997**. The **1997 Act** makes it an offence and a tort to pursue a course of conduct which amounts to harassment of another, where the harasser knows or ought to know that this will be its effect. However, it has severe limitations as a general weapon against intrusion on privacy. Most significant is the requirement of a 'course of conduct', which means that a single intrusion would not engage the Act's provisions (see *Sai Lau v DPP* (2000)).

These days, surveillance is often conducted by CCTV. There is surprisingly little regulation, although the Information Commissioner has produced a Code of Practice dealing with the requirements of the **Data Protection Act 1998** as regards CCTV in public places. The use of CCTV in public places may not, in itself, raise major privacy questions in the eyes of the law. **Article 8** of the **ECHR**, for example, does not provide for a right not to be photographed in the street (*Freidl v Austria* (1996), but see comments in *Von Hannover v Germany* (2006) to the effect that private life may in appropriate circumstances extend to the public realm). However, misuse of the resulting film will raise privacy issues. In *Peck v UK* (2003), the applicant's suicide attempt was recorded on CCTV and distributed to the media by the local council involved. There was held to be a violation of **Art 8** due to the lack of safeguards involved in the management and use of the CCTV footage. This should influence any future judicial review by the English courts about the use of CCTV.

---

18   This use of the *Skyviews* case shows how to use cases actively and effectively to set the law out.

The law of defamation is often thought to be closely linked to the protection of privacy. The difficulty with the use of defamation, however, is that the defence of justification means that it will not usually affect the situation where true facts are revealed. Moreover, the interest protected by defamation – the interest in preserving reputation – is not synonymous with the interest in preserving privacy.[19]

A further possible candidate for the development of a common law remedy for privacy is breach of confidence. It has a wider ambit than defamation, in that it prevents truthful communications and appears to protect confidential communications, whether or not their unauthorised disclosure causes detriment to the reputation of any person. At one time it was thought that breach of confidence was actionable only where there was a prior relationship implying confidentiality, such as between master and servant, husband and wife or medical practitioner and patient. However, cases such as *Stephens v Avery* suggest that a relationship of confidence can be found, despite the absence of a formal relationship. An important point about breach of confidence is that any remedy requires a consideration of the public interest – whether, on balance, the public interest favours disclosure over secrecy; the law will not protect infamous conduct from disclosure. In *R v Chief Constable of North Wales ex p AB* (1999), for example, the disclosure by the police of confidential information about the whereabouts of child sex offenders was upheld on public interest grounds.

The use of breach of confidence, with the **HRA** as a catalyst, as a means for protecting privacy has seen major strides in recent years. Step by step the courts have asserted their obligation to ensure that the ambit of the tort adequately protects privacy interests in **Art 8** of the **European Convention**. This culminated in *Campbell v MGN* (2004) where the House of Lords dealt with a dispute over the revelation of Narcotics Anonymous therapy by a leading model on the basis of the law of confidence without the need to develop a separate privacy law. Nevertheless, Lord Nicholls acknowledged the awkward fit when he suggested that the essence of the tort is now better encapsulated as 'misuse of private information'. What is not clear is whether the courts take the view that all reasonable privacy claims involving personal information can be met through a flexible interpretation of the rules of breach of confidence. In a different context the decision in *Wainwright* arguably shows that a more general remedy for breach of privacy is needed.

As well as the common law, the impact of statute on the protection of privacy should also be noted. The **Data Protection Act 1998** provides a statutory regime governing the holding of personal information. It applies to both public and private organisations and has its principal effect on the keeping of personal information. Such information must be processed in accordance with the data protection principles and this is enforced by the

---

19 These comments about defamation could only be made by having a deep understanding of the area, and as such will be given great credit by the examiner.

Information Commissioner and a tribunal; data subjects also have legal rights enforceable in the courts, for example, a right to have errors corrected. Privacy rights over personal information are limited, however, because of the wide range of exemptions in the Act.[20]

Thus, the common law currently offers only a partial protection of privacy and it no longer seems likely that the concept of breach of confidence will develop into a general right to privacy. **Article 8** of the **ECHR** may be the most satisfactory way forward. It gives each individual a right to respect for his or her private and family life, and the ECtHR has developed these rights fairly broadly. For example, the State has a positive duty to ensure respect for individuals' private and family lives (*X and Y v The Netherlands* (1986)); searches of the home or office are open to special scrutiny (*Niemietz v Germany* (1993)); there is a right to peaceful enjoyment of the home (*Sporrong and Lonnroth v Sweden* (1983) and *Powell and Rayner v UK* (1990)); and surveillance of the home by police or others at least requires safeguards (*Khan v UK* (2000)). However, the effect of **Art 8** is limited. **Article 8(2)** allows public authorities to invade or limit privacy for a number of reasons, including the interests of national security and protecting the rights and freedoms of others. These exceptions could be interpreted broadly. The ECtHR has, for example, been particularly cautious in cases related to personal information (see *Leander v Sweden* (1987)). Thus, much depends upon the attitude taken by future courts and governments.

Article 8 applies directly in English law only through the provisions of the **HRA**. The main point here is that the direct impact will be on the interpretation of statutes and the actions of public authorities, identified by **s 6** of the Act. The latter means that cases such as *Wainwright* should now be decided with proper reference to privacy. Whether **Art 8** has a major impact on privacy questions that do not involve public authorities depends on the extent to which the article is interpreted as imposing positive duties on the State to change the law affecting private parties, and the extent to which the 'horizontal effect' of the Act means that the courts, as public authorities themselves, use the **Convention** as a source of values inspiring the development of the common law. Of great importance also will be the way **Art 8** is related to **Art 10**, freedom of expression, including media freedom. The early decisions of the courts show that the courts are willing to engage in detailed and rigorous balancing of the right of the media to publish information of public interest against the rights of public figures to some degree of privacy in their lives. Where **Art 8** exposes gaps in the legal protection of privacy the way forward, it is suggested, is by specific regulation. In light of the existing protection and given the direct applicability of **Art 8** via the **HRA**, a general tort protecting privacy is unnecessary.

....

20 This reference to the **DPA** provides depth of coverage to the question, which was required by the set question and demonstrates a good grasp of the area.

Police Powers and Counter-Terrorist Measures
The Rights of Suspects

INTRODUCTION

This area concerns the balance struck by the law between powers conferred on the police, counter-terrorist measures, and the maintenance of individual freedom and of due process. That balance has been affected by the **HRA**, and the relevant **HRA** jurisprudence is gradually becoming a significant part of the law in this area.

Examiners often set problem questions in the area of 'ordinary' police powers, since the detailed rules of the **Police and Criminal Evidence Act 1984** (hereafter **PACE**), as amended, and the **Codes of Practice**) made under it lend themselves to such a format. (Note also the power to stop and search arising under the **Misuse of Drugs Act 1971 s 23(2)**.) The questions usually concern a number of stages from first contact between police and suspect in the street up to the charge. This allows consideration of the rules governing stop and search, arrest, searching of premises, seizure of articles, detention, treatment in the police station and interviewing. (It must be borne in mind that interviews do not invariably take place in the police station; an important area in the question may concern an interview of the suspect which takes place in the street or in the police car.) You need to be aware of key changes made to the **PACE** Codes (the most recent changes to which took place in 2011). In particular, a new arrest Code, Code G, and a special new Code, Code H (covering police detention of terrorist suspects) were introduced in 2006. The Codes, especially Code C, are very long and detailed; you only need, however, to be aware of the key provisions – the ones mentioned in the questions below. You also need to be aware of **ss 34–37** of the **Criminal Justice and Public Order Act 1994**, as amended, which curtail the right to silence and therefore affect police interviewing. (In freedom of assembly questions involving police powers, covered in Chapter 3, you also need to be aware of the extension of police powers in the public order context, contained in **Part V** of the **1994 Act**.) The common law power to arrest to prevent a breach of the peace is still extensively used and may need to be considered.

The rules governing obstruction and assault on a police officer in the execution of his duty under **s 89** of the **Police Act 1996** may be relevant as necessitating analysis of the legality of police conduct, in order to determine whether or not a police officer was in the execution of his duty. Finally, the question may call for an analysis of the forms of redress available to the suspect in respect of any misuse of police power. If essay questions are set, they often tend to place an emphasis on the balance struck by **PACE** between the suspect's rights and police powers.

Police powers to deal with 'ordinary' suspects differ from those available to deal with terrorist suspects; in general the level of due process available in relation to terrorist suspects is lower. Also, post-9/11, special measures were introduced to deal with terrorist suspects outside the normal criminal justice process – these were and are proactive measures, including detention without trial, designed to deal with terrorist activity before it occurs. At present detention without trial is not being used, but TPIM Notices (from the **Terrorism Prevention and Investigation Measures Act 2011**) can impose regimes on suspects that are close to house arrest. So this chapter deals with a range of police powers applicable to 'ordinary' suspects and also aspects of the current counter-terrorist scheme. The **Codes of Practice** made under **PACE** reflect the differences between terrorist suspects and non-terrorist suspects since terrorist suspects are no longer covered by Code C (the Code covering interviews and police detention) but by Code H. Police powers in relation to terrorist suspects, special terrorism offences and sanctions operating outside the criminal justice system are contained in the **Terrorism Act 2000**, as amended, especially by the **Terrorism Act 2006**, and the **Terrorism Prevention and Investigation Measures Act 2011** (which abolished the **Prevention of Terrorism Act 2005**). **Part 4** of the **Anti-Terrorism, Crime and Security Act 2001** – the key UK counter-terrorist response to 9/11 – has been repealed. However, this chapter takes account of it in order to place its successor, the **2005 Act**, and in turn, its successor, the **Terrorism Prevention and Investigation Measures Act 2011** in their proper context. Counter-terrorism powers are most likely to be discussed in essay question format. It should be noted that some Public Law courses may not cover counter-terrorism powers, or may cover only the 'police powers' aspects.

Articles 5 and **6** of the **European Convention on Human Rights** (hereafter the **ECHR**), which provide guarantees of liberty and security of the person and of a fair trial respectively, were received into UK law once the **Human Rights Act (HRA) 1998** came fully into force in 2000. It should be noted that **Art 6** protects a fair hearing in the civil and criminal contexts, but our concern is with the criminal context, and in particular with pre-trial procedures which may affect the fairness of the trial and which, therefore, may need to be considered under **Art 6** (*Teixeira v Portugal* (1998), *Khan v UK* (2001)). Under the **HRA, Arts 5** and **6** and other **Convention** articles relevant in this area, such as **Art 8** (which provides a right to respect for private life and for the home), are directly applicable in UK courts since the courts are bound by them (**s 6 HRA**). The police and other authorities involved in the criminal justice process are also so bound. The rights should also be taken into account in relation to interpreting and applying common law and statutory provisions affecting the powers of State agents, including the police, and counter-terrorist powers. **Section 3** of the **HRA** requires that: 'So far as it is possible to do so, primary and subordinate legislation must be read and given effect in a way which is compatible with the **Convention** rights.' **Section 3(2)(b)** reads, 'this section does not affect the validity, continuing operation or enforcement of any incompatible primary legislation'. This goes well beyond the previous obligation to resolve ambiguity in statutes by reference to the **Convention**. All statutes affecting this area, in particular **PACE**, the **Terrorism Act 2000** and the **Terrorism Prevention and Investigation Measures Act 2011**, will therefore have to be interpreted so as to be in harmony with the **ECHR**, if that is at all possible.

So the application of the powers under all these statutes, in specific instances, should be in harmony with all the **Convention** rights, since those applying the powers, including the courts, are bound by those rights, under **s 6 HRA**. As Chapter 9 explains, under **s 6**, **Convention** guarantees are binding only against public authorities. In this context, if the police or other State agents use powers deriving from any legal source in order to interfere with the liberty or privacy of the citizen, this means not only that the rights should be adhered to, but that the citizen may be able to bring an action against them under **Art 5, 6** or **8** (and/or any other relevant article). Within the criminal process, citizens can rely on **Art 6** in order to ensure the fairness of the procedure under **s 7(1)(b)** of the **HRA**. Also, in a hearing relating to interference with the liberty of terrorist suspects *outside* the normal criminal process **Art 6** will be applicable. Exam questions therefore demand awareness of the **Arts 5, 6** and **8** jurisprudence and of the impact of the **HRA** in this area. It is not good practice merely to refer to the **HRA** in answers; you should refer to specific sections of the **HRA**, usually **ss 3** or **6** and to the relevant **Convention** right; reference should also be made to the **Convention** jurisprudence and to the domestic use of the **Convention** in relevant post-**HRA** cases.

Checklist ✔

Students must be familiar with the following areas:

- the key provisions under **PACE**, as amended, in particular by **s 110 Serious and Organised Crime Act 2005**;

- key aspects of the **PACE** Codes of Practice affecting the areas mentioned above, especially Codes A (2011) and C (2008), and **ss 1, 2, 17, 18, 24, 28, 32, 58, 76** and **78 PACE**;

- **s 23(2) Misuse of Drugs Act 1971**;

- key cases on **PACE** and related provisions, especially *R v Samuel* (1988), *R v Loosely* (2001), *R v Khan* (1996), *Osman* (1999), *DPP v Hawkins* (1988), *R v Beckles* (2004), *R v Condron* (1997), *R v Delaney* (1988), *R v Parris* (1993) and *Gillan* (2006);

- the provisions under the **Criminal Justice and Public Order Act 1994**, as amended, relevant to police powers, especially **ss 34, 36, 37** and **60**;

- **s 58** of the **Youth Justice and Criminal Evidence Act 1999** – inserts **s 34(2A)** into the **Criminal Justice and Public Order Act 1994**;

- the offences of obstruction and assault on a police officer in the execution of his duty under **s 89** of the **Police Act 1996**;

- the issues raised by the revisions of the Codes of Practice made under **PACE**; latest revisions 2011; new arrest Code, Code G, introduced in 2006;

- the **PACE** rules governing exclusion of evidence, particularly **s 78**;

- the relevant tortious remedies;

- the police complaints mechanism under **Police Reform Act 2002 Part 2** and **Sched 3**;

- police powers contained in the **Terrorism Act 2000**, as amended, especially by the **Terrorism Act 2006; PACE** Code H 2006;

- counter-terrorist offences under the **Terrorism Act 2000** as amended;

- counter-terrorist measures under the **Prevention of Terrorism Act 2005** – Control Orders (now repealed)

- key control order cases;

- **Part 4 Anti-Terrorism, Crime and Security Act 2001** (now repealed);

- counter-terrorist measures under the **Terrorism Prevention and Investigation Measures Act 2011**

- **Arts 3, 5, 6** and **8** of the **ECHR**; relevant ECtHR case law, especially *Khan v UK* (2001), *Condron v UK* (2001) and *Beckles v UK* (2003); *Gillan v UK* (2010);

- the **HRA**, especially **ss 2, 3, 6**.

QUESTION 24

Barneveld had been out with his friends one evening for a meal and some drinks and he returned home at 2 am. Unfortunately he had lost his house keys and he did not want to wake his wife and children up. He remembered that he kept a spare key in the garden shed so he went into the shed to get it. The shed door was locked though and the key to the shed was inside the house. Barneveld decided to force entry into the shed and he broke the lock to do so. Once inside the shed he managed to find the key and he came out of the shed and put the house key into his pocket.

Two police officers had been watching Barneveld throughout all of this activity as they were parked in a police car in the street. They watched him enter the garden and they saw him skulking about for a few minutes and he appeared to be looking around frantically all over the garden and through the windows. They then saw him walking around the shed, break into it and re-appear putting something into his pocket.

They approached Barneveld as he came out of the shed and asked him what he thought he was doing. Barneveld ignored them and pushed his way past the officers and walked towards the house.

The two officers immediately grabbed Barneveld's arms and twisted them up his back and forced him onto the floor. They searched Barneveld's pockets and found his wallet and the house keys he had located from the garden shed. One of the officers said to Barneveld 'So, thought you'd do a bit of house-breaking did you? We'll see about that!'.

Barneveld told the officers that he was not house breaking and that he actually lived at the house and merely did not want to wake his family up. The officers did not believe Barneveld so they rang the doorbell of the house and Barneveld's wife answered. She confirmed Barneveld's story so the police officers told Barneveld to watch what he was doing in the future and then left.

▶ **Comment upon the legality of the police conduct in the above scenario.**

How to Answer this Question

This is a classic police powers problem question. Rather than requiring students to briefly cover many different areas of law relating to police powers, this question requires a specific focus upon one area of law, namely stop and search. With a narrow focus students will be expected to go into a good deal of depth in their answer. Police powers of stop and search have been making headlines again lately, the recurring allegation of them being used in a discriminatory way raising serious questions about their use. It is therefore vitally important that students can demonstrate good understanding of police powers of stop and search as governed by **ss 1–3** of the **Police and Criminal Evidence Act 1984** (**PACE**).

Applying the Law

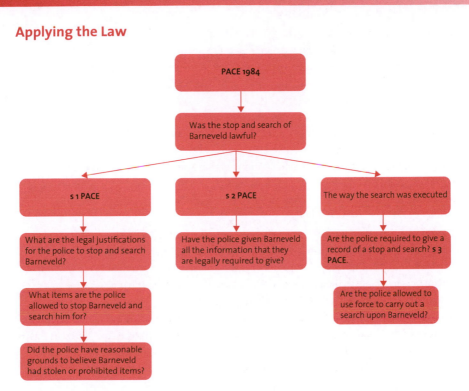

This diagram shows how to apply the law relating to stop and search under the **Police and Criminal Evidence Act 1984** *to Barneveld's circumstances.*

Aim Higher ★

To get the best possible marks from a problem question the correct law needs to be identified and explained accurately and then good application of the law to facts is required with firm conclusions given.

Common Pitfalls ✗

Weak answers to problem questions merely describe the law without applying it to the facts of the scenario.

ANSWER

Police powers are mainly governed by the **Police and Criminal Evidence Act 1984** (**PACE**). **PACE** is a very wide ranging statute with governs police powers in relation to stop and searches, arrest, detention and questioning, and entry search and seizure amongst others. In addition to the statute itself, **PACE** also has **Codes of Practice**, which are documents that give guidance to both police officers and citizens about the extent of the powers set out in **PACE** and what safeguards there are in place to protect the rights of citizens. The area of police powers that is relevant to the given scenario is police powers of stop and search, which are set out in **ss 1–3** of **PACE** and guidance is given about these powers in **Code of Practice A**.

The first actions of the police that need to be considered are when they approach Barneveld and ask him what he is doing. The police are allowed to ask people questions in order to fulfil their duties of crime prevention and detection. Individuals are not under any legal obligation to answer police questions though *Rice v Connolly* (1966), so Barneveld is not acting unlawfully when he ignores the questions put to him by the police.

The officers then grab hold of Barneveld, twist his arms up his back and take him down to the ground and conduct a search of his pockets. As the police are conducting a search the relevant area of law here is police powers of stop and search. **Section 1** of **PACE** sets out the powers available to the police to conduct stop and searches. The police can search anyone, in a public place, whom they have reasonable grounds of suspecting to be in possession of items such as stolen or prohibited articles. Barneveld is a person, so he can be stopped and searched, but the other key legal areas that need to be considered at this stage are whether the search took place in a public place and whether the officers had reasonable grounds to suspect Barneveld was in possession of stolen or prohibited articles.

Section 1(1)(a) and **(b)** of **PACE** states where a stop and search can take place. Essentially the rule is that it must be a public place. Dwellings are specifically mentioned as places where a stop and search cannot be carried out. **Section 1(4)** then goes on to expand further upon dwellings in relation to yards or gardens. The sections state that a stop and search cannot take place in a yard or garden that is used as part of a dwelling. It initially appears then that a stop and search could not lawfully take place upon Barneveld as he is in his own garden, and therefore it is not a public place and is an extension of his dwelling. However, **s 1(4)(a)** and **(b)** go on to give exceptions to this rule. They say that if an officer has reasonable grounds to believe that the individual does not live in the dwelling in relation to the garden, or if they have reasonable grounds to believe that he is there without the owner's permission, then they can conduct a stop and search upon the individual. From the scenario, it seems likely that the officers would have reasonable grounds for believing that Barneveld did not live at the property given his behaviour in the garden and his breaking into the shed. It is therefore likely that it would be lawful for the officers to conduct a stop and search upon Barneveld in the garden. It does not matter that the garden actually does belong to Barneveld, as the key issue is whether the police officers had reasonable grounds to believe that he did not at the time they conducted the stop and search.[1]

....

1   This application of the law surrounding reasonable grounds of suspicion is the kind of application of law to the facts that examiners are looking for.

The next issue that needs to be discussed is whether the police officers had reasonable grounds to suspect that Barneveld had stolen items in his possession. **Section 1(2) PACE** gives officers a power to stop and search someone for certain types of items only, such as stolen or prohibited articles, which includes articles that can be used in relation to a number of offences listed in **s 8**, such as burglary. The relevant items that the officers are searching for here appear to be stolen articles or prohibited articles that could be used to help commit burglary, as they suspect Barneveld to be breaking into houses. The key issue that needs to be discussed here is whether the 'reasonable grounds' test is satisfied.

Section 1(3) of **PACE** states that officers can only conduct a stop and search if they have the requisite reasonable grounds of suspicion that they are going to find an article that they are allowed to search for. This is a key safeguard to make sure that the powers of stop and search are not used in a discriminatory or arbitrary way.[2] No guidance is given in **s 1** about what can or cannot amount to reasonable grounds. In order to explore this are further we need to look at the Code of Practice A which gives us guidance about the police powers of stop and search. Code A gives very good guidance about reasonable grounds (paras 2.2–2.11). The general rule about reasonable grounds is that officers must have some objective facts that have given rise to the grounds of suspicion. Objective here means some evidence that is external to the mind of the officer, such as known information from a witness or intelligence in the form of CCTV footage which the officer is aware of which forms the basis of suspicion for the relevant individual. The requirement of objective grounds is an important safeguard to protect individuals from discrimination and arbitrary use of the powers.

There are exceptions to this general rule though. Para 2.3 of Code A states that behaviour alone can sometimes give rise to reasonable grounds of suspicion in the absence of external intelligence, and the Code specifically gives the example of someone acting suspiciously at night trying to hide something. The Code says it is reasonable in such circumstances for officers to believe that such behaviour can be linked to someone trying to hide stolen or prohibited articles. In the given scenario, Barneveld is acting suspiciously as he is 'skulking' around a garden at 2 am and then he breaks into a shed and emerges putting something into his pocket. This accords with exactly the kind of scenario envisaged by Code A para 2.3 and suggests that Barneveld's behaviour alone is sufficient to give rise to reasonable grounds of suspicion that he is carrying stolen or prohibited articles. It appears therefore that the officers are acting lawfully in wanting to carry out a stop and search of Barneveld.

....

2   Examiners give credit to remarks such as this one about using stop and search powers in a discriminatory way, as it shows an awareness and understanding of the law and demonstrates you have a contextual understanding of the law.

Another issue that needs to be discussed is the use of force by the officers in conducting the stop and search. Para 3.2 of Code A states that force may be used to conduct a search but only when it is clear that the person refuses to comply or where they resist a search. The officers have not given Barneveld any opportunity to comply with the search and even though he pushed past the officers, this does not amount to an indication that he was refusing to comply with a stop and search or that he was resisting a stop and search as the officers had not made it clear that they wanted to conduct a stop and search. **Section 117 PACE** gives the police a general power to use force whenever they are exercising any of their powers. The application of this section is still subject to the requirements of Code A though as this is a stop and search and as Barneveld has not been given an opportunity to comply with a stop and search first, the use of force by the officers here will not be reasonable, and as such, it will be an unlawful use of force which may give rise to tortious issues.[3]

Whilst **s 1** of **PACE** governs when a stop and search can take place, that section is not enough in order to conclude whether the police actions were lawful. **Section 2** of **PACE** is of crucial importance. It states that before a stop and search is carried out, certain information must be given to the individual. Again, this is a safeguard to prevent arbitrary use of the powers and allows transparency in the process. Stop and searches are an inconvenience to the individual so they need to know exactly what is happening and why it is happening. **Section 2(1)(b)** says that it is the duty of officers to take reasonable steps to tell the individual, before a search take places, their name and station, why the person is being searched, what objects they are looking for, and what grounds the officer has for doing the search. The UK courts have given a very strict meaning to **s 2** and have stated that any failings under section will render the stop and search unlawful *Osman v Southwark Crown Court* (1999). In the given scenario the officers have not complied with these requirements. There is no reason why it was not practicable for the officers to give this information to Barneveld before they conducted the search, so the officer's failings will render the stop and search unlawful.

In addition to the requirements under **s 2** of **PACE**, **s 3** also sets out some requirements. Officers must make a record of the search at time of the search unless it is not practicable for them to do so (**s 3(1)**). If a person is arrested after they have been searched then the record of the search must form part of the individual's custody record at the police station. If they are not arrested after the search then a record must be made immediately unless it is not practicable for the officer to do so. The person must then be asked whether they want a copy of the record and if they do they must be given a copy or given a receipt which tells them how they can obtain a full copy at a later time. As Barneveld has not been arrested after the search a record should have been made at the time. There

---

3   This reference to what will practically happen as a result of the unlawful search again demonstrates wider understanding and shows 'joined-up' thinking which will be looked upon favourably by examiners.

were no reasons for the officers not to make a record at the time so if no record has been made then this will be a further breach of **PACE**. However, it is important to note that the UK courts have drawn a distinction between breaches of **ss 2** and **3** of **PACE**. Whilst the courts have said that breaches of **s 2** will render a stop and search unlawful *Osman v Southwark Crown Court* (1999), they have said that a breach of **s 3** will not necessarily render a stop and search unlawful *Basher v DPP* (1993).

After examining the law in this area we are able to conclude that the police officers have acted unlawfully in their stop and search of Barneveld. They did have grounds to stop and search him but the way the search was executed will render the search unlawful. The officers should have given Barneveld all the required information as set out in **s 2** of **PACE** and they should have given him a chance to comply with the search before using force. If they had done this then they would have found out sooner that Barneveld lived at the house in question and no stop and search would have been required at all. The result of this unlawful activity by the police officers is that Barneveld can consider legal action against the police to seek damages.[4]

QUESTION 25

- -

Toby, who has a history of mental disorder and has two convictions for possessing cannabis, is standing on a street corner at 2.00 am on Sunday when he is seen by two police officers in uniform, Andy and Beryl. Andy says: 'What are you up to now, Toby? Let's have a look in your pockets.' Toby does not reply, but turns out his pockets and produces a small quantity of Ecstasy. Andy and Beryl then ask Toby to come to the police station; he agrees to do so.

They arrive at the police station at 2.20 am. Toby is cautioned, informed of his rights under Code C by the custody officer and told that he is suspected of dealing in Ecstasy. He asks if he can see a solicitor, but his request is refused by Superintendent Smith, on the ground that this will lead to the alerting of others whom the police suspect are involved. Toby is then questioned for two hours, but makes no reply to the questions. He then has a short break; when the interview recommences, he is re-cautioned and reminded of his right to legal advice although he is again told that he cannot yet exercise the right. After another hour, he admits to supplying cannabis. The interviews are tape recorded. He is then charged with supplying cannabis.

Toby now says that he only confessed because he thought he had to in order to get home.
▶ **Advise Toby as to any means of redress available to him.**

· ·

4   It is important to give a concluding paragraph like this, even for problem questions, as it allows you to draw together all of your findings to allow you to demonstrate understanding. It also allows you to ensure that you specifically answer the question that has been set.

How to Answer this Question

This question is fairly demanding and quite tricky, since it covers the problem of apparently voluntary compliance with police requests and the particular difficulties created when the police are dealing with a mentally disordered person. The most straightforward approach is probably to consider the legality of the police conduct at every point. Once this has been done, the applicability of the possible forms of redress in respect of each possible breach can be considered. As special problems arise in respect of each, they should be looked at separately. It should be noted that the examinee is merely asked to 'advise Toby as to any means of redress'; therefore, all relevant possibilities should be discussed. It is important to remember to consider whether adverse inferences are likely to be drawn at trial from Toby's silence under **ss 34** and **36** of the **Criminal Justice and Public Order Act 1994**, as amended.

Essentially, the following issues should be considered:

- ❖ the legality of the search under **s 23(2)** of the **Misuse of Drugs Act 1971** and Code A of the **Police and Criminal Evidence Act (PACE) 1984** (2011);
- ❖ is this a voluntary detention or an arrest under **s 24** of **PACE**? – legality of the arrest;
- ❖ access to legal advice under **s 58** of **PACE** – exceptions under **s 58(8)** – the legality of the refusal of advice;
- ❖ the failure to ensure that an appropriate adult was present during the interview as required under **s 11.15** of Code C and Annex E;
- ❖ exclusion of evidence under **ss 76** and **78** of **PACE** – relevance of **ss 34** and **36** of the **Criminal Justice and Public Order Act 1994**; **Art 6** of the **Convention** under the **HRA 1998**; *Khan v UK (2000)*;
- ❖ inferences to be drawn at trial from Toby's silence under **s 34** of the **Criminal Justice** and **Public Order Act 1994**;
- ❖ relevance of **ss 34(2A)** and **36**; **Art 6** of the **ECHR** under **HRA**; *Murray v UK (1996)*;
- ❖ relevant tortious remedies;
- ❖ police complaints and disciplinary action.

Applying the Law

This diagram shows how to apply the relevant law relating to police powers raised by Toby's situation.

ANSWER

The legality of the police conduct in this instance will be considered first; any possible forms of redress open to Toby will then be examined. In both instances, the impact of the **Human Rights Act (HRA) 1998** will be taken into account.[5]

When Toby is asked to turn out his pockets, this appears to be a request. He cannot be subject to a voluntary search under **s 1.5** Code A (2006). Thus, the search should not have taken place unless the police officers can show reasonable suspicion as the basis for the exercise of the power. In order to do so, it must be shown that the police officers complied with the provisions of **s 23(2)** of the **Misuse of Drugs Act 1971** and of Code A. Under **s 23(2)**, a police officer may search for controlled drugs if he has reasonable grounds for believing that he will find such articles. The necessary reasonable suspicion is defined in ss 2.2 and 2.3 of Code A (2006). There must be some objective basis for it, which might include various objective factors, including the time and place and the behaviour of the person concerned. In the instant situation, the lateness of the hour might give rise to some suspicion, but it is apparent that the suspicion does not relate specifically enough to the possibility that Toby is in possession of drugs (*Black v DPP* (1995)). In *Slade* (1996) the suspect's demeanour gave rise to suspicion; here Toby has done nothing that might arouse suspicion, since he is merely standing on a corner. His convictions cannot be viewed as relevant under s 2.2 Code A. Following this argument, no power to stop and search arises; the search itself and the seizure of the Ecstasy are therefore unlawful. It should further be noted that the procedural requirements of **s 2 PACE** are breached since the officers do not identify themselves or give the other required information (see *Osman*

5   Whilst this passage is quite brief, it serves the useful purpose of proving a key to the structure the answer is going to take, which helps to provide clarity for the examiner.

v DPP (1999), in which it was found that **s 2** is mandatory). There are therefore two bases on which to find that the search is unlawful.[6]

The request made to come to the police station appears to assume that Toby will come on a voluntary basis; however, it might be argued that if Toby is deemed incapable of giving consent to a stop and search, he cannot be viewed as capable of consenting to a voluntary detention.

Arguably, since the police must abide by **Art 5** of the **ECHR** under **s 6** of the **HRA**, the better view is that he has not given a true consent to the detention, on the ground that where there is a doubt as to consent to a deprivation of liberty, a strict view should be taken giving the emphasis to the primary right (*Murray v UK* (1994)).

Again, the demands of **Art 5(1)** would favour this view. If this assumption is correct, it is necessary to consider whether a power to arrest arises. Toby is presumably arrested for possessing Ecstasy, an offence arising under **s 5(3)** of the **Misuse of Drugs Act 1971**. In order to arrest under **s 24 PACE**, it is necessary to show that Andy and Beryl had reasonable grounds for suspecting that Toby was in possession of the Ecstasy. Clearly, this is the case. Nevertheless, even assuming that reasonable suspicion is present, the 'arrest' (if it may be characterised as such) is clearly unlawful due to the failure to state the fact of the arrest and the reason for it as required under **s 28** of **PACE** and **Art 5(2)** of the **ECHR** (see *Wilson v Chief Constable of Lancashire Constabulary* (2000)).

At the police station, Toby is not afforded access to legal advice. Delay in affording such access will be lawful only if it is the case that one of the contingencies envisaged under **s 58(8)** will arise if a solicitor is contacted. In this instance, the police will wish to rely on the exception under **s 58(8)(b)**, allowing delay where contacting the solicitor will lead to the alerting of others suspected of the offence. Leaving aside the lack of any substantial evidence that others are involved at all, it will be necessary for the police to show, following *Samuel* (1988), that some quality about the particular solicitor in question could found a reasonable belief that he/she would bring about one of the contingencies envisaged if contacted. There is nothing to suggest that the police officers have any basis for this belief, especially as Toby has not specified the solicitor he wishes to contact. He may well wish to contact the duty solicitor. A further condition for the operation of **s 58(8)** is that Toby is being detained in respect of an indictable offence. He is in detention at this point in respect of possession of Ecstasy. As supplying Ecstasy is an indictable offence, this condition is fulfilled. However, the lack of any basis for the necessary reasonable belief under **s 58(8)** means that there has been a breach of **s 58**. This strict approach to **s 58** is supported by *Samuel* (1988) and by the approach of the European Court of Human

....

6   This application of stop and search law is an excellent example of how to effectively apply the law by using authority.

Rights to the right of access to legal advice under **Art 6**. It has placed considerable importance on the right in cases such as *Murray (John) v UK (1996)* and *Averill v UK (2000)*. It has held that delay in access where the defendant faces the possibility that adverse inferences may be drawn from silence is likely to amount to a breach of **Art 6** of the **ECHR**. That strict approach should be followed under the **HRA**.[7]

Since Toby is mentally disordered, he should not have been interviewed except in the presence of an 'appropriate adult' as required under para 11.15 of Code C. Under s 1.4 Code C, if an officer has any suspicion that a person may be mentally disordered or mentally vulnerable then he should be treated as such for the purposes of the Code (see also Annex E). Therefore, a further breach of **PACE** has occurred, unless it could be argued that the officers were not aware of his disorder; if so, following *Raymond Maurice Clarke (1989)*, no breach of the Code provision occurred. The behaviour of Andy suggests, however, that the officers were aware of Toby's condition.

Having identified a series of breaches of **PACE** and the Codes on the part of the police, it will now be necessary to consider any redress available to Toby in respect of them. The first such act was the unlawful seizure of the Ecstasy. The appropriate cause of action in this instance will be trespass to goods; damages will, however, be minimal.

Will the Ecstasy be excluded from evidence under **s 78**? According to the analysis above, the stop and search was unlawful. Following the decision of the House of Lords in *Khan (1997)*, evidence other than involuntary confessions obtained improperly is nevertheless admissible, subject to a narrow discretion to exclude it. In *Khan* itself, it was found that the trial judge had properly exercised his discretion to include the improperly obtained evidence under **s 78**. This position has been unaffected by the reception of **Art 6** into domestic law under the **HRA** (*AG's Reference (No 3 of 1999) (2001)* and *Loosely (2001)*) on the basis that the admission or exclusion of evidence is largely a matter for the national courts (*Khan v UK (2000)*). The courts have therefore taken the view that the position that had developed under **s 78** pre-**HRA** regarding exclusion of non-confession evidence need not be modified. It may be concluded that the Ecstasy would not be excluded from evidence.

Toby could make a complaint under the provisions of the **Police Reform Act 2002** in respect of the illegal seizure of the Ecstasy, since it can be characterised as resulting from an unlawful search in breach of **s 23(2)** of the **Misuse of Drugs Act 1971** and of **s 2 PACE** and Code A.[8]

---

7   The application of the law to the **ECHR** and the **HRA** provides an extra layer of understanding which will be given credit by the examiner.
8   This additional passage about making a police complaint shows a good understanding of the area and consideration of multiple factors, rather than just focusing solely upon **PACE**.

Assuming that the arrest was unlawful (which cannot be determined with certainty), Toby could bring an action for false imprisonment for the whole period of his detention. A further option might be to make a complaint in respect of the failure to observe the provisions of **s 28** of **PACE**.

Can a reasonable argument be advanced that the admissions made by Toby will be excluded from evidence under **s 76**? Following *Alladice and Hughes* (1988), unless it can be shown that the custody officer acted in bad faith in failing to allow Toby access to a solicitor, it seems that **s 76(2)(a)** will not apply. However, following *Delaney* (1989), which was concerned with the operation of **s 76(2)(b)**, if the defendant was in some particularly difficult or vulnerable position, the breach of **PACE** may be of special significance. Toby may be said to be in such a position due to the fact that he is mentally disordered. On this basis, it seems that **s 76(2)(b)** may be invoked to exclude the admissions from evidence.

The admissions may also be excluded from evidence under **s 78**, on the basis that the police breached **s 58**. If so, following *Samuel* (1988) and *Alladice* (1988), it must be shown that the breach of **s 58** was causally related to the admissions made in the second interview. It may be that Toby would have made admissions in any event had he had advice. The adviser might have considered that he should make admissions, since a failure to account for the Ecstasy would be commented on adversely in court under **s 36** of the **Criminal Justice and Public Order Act 1994**. On the other hand, the adviser might have considered that this risk should be taken, especially as it could probably be established that the wrong caution had been used; the correct caution is in Annex C para 2 and the adviser might have been aware of this. This seems the stronger argument, bearing in mind Toby's mental disorder. On this analysis, the requisite causal relationship exists and the admissions may also be excluded from evidence under **s 78**. This approach is given additional weight by the importance attached to access to legal advice by the European Court in cases such as *Murray (John) v UK* (1996) and *Averill v UK* (2000). Under **ss 2** and **6** of the **HRA 1998**, those decisions need to be taken into account in considering whether the evidence should be excluded; they would be likely to tip the balance in favour of exclusion.

It could further be argued that a breach of s 11.15 of Code C occurred, in that Toby was interviewed, although no appropriate adult was present. The breach of **s 58** could also be the subject of a complaint, as could the breach of s 11.15 of Code C.

It follows from the above analysis that the first interview, which may be said to be causally related to the breach of s 6.6 Code C and **s 58**, may be excluded from evidence under **s 78**, since had Toby had legal advice, he might *not* have decided to remain silent. On the other hand the courts, as indicated, are very reluctant to use the discretion under **s 78** to exclude non-confession evidence (*Khan*).

Since there is a strong possibility that the interview will not be excluded, it must be considered whether adverse inferences would be likely to be drawn from Toby's silence during it. **Section 34(2A)** of the **Criminal Justice and Public Order Act 1994**, introduced in order to satisfy **Art 6** of the **ECHR** under the **HRA**, applies (see *Murray v UK*). Under **s 34(2A)**, inferences cannot be drawn if the defendant has not had the opportunity of having legal advice. This appears to apply to Toby, especially as he has been unlawfully denied the opportunity, as argued above. Thus, no adverse inferences can be drawn.

QUESTION 26

It is now over 25 years since the **Police and Criminal Evidence Act (PACE) 1984** was enacted. **PACE** and the **Codes of Practice** made under it were supposed to strike a fair balance between increased police powers and greater safeguards for the suspect. Taking into account the effect of the **Human Rights Act (HRA) 1998**, amendments to **PACE** and the Codes, **ss 34–37** of the **Criminal Justice and Public Order Act (CJPOA) 1994**, and relevant aspects of the **Police Reform Act 2002**, how far would it be fair to say that such a balance is still evident?

How to Answer this Question

This is a reasonably straightforward essay question, which is commonly set on **PACE**. It is clearly very wide-ranging and therefore needs care in planning in order to cover provisions relating to the key stages in the investigation. Note that it does not ask you to comment on the treatment of terrorist suspects in the pre-trial investigation governed by the **Terrorism Act 2000** as amended. It is clearly necessary to be selective in your answer. Essentially, the following points should be considered, mentioning relevant case law, including post-**HRA** cases at the various points:

- ❖ the arrest provision under **s 24** of **PACE**, as amended in 2005;
- ❖ **Art 5** of the **ECHR**; Code G (2006);
- ❖ the stop and search provision under **s 1 PACE** and Code of Practice A (2011) and the efficacy of the procedural safeguards; **s 60** of the **Criminal Justice and Public Order Act (CJPOA) 1994**;
- ❖ the detention provisions under **Pt IV PACE**; **Art 5** of the **Convention**;
- ❖ the safeguards for interviews under **Pt V** and Codes C (2008) and E (2010) – relevance of **ss 34–37** under the **CJPOA**, as amended; **Art 6** of the **Convention** under the **HRA**;
- ❖ a brief overview of the redress available for breaches of these provisions – tortious remedies; the police complaints mechanism (**Police Reform Act 2002**); exclusion of evidence; the impact of the **HRA**, especially **Art 6** of the **Convention**.

Answer Structure

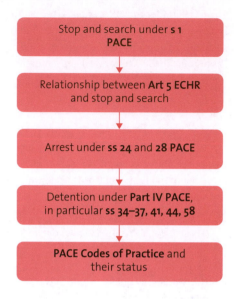

ANSWER --

It will be argued that although the **Police and Criminal Evidence Act (PACE) 1984** and the Codes of Practice contain provisions capable of achieving a reasonable balance between increasing the power of the police to detain and question and providing safeguards for the suspect, that balance is not maintained in practice. Moreover, it has changed significantly since **PACE** came into force. **PACE** has been amended, most significantly by **s 110** of the **Serious and Organised Crime Act 2005**; the Codes have gone through a number of revisions, most recently in 2011; new Codes have been introduced, including new Code G, the Arrest Code. Other provisions, including in particular **s 34** of the **Criminal Justice and Public Order Act (CJPOA) 1994**, and the **Police Reform Act 2002**, have been introduced. The safeguards in the Codes have been increased, but those in **PACE** itself have diminished, while the powers have increased. The curtailing of the right to silence had a significant impact on the balance that was originally created under **PACE**.[9]

In **s 1 PACE**, a general power to stop and search persons is conferred on the police if reasonable suspicion arises that stolen goods or prohibited articles may be found. This general power is balanced in two ways. First, the concept of reasonable suspicion, which is defined in s 2 of Code A (2011), appears to allow it to be exercised only when quite a high level of suspicion exists. However, the level of reasonable suspicion needed is not very high in practice (see *Slade* (1996)). Second, the police must give the person to be searched certain information. It now appears unlikely that the **HRA** will tend to

....

9   This is a good introduction as it provides an overview of **PACE** and other relevant legislation and provides some context.

encourage a stricter adherence to the rules providing safeguards for suspects who are stopped and searched. **Article 5**, contained in **Sched 1** to the **HRA**, provides a guarantee of liberty and security of person. Deprivation of liberty can occur only on a basis of law and in certain specified circumstances, including, under **Art 5(1)(b)**, the detention of a person in order to secure the fulfilment of any obligation prescribed by law and, under **Art 5(1)(c)**, the 'lawful detention of a person effected for the purpose of bringing him before the competent legal authority on reasonable suspicion of having committed an offence'. The House of Lords decided in *Gillan* (2006) that **Art 5(1)** does not cover temporary detention for the purposes of a search. In *Gillan v UK* (2010), however, the Strasbourg Court came closer to finding a breach of **Art 5**, while deciding the case under **Art 8**. This may lead to a stricter stance towards stop and search.

Originally, the police also acquired a general power of arrest under **s 25**. This power did not merely allow an officer to arrest for any offence so long as reasonable suspicion could be shown. It was balanced by what were known as the general arrest conditions, which also had to be fulfilled. The inclusion of those provisions implied that the infringement of civil liberties represented by an arrest should be resorted to only where no alternative exists.[10] However, **s 25** was repealed in 2005 by **s 110** of the **Serious and Organised Crime Act 2005** and **s 24** of **PACE** was amended, making the arrest powers available much broader. Under **s 24**, a person can be arrested on reasonable suspicion of having committed or being about to commit an offence – any offence. The arrest conditions originally under **s 25** also have to be satisfied under **s 24** but, crucially, two new ones have been added. The police can also show that the arrest is needed to allow the prompt and effective investigation of the suspected offence in question or to prevent prosecution of the offence from being hindered by the suspect's disappearance (**s 24(5)(e)** and **(f)**).

It is highly probable that one of these conditions will be found to be satisfied in relation to most arrests. Thus the police now have a broad power of arrest that would have been viewed as too draconian had it been introduced in 1984. Some attempt at balancing this power with increased safeguards for arrestees was made by the introduction of Code G, the Arrest Code, in 2006. The concept of reasonable suspicion, which should ensure that the arrest takes place at quite a late stage in the investigation, limits the use of the **s 24** power, although the concept tends to be flexibly interpreted. This can be found if the leading post-**PACE** case on the meaning of the concept, *Castorina v Chief Constable of Surrey* (1988), is compared with the findings of the Strasbourg Court in *Fox, Campbell and Hartley v UK* (1990). It is debatable whether the UK courts are in general applying a test of reasonable suspicion under **PACE** or other provisions for arrest that reaches the standards that the European Court had in mind in *Fox, Campbell* (1990), especially where

---

10 Whilst it may seem irrelevant to mention the old law in relation to arrest, this clearly shows how it can add value to your answer by providing depth of knowledge and context.

terrorism is not in question. The departure that the HRA brings about is to encourage stricter judicial scrutiny of decisions to arrest.[11]

Detention under PACE can be for up to 24 hours. In the case of a person in police custody for an indictable offence it can extend to 36 hours with the permission of a police officer of the rank of Superintendent or above, and may extend to 96 hours under s 44 after an application to a magistrates' court. These are very significant powers. However, they are supposed to be balanced by all of the safeguards created by Pt V of PACE and by Codes C and E. The most important safeguards available inside the police station include contemporaneous recording under s 11.7 of Code C, tape recording under s 3 of Code E, the ability to read over, verify and sign the notes of the interview as a correct record under subss 11.9 and 11 Code C, notification of the right to legal advice under s 58 and s 3.1 of Code C, the option of having the adviser present under s 6.6 of Code C and, where appropriate, the presence of an appropriate adult under s 11.15 of Code C.

The right of access to legal advice was intended to bolster the right to silence. That right, originally included in the PACE scheme since it was reflected in the Code C caution, was severely curtailed by ss 34–37 of the CJPOA, thereby disturbing the 'balance' that was originally created. However, s 34(2A) was inserted into the CJPOA by s 58 of the Youth Justice and Criminal Evidence Act 1999. The amendments provide that if the defendant was at an authorised place of detention and had not had an opportunity of consulting a solicitor at the time of the failure to mention the fact in question, inferences cannot be drawn. This is a very significant change to the interviewing scheme, which was introduced as a direct response to the findings of the European Court of Human Rights in *Murray v UK* (1996). Had this change not been made, ss 34–37 might have been found to be incompatible with Art 6 under s 4 of the HRA.

Damages will be available at common law in respect of some breaches of PACE. For example, if a police officer arrests a citizen where no reasonable suspicion arises under s 24 of PACE, an action for false imprisonment arises.[12] Equally, such a remedy would be available if the provisions governing time limits on detention were breached. However, tortious remedies are inapplicable to the provisions of the Codes under s 67(10) and seem to be inapplicable to the most significant statutory interviewing provision, the entitlement to legal advice.

The police complaints mechanism covers any breaches of PACE, including breaches of the Codes under s 67(8), but it is generally agreed that it is defective as a means of redress. Despite the involvement (albeit limited) of the Independent Police Complaints

---

11   This brief analysis of the impact the HRA has made in this area adds extra quality to the answer.
12   This reference to false imprisonment will be given credit by the examiner as it shows an ability to 'join the dots up'.

Commission, introduced by the **Police Reform Act 2002**, with a view to creating a stronger independent element in the system, the complaints procedure is still largely administered by the police themselves. The context in which many breaches of **PACE** have been considered is that of exclusion of evidence. In *Samuel* (1988), the police unlawfully denied the appellant access to legal advice; the court took the view that if a breach of **s 58** had taken place that was causally linked to the confession, **s 78** should be invoked. However, the provisions of **ss 34–37** of the **CJPOA**, reflected in the caution introduced under the 1995 revision of Code C, and continued in the 2006 version (unless the detainee has had no opportunity to have legal advice, in which case the 'old' caution should be used) make it less likely that advisers will advise silence, since adverse inferences may be drawn at trial from silence. Thus, it may be more difficult to establish the causal relationship in question relying on the method used in *Samuel*. **Section 78** may become less effective as a means of maintaining the balance between police powers and suspects' rights.

Following the decision of the House of Lords in *Khan* (1997), evidence other than involuntary confessions obtained improperly is nevertheless admissible, subject to a narrow discretion to exclude it. This position has been unaffected by the reception of **Art 6** into domestic law under the **HRA** (*AG's Reference (No 3 of 1999)* (2001); *Loosely* (2001)) on the basis that the assessment of evidence is largely a matter for the national courts. The courts have therefore taken the view that the position that has developed under **s 78** regarding exclusion of non-confession evidence need not be modified under the **HRA**.

The relevant decisions so far under the **HRA** do not indicate that the **HRA** is having or is likely to have a significant impact in this context. This is particularly the case in relation to the decisions in *Gillan* (2006) and *Beckles* (2004), although the earlier decisions in *Osman* (1999) (in relation to adopting a strict view of the identification requirement of **s 2 PACE**) and *R v Chief Constable of Kent* (2000) (demanding that to accord with **Art 5** reviews of detention should be in person, not by video link; the decision was reversed by **s 73 Criminal Justice and Police Act 2001**) suggested otherwise.

In conclusion, it is therefore argued that the balance originally struck is no longer being maintained. This failure arguably arises partly due to the changes that have occurred since 1984, partly because many of the safeguards can be evaded quite readily, and partly because there is no effective sanction available for their breach. It is contended that while the relevant Articles of the **Convention**, afforded further effect in domestic law under the **Human Rights Act 1998 (HRA)**, are having some impact in encouraging adherence to the rules intended to secure suspects' rights, they are not having a radical effect, especially in terms of encouraging the exclusion of evidence where the rules have not been adhered to.

QUESTION 27

Yasmin has been arrested upon suspicion of committing burglary and has been taken to a police station. Upon arrival at the station at 11:00 pm on Friday night Yasmin is presented to the Custody Officer to be booked in. The arresting officer, Inspector Montego, instructs the Custody Officer to put Yasmin in a cell immediately as the night is getting late and he needs to arrange for Yasmin to be interviewed.

After being put in the cell Yasmin is left there until 6:00 am on Saturday morning when she is taken to an interview room. Inspector Montego questions Yasmin about her suspected involvement in a series of burglaries. Yasmin tells him that she wants to speak to a solicitor first before answering any questions. The Inspector tells her that as it is the weekend she will not be able to get a solicitor for quite a while and he asks Yasmin whether she wants to wait that long. Yasmin does not want to be in the police station any longer than is necessary so she agrees to answer his questions.

The Inspector finishes interviewing Yasmin at 10:00 am on Saturday morning and decides that he wants to search Yasmin's premises to see if any of the stolen items are stored there. He takes her keys, which they seized from her before she was put in her cell, and goes to her property to search it.

Inspector Montego did not find any stolen items in Yasmin's premises. She is released on bail at 11:30pm on Saturday night pending further enquiries.

▶ **Comment upon the legality of the police conduct in the above scenario.**

How to Answer this Question

Many problems questions are set on police powers. This question is a very traditional type of problem question on police powers and focusses upon two areas of police powers:

1. Powers of detention and questioning at the police station.
2. Powers of entry, search and seizure.

The following matters should be discussed:

- ❖ the role of the Custody Officer (**s 36 PACE**);
- ❖ what should happen upon arrival at the police station;
- ❖ the 'rights' of suspects at the station:
  - ❖ the right to tell someone where they are (**s 56 PACE**);
  - ❖ the right to free and independent legal advice (**s 58 PACE**);
  - ❖ the right to consult the Codes of Practice;
- ❖ tests the Custody Officer needs to carry out (**s 37 PACE**);
- ❖ the duties of the Custody Officer (**s 39 PACE**);
- ❖ review of detention (**s 40 PACE**);
- ❖ time-limits of detention (**s 41 PACE**);
- ❖ various conditions of detention and questioning;
- ❖ powers of entry and search under **s 18 PACE**.

Applying the Law

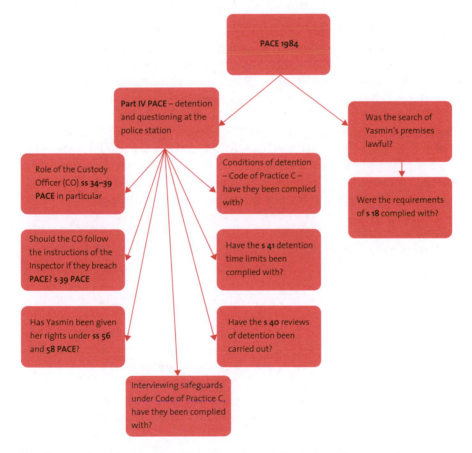

This diagram shows how to apply the relevant law relating to the detention and questioning of Yasmin and the search of her premises.

Aim Higher ★

To get the best possible marks from this problem question the correct focus needs to be achieved by identifying the relevant law relating to the powers of detention and questioning at the police station. That law then needs to be applied coherently and confidently to the facts of the given scenario in order to reach firm conclusions about the legality of the police conduct.

Common Pitfalls ✗

Weak answers to problem questions merely describe the law without applying it to the facts of the scenario.

ANSWER

Yasmin has been taken to the police station following her arrest. As we are given no details of her arrest we cannot comment upon the legality of this aspect of the police conduct. The area of police powers that we can comment upon in relation to their legality is her detention and questioning at the police station and the entry and search of her premises.

Police powers of detention and questioning are governed by **Part IV** of the **Police and Criminal Evidence Act 1984** (**PACE**) and there is an accompanying Code of Practice, Code C, which gives guidance about the extent of the powers and how they should be exercised. It is important to bear in mind the status of the Codes of Practice. **Section 67 PACE** states that breaches of the Codes do not give rise to criminal or civil liability, but it goes on to say that courts can take breaches of the Codes into account if they think it is relevant when determining a question. Even though the Codes are merely guidance, they are very influential rules and the courts can and do take breaches of the Codes into account.[13]

The first thing that should happen to a suspect when they arrive at the police station is that they should be presented to the Custody Officer (CO). The CO is a creation of **PACE** and is there as a safeguard for suspects to ensure that **PACE** and the Codes of Practice are complied with. **Section 36** of **PACE** creates the CO and **s 39** puts them under a legal duty to ensure that **PACE** and the Codes of Practice are complied with.

Once a suspect has been presented to the CO they should open a Custody Record (CR) for the suspect. The CR is a very important document which is individual to each suspect and

---

13 These comments about the status of the codes show the examiner that you are aware of the difference between the codes and the Act, something which many students sometimes find difficult to appreciate.

records everything that happens to that suspect whilst they are in detention. It also records key times when things happen, such as time of arrest, the time a suspect was brought to the station and the time when detention was authorised.

Section 37 PACE sets out the duties of the CO before charge and contains the key duties the CO must perform as soon as the suspect is brought before them. **Section 37(1)** sets out the first duty of the CO and says that if there is sufficient evidence to charge the suspect then they should be charged immediately. The significance of this is that the suspect then ceases to be a suspect and becomes a 'defendant' and passes into the hands of the court system and as such they cannot be questioned about the offence by the police.

Section 37(2)[14] sets out the second duty of the CO which arises if there is not sufficient evidence to charge the suspect. It says that the CO must decide whether detention is necessary to secure or preserve evidence or to obtain such evidence by questioning. These have become known as the detention conditions or detention grounds. It is a key test and a suspects detention will only be lawful if this test is satisfied.

There are major concerns with these matters for Yasmin. The tests set out in **s 37** have not been complied with by the CO. This means that Yasmin's detention will be unlawful as detention is only lawful if the detention conditions are satisfied. The CO has not applied this test and so has not determined whether detention is necessary or not; a key failure which will render the detention unlawful.

The fact that **s 37** was not complied with by the CO appears to be due to a superior officer, Inspector Montego, ordering the CO to put Yasmin in a cell immediately. Could the CO evade legal liability for the breaches of **PACE** by saying they were merely following order from a superior officer? **Section 39(6)** of **PACE** specifically caters for such matters. It says that if a superior officer gives an instruction to a CO that would result in a breach of **PACE** then the CO must immediately refer the matter to an officer of the rank of superintendent or above who is responsible for that police station. This is a safety mechanism designed to prevent breaches of **PACE** being committed by instructions such as Inspector Montego gives here. As the CO in our scenario has not reported this to the superintendent the CO is still legally responsible for the breaches in **PACE** as governed by **s 39** of **PACE**.

If **s 37** had been complied with and the CO had determined that detention was necessary the CO then needs to make sure that the suspect is aware of their 'rights' whilst at the station. **Section 56 PACE** states that suspects must be given the opportunity to have someone notified of their situation; this is often known as the right not to be held

---

14 By taking specific issues in turn the answer is taking a very methodical approach to answering the question. This structural technique provides clarity and makes the answer easy for the examiner to read.

incommunicado. **Section 58** states that suspects must be given the opportunity to consult privately with a solicitor to receive free and independent legal advice. Para 3.1 of Code C confirms the above two rights and also adds that suspects must be allowed to consult the Codes of Practice at any time whilst in detention.

As the CO has put Yasmin straight into a cell none of these three rights have been given to her. This amounts to further serious breaches of **PACE** and unlawful activity by the police (*Samuel* (1988)). These rights can be delayed for indictable offences (which robbery is) in certain circumstances which are set out in **s 56** and **58**, such as if the relevant officer believes that allowing the rights to be exercised would lead to the destruction of evidence. No such justifications have been relied upon here though in our scenario to delay these rights for Yasmin. They have simply not been given which is a clear breach of **s 56** and **58** and Code of Practice para 3.1.

There are many rules given in **PACE** itself and in Code C in relation to interviews. Interviewing is a key area of the police investigation and **PACE** and the Codes introduced numerous safeguards to protect both the police (to ensure evidence is obtained properly and can be used in court) and suspects (to make sure they are treated fairly) at this crucial stage. For example, **s 60 PACE** states that all interviews must be tape recorded. This ensures that an exact record of interviews takes place to prevent any dispute about what was or was not said during interview.

Further safeguards in relation to interviews are such as those contained in para 6.4 of Code C,[15] which states that officers should not say or do anything with the intention of dissuading a detained person from seeking legal advice, and para 6.6 of Code C, which states that a detainee who wants legal advice may not be interviewed or continue to be interviewed until they have received such advice. Inspector Montego has clearly breached these requirements by telling Yasmin that she will have to wait quite a while for a solicitor as it is a weekend (not a true statement at all) and he then conducts an interview without her obtaining advice from a solicitor when she clearly said she wanted one. Inspector Montego appears to be playing on Yasmin's emotions and her desire to want to get out of the police station as soon as possible. Such breaches of **PACE** and Code C would be looked upon very unfavourably by the courts.

Yasmin is taken to be interviewed at 6:00 am. Paragraph 12.2 of Code C states that in any 24 hour period detainees must be given a continuous period of at least 8 hours rest, free from questioning, and this should normally be given at night. The Code does permit exceptions to this requirement, but only in circumstances such as to avoid unnecessary

---

15 These references to the provisions of the Codes of Practice show the examiner that you have a confident grasp of the fine details of the area and that you can confidently use and incorporate these fine details into a practical approach.

delay or to prevent harm to a person or property. No such exceptions appear to be relevant here so this requirement has been breached as Yasmin is only given 7 hours rest.

In addition to this, para 12.8 of Code C states that short refreshment breaks must be provided at approximately 2 hour intervals when a suspect is being interviewed. Yasmin was questioned for 4 hours without a break, between 6:00 am and 10:00 am, which clearly breaches this requirement.

After the interview takes place Inspector Montego decides to search Yasmin's premises. This gives rise to issues in relation to police powers of entry, search and seizure, which are governed by **Part II** of **PACE** and Code of Practice B. For any search to be lawful, lawful authority must exist for the search. Lawful authority can derive from a number of different sources, such as with consent, statutory authority, or with common law powers. The only one of these powers which could be relevant in the given scenario is a **s 18 PACE** search, as that allows searching of an arrested person's premises after they have been arrested.

For the search to executed in accordance with **s 18 PACE** the offence the person is arrested for must be an indictable offence, an Inspector or above needs to authorise the search in writing, and there must be reasonable grounds to suspect that there is evidence on the premises relating to the offence the person has been arrested for, or a connected or similar offence.

Yasmin has been arrested for burglary, which is an indictable offence, and the officer carrying out the search is an Inspector. There is nothing in **s 18** or Code of Practice B that expressly requires the Inspector not to be involved in the offence, even though this would be expected. However, There does need to be written authorisation and this does not seem to have taken place; the Inspector merely appears to have gone off on his own authority. The absence of written authority would render the search unlawful as it is an express requirement laid out in **s 18**. Details of what was discussed in the interview are not given so no conclusions can be reached about whether the Inspector had reasonable grounds to suspect he would find evidence on the premises. Given the absence of the written authority though the search by Inspector Montego would be an unlawful one.

After the search has taken place Yasmin is released at 11:30am the day after she was initially detained. **Section 41 PACE** states that there is a 24-hour limitation upon detention. The time for this calculation starts at the time Yasmin arrived at the station as she was under arrest when she arrived there. As she arrived at the station at 11:00am the latest time she could lawfully be detained without any extensions of detention (catered for in **ss 42–44**) would be 11:00 am the following day. Yasmin has been detained for 30 minutes longer than this which amounts to unlawful detention. Any unlawful detention will give rise to tortious liability (such as false imprisonment) and will also amount to a breach of **Article 5 ECHR** (right to liberty).

A further safeguard introduced by **PACE** is the detention review requirement. **Section 40** states that a suspect's detention must be reviewed at certain intervals to ensure that detention is still necessary. The first review must take place no later than 6 hours after detention was first authorised. Thhis never happened to Yasmin as she was placed straight in a cell, but it should have happened shortly after 11:00am. Subsequent reviews must take place no later than at 9-hourly intervals after that. No such reviews appear to have taken place in relation to Yasmin which would also render her detention unlawful (*Roberts v Chief Constable of Cheshire* (1999)).

There have been multiple breaches of **PACE** itself and of the Codes of Practice by the officers in this case. This unlawful activity will mean that Yasmin's detention is unlawful for which will be able to take action against the police. She will have tortious causes of action available to her in addition to a cause of action under **s 7 of the Human Rights Act 1998**, as the police have failed in their duty (under **s 6 HRA**) not to act incompatibly with Yasmin's **ECHR** rights (namely **Art 5**).[16]

QUESTION 28

Albert and Bill, two policemen in uniform and driving a police car, see Colin outside a factory gate at 11.30 pm on a Saturday. Albert and Bill know that Colin has a conviction for burglary. Colin looks nervous and is looking repeatedly at his watch. Bearing in mind a spate of burglaries in the area, Albert and Bill ask Colin what he is doing. Colin replies that he is waiting for a friend. Dissatisfied with this response, Bill tells Colin to turn out his pockets, which he does. Bill seizes a bunch of keys that Colin produces and, still suspicious, tells Colin to accompany them to the police station. Colin then becomes abusive; Bill takes hold of him to restrain him, and Colin tries to push Bill away. Albert and Bill then bundle Colin into the police car, telling him that he is under arrest. Colin does not resist them. They proceed to Colin's flat and search it, discovering a small amount of cannabis, which they seize.

Albert and Bill then take Colin to the police station, arriving at 12.20 am. He is cautioned under s 10.5 Code C, informed of his rights under Code C by the custody officer, and told that he is suspected of dealing in cannabis. Colin asks if he can see a solicitor, but his request is refused 'for the time being'. Colin is then questioned and eventually admits to supplying cannabis. The interview is tape-recorded. He is then charged with supplying cannabis and with assaulting a police officer in the execution of his duty.

▶ **Advise Colin.**

---

16 By mentioning the different causes of action available to Yasmin you are showing the examiner that you have a good understanding of law in general which shows an ability to be able to properly advise a client.

How to Answer this Question

This is a reasonably straightforward question, but it does cover a very wide range of issues. The most significant and difficult issue is that of the arguably unlawful arrest(s) – so that should form a large part of the answer. The most straightforward approach is to consider the legality of the police conduct at every point. Once this has been done, the applicability of the possible forms of redress can be considered. It should be noted that the examinee is merely asked to 'advise Colin'; therefore, all relevant possibilities should be discussed – albeit briefly due to the time constraint. European Court of Human Rights (ECtHR) cases should be considered in relation to the relevant Articles of the **ECHR**, contained in **Sched 1** to the **HRA**, and the effects of **ss 3** and **6** of the **HRA** should be mentioned where relevant.[17]

Essentially, the following issues should be considered, using case law to support your points and mentioning the **HRA**, with relevant cases, where applicable at various points:

❖ the legality of the search under **ss 1** and **2** of the **Police and Criminal Evidence Act (PACE) 1984** and Code of Practice A (2011); **Art 5** of the **Convention**;

❖ assaulting a police officer in the execution of his duty under **s 89(1)** of the **Police Act 1996**;

❖ the legality of the arrest under **s 24** of **PACE**, as amended 2005; mention Code G (2006);

❖ the legality of the search of premises and the seizure of the cannabis under **ss 18** and **19** of **PACE**; **Art 8** of the **Convention**;

❖ access to legal advice under **s 58** of **PACE** – legality of the refusal of advice; **Art 6** of the **Convention** under **HRA**;

❖ exclusion of evidence under **ss 76** and **78** of **PACE**; relevance of **Art 6** of the **Convention** under **HRA**;

❖ possible free-standing action under **s 7(1)(a)** of the **HRA** relying on **Art 8**;

❖ relevant tortious remedies;

❖ the police complaints procedure under the **Police Reform Act 2002**.

---

17 This is a good introduction as it picks out the most important parts of the question and provides the examiner with a clear focus and structure.

Applying the Law

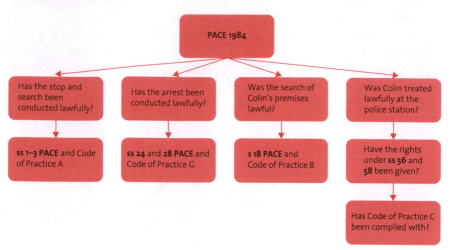

This diagram shows how to apply the relevant law under the **Police and Criminal Evidence Act 1984** to Colin's circumstances.

ANSWER -

The legality of the police conduct in this instance will be considered first; any possible forms of redress open to Colin will then be examined. The impact of the **Human Rights Act (HRA) 1998**, which affords the **European Convention on Human Rights (ECHR)** further effect in domestic law, will be taken into account at a number of significant points.

When Colin is asked to turn out his pockets, this appears to be part of a voluntary search. However, such searches are now forbidden under Code A s 1.5 (2011). Thus under s 1.5 the search and seizure of the keys should be part of a lawful stop and search. Thus, it must be shown that the police officers complied with the provisions of **ss 1** and **2** of **PACE** and of Code A. Under **s 1(2)**, a police officer may search for stolen or prohibited articles if he has reasonable grounds (**s 1(3)**) for believing that he will find such articles.

The necessary reasonable suspicion is defined in **s 2** of Code A, especially s 2.2. There must be some objective basis for it that will relate to the nature of the article suspected of being carried. Various factors could be taken into account including the time and place, the behaviour or demeanour of the person concerned (see *Slade* (1996)) and the carrying of certain articles in an area that has recently experienced a number of burglaries. In the instant situation, the lateness of the hour and the fact that Colin is outside a factory in an area that has recently experienced burglaries, coupled with his nervous behaviour, might give rise to a generalised suspicion, but it could be argued that the suspicion does not relate specifically enough to a particular article, since there is very little to suggest that Colin is carrying any particular article (this was found in *Black v DPP* (1995) and in *Francis*

(1992)).[18] Following this argument, it is doubtful whether a power to stop and search arises. But in any event, even if it could be established that reasonable suspicion is present, the search is unlawful, since the procedural requirements of **s 2** of **PACE** are breached (*Osman* (1999)); the seizure of the keys is therefore also unlawful. After Colin becomes abusive, Bill takes hold of him to restrain him. If this restraining is not part of a lawful arrest and therefore lawful under **s 117** of **PACE**, it could be characterised as an assault on Colin. Even if **s 24 PACE** is satisfied on the basis that reasonable suspicion of burglary may be present, **s 28** is not, since no reason is given for the arrest and the fact of the arrest is not stated, although it is later. At this point, before Colin becomes abusive, it would be practicable to state the fact of and reason for the arrest as required by **s 28** since Colin has been cooperative so far; therefore the arrest becomes unlawful at that point (*DPP v Hawkins* (1988)). Therefore, since no power to arrest arises, the restraint of Colin is unlawful. Under s 2.2 Code A, officers need to inform the suspect of the fact of the arrest even if it is obvious; they also need to inform of the reason for the arrest. A strict approach to s 28 PACE also accords with the demands of **Art 5(2)**, under the **HRA**.

The arrest may be for simple assault or for assault on a police officer in the execution of his duty, an offence arising under **s 89(1)** of the **Police Act 1996**, but this reason is not given. If it is to arise under **s 24**, two tests must be satisfied. First, it must be shown that one of the general arrest conditions under **s 24** arises: the police need to show that the arrest is needed to allow the prompt and effective investigation of the suspected offence in question or to prevent prosecution of the offence from being hindered by Colin's disappearance (**s 24(5)(e)** and **(f)**). It is probable that one of these conditions will be found to be satisfied in relation to most arrests, and an offence has already occurred. Second, Albert and Bill must be able to show that Colin is suspected of an offence – that the assault has been perpetrated or that they have reasonable suspicion that he is guilty of the offence (s 24(2)(3)). It may be argued, following *Marsden* (1868) and *Fennell* (1970), that since Bill had exceeded his authority in restraining Colin, Colin was entitled to resist by way of reasonable force; any such resistance would be lawful and therefore could not amount to an assault on an officer in the execution of his duty, so on this argument the offence under **s 89 Police Act** is not made out. Simple assault would not be made out either since he was entitled to resist. Even assuming that reasonable suspicion is present of assault or burglary, no reason is given for the arrest.

Thus, it is arguable that the arrest was unlawful for a period of time, before Colin pushed Bill. It arguably became lawful for a period of time, but then again became unlawful when the point came and passed at which Colin could have been given the reason (under **s 28** and s 2.2 Code G) – in the police car. On this argument, when Colin is bundled into the car, Albert and Bill are entitled to use reasonable force under **s 117**, as they are in the

---

18 This application of the law relating to reasonable suspicion shows how to effectively apply the law, which requires a judgment call from you to do so effectively. Do not sit on the fence if you can help it.

exercise of an arrest power. But they are not entitled to use force before Colin pushes Bill. The subsequent detention – after the point when they could have informed Colin of the reason for the arrest – is also unlawful. These findings as to the arrest would appear to accord with the demands of **Art 5(1)** and **(2)** under the **HRA**.[19]

The search of Colin's flat also appears to be unlawful. Under **s 18**, a power to enter and search premises after arrest arises in instances covered by **s 24**. Since the arrest appears to be unlawful at this point, this condition is not satisfied. It follows from this that the power of seizure under **s 19(2)** does not arise, as it may only be exercised under **s 19(1)** by a constable lawfully on the premises. The seizure of the cannabis is therefore unlawful. The search of the home also appears to breach **Art 8** under the **HRA** and gives rise to an action in trespass. The search should also comply with Code B, but Colin is not given a notice of powers and rights as the Code requires. **Section 30(1) PACE** requires that Colin should be taken to the police station as soon as practicable after arrest; since there is no basis for the search, it appears that **s 30(1)** has not been complied with.

At the police station, Colin is denied access to legal advice. Delay in affording such access will only be lawful if one of the contingencies envisaged under **s 58(8)** of **PACE** will arise if a solicitor is contacted. Following *Samuel* (1988), the police must have a clear basis for this belief. In this instance, the police made no effort to invoke one of the exceptions and have therefore breached **s 58** and para 6 of Code C (2008), which provides that once a suspect has requested advice, he must not be interviewed until he has received it.

Having identified a series of illegal acts on the part of the police, it will now be necessary to consider the redress, if any, available to Colin in respect of them. The first such act was the unlawful seizure of the keys. The appropriate tortious cause of action in this instance will be trespass to goods; damages will, however, be minimal.[20]

In taking hold of and then detaining Colin outside the context of a lawful arrest, Bill commits assault and battery and breaches **Art 5** of the **ECHR**. The facts of the instant case closely resemble those of *Collins v Willcock* (1984) or *Kenlin v Gardner* (1967), which established this principle. Further, the unlawful arrest and the subsequent unlawful detention in the car and police station will support a claim of false imprisonment. The search of the home, based on an unlawful arrest, will give rise to an action in trespass to land. The seizure of the keys was part of an unlawful search; Colin could therefore sue the police authority for trespass to land and to goods. Colin may hope that the keys and cannabis will be excluded from evidence under **s 78** of **PACE**, as found during the course of unlawful searches. However, according to *Thomas* (1990) and *Effick* (1992), and

---

19 This passage demonstrates how to effectively make clear conclusions as you go along.

20 By adding in advice about redress, rather than just focussing upon the breaches, this answer is much more comprehensive.

confirmed in *Khan* (1997) and *Loosely* (2001), physical evidence is admissible subject to a very narrow discretion to exclude it. It appears that no strong argument for exclusion of the cannabis or keys from evidence arises, and this outcome appears to be in accordance with the demands of **Art 6** under **s 3** of the **HRA. Section 78** must be interpreted in accordance with **Art 6**, under **s 3 HRA**, but no change in the current interpretation appears to be required due to the findings in *Khan v UK* (2000).

Can a reasonable argument be advanced that Colin's admissions in the police station interview should be excluded from evidence under **s 76**? Following *Alladice* (1988) and *Hughes* (1988), unless it can be shown that the custody officer acted in bad faith in failing to allow Colin access to a solicitor, it seems that **s 76(2)(a)** will not apply. Following *Delaney* (1989), it is necessary to show under **s 76(2)(b)** that the defendant was in some particularly difficult or vulnerable position, making the breach of **PACE** of special significance. Since this does not appear to be the case here, it seems that **s 76(2)(b)** cannot be invoked.

On the other hand, Colin's admissions may be excluded from evidence under **s 78** on the basis that the police breached **s 58**. Following *Samuel* (1988), it must be shown that the breach of **s 58** was causally related to the admissions made in the second interview. (It should be noted that the wrong caution was given; the caution should have been that of Annex C para 2 Code C, since the restriction on drawing adverse inferences from silence applied as he had been denied access to legal advice.) Since he was not afforded an opportunity to have legal advice (**s 34(2A) Criminal Justice and Public Order Act 1994**), the adviser could have warned him that there was probably no risk involved in staying silent under **s 34 CJPOA**. On this analysis, it is possible that the requisite causal relationship exists and the admissions might, therefore, be excluded from evidence under **s 78**.

A further possibility is that the actions of the police in breaching the **PACE** Codes and **PACE** itself could be the subject of a complaint, as could the other unlawful actions mentioned, under the **Police Reform Act 2002**.

Finally, Colin may want to know whether the charge of assaulting a police officer in the execution of his duty will succeed. Clearly, it will fail on the argument that Colin's actions did not amount to an assault, as he was entitled to resist Bill. Moreover, it has been determined that Bill was outside the execution of his duty since he was in the course of perpetrating an unlawful arrest.

QUESTION 29

'The interviewing scheme under the **Police and Criminal Evidence Act 1984** is wholly inadequate as a means of preventing miscarriages of justice.'

▶ **Do you agree?**

How to Answer this Question

It should be noted that the question is only concerned with the interviewing scheme under **PACE 1984**, not with other methods of addressing the problem of miscarriages of justice. It is obviously important to take the **Human Rights Act (HRA) 1998** fully into account in your answer, since the **ECHR** may provide greater safeguards for police interviews.

Essentially, the following matters should be considered:

- ❖ the nature of the safeguards available under **Pts IV** and **V** of **PACE** and Codes of Practice C (2008) and E (2011);
- ❖ **Art 6** under **HRA**;
- ❖ the provisions determining when the safeguards come into play – definition of an 'interview' – interviewing inside or outside the police station;
- ❖ the legal advice provisions;
- ❖ the recording provisions;
- ❖ the value of exclusion of evidence as a form of redress for breaches of the interviewing scheme – the relevance of **ss 34–37** of the **Criminal Justice and Public Order Act (CJPOA) 1994; Art 6 ECHR** under **HRA**;
- ❖ the possibilities of invoking the **HRA 1998** to improve the protection for suspects;
- ❖ the scope for miscarriages of justice which remains.

Answer Structure

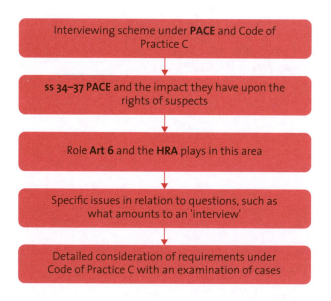

Interviewing scheme under **PACE** and Code of Practice C

↓

ss 34–37 PACE and the impact they have upon the rights of suspects

↓

Role **Art 6** and the **HRA** plays in this area

↓

Specific issues in relation to questions, such as what amounts to an 'interview'

↓

Detailed consideration of requirements under Code of Practice C with an examination of cases

ANSWER

Our criminal justice process relies heavily on the use of confession evidence but, at the same time, is wedded to a system in which a suspect is interviewed by a body, the police, who have a strong interest in securing a conviction, under conditions which are entirely under police control. In such circumstances, what can be done to ensure that a confession so acquired can be relied on by a court?

A body of rules can be devised, intended *first* to alter the balance of power between interviewers and interviewee, reducing the vulnerability of the interviewee and making it more likely that any confession is reliable. This process began in this country with the Judges' Rules, which were replaced by the more complex interviewing scheme under **PACE 1984** and Code C. A revised Code C was introduced in 2003 and then revised again in 2006 and 2008. Code E deals with audio recording. These developments notwithstanding, the pressure which originally led the police to circumvent the rules is still unchanged.[21]

These changes represent an attempt to obtain greater control of the interviewing process, to address the inherent limitations of police interviews. If an interview is conducted in compliance with sound interviewing rules, it should be possible to feel confident that a conviction based on it will be safe and therefore miscarriages of justice should be less likely. In order to place the changes in their context, the general nature of the interviewing scheme, which **PACE** brought into being, should be considered, as well as any impact that the **HRA** has had or could have. The **PACE** scheme consists of a web of provisions which derive from three sources of differing legal status: the Act itself, Codes C and E made under it and the Notes for Guidance accompanying the Codes.

A radical change to the balance between police and interviewee was made by curtailment of the right to silence under **ss 34–37** of the **CJPOA 1994**. This was reflected in the complex caution introduced under the 1995 revision of Code C. It meant that, even where all the safeguards are in place, there may be great pressure on the suspect to speak, bearing in mind the disadvantage which silence may create, and this may result in an increase in the number of false confessions. However, ECtHR cases make it clear that a suspect must not be compelled to speak (*Funke v France* (1993)), and that adverse inferences should not normally be allowed when the detainee was not allowed independent legal advice (*Murray v UK* (1996)), and that inferences may not be drawn from silence unless that silence 'could only sensibly be attributed to their having no answer or none that would stand up to cross-examination', as to the question originally asked (*Condron v UK* (2000)). So, any silence which can later be explained plausibly should no longer trigger inferences or **Art 6** will be breached. These **Convention** requirements have been adopted into the law under

---

21 By setting out the developments of the Judges' Rules up to **PACE** and the Codes, this shows the examiner you have an excellent knowledge of the area.

s 34(2A) of the **CJPOA 1994**, and the later revisions to Code C makes appropriate changes to the caution in respect of interviews from which adverse inferences cannot lawfully be drawn. The old caution, maintaining the full right to silence, must be used where the suspect has not had an opportunity of having legal advice, under para 10.6. The 2006 revision, in line with the **Convention** rights under the **HRA**, emphasises the importance of the right to legal advice. There is still room for argument, however, as to the meaning of the term 'opportunity'. Also, it seems that adverse inferences can be drawn from silence in interviews under caution outside the police station, even though the suspect has had no real and effective opportunity to have access to legal advice and has not been notified that it will be available later.

The correct interpretation of the term 'interview' used in Code C as originally drafted was a matter of great importance, because the relevant safeguards only came into play once an exchange between police officer and suspect was designated an interview. The term 'interview' therefore tended to be given a wide interpretation and eventually the definition given to it by the Court of Appeal in *Matthews* (1990), 'any discussion or talk between suspect and police officer', brought within its ambit many exchanges far removed from formal interviews.[22]

However, assuming that an exchange could be called an interview, the safeguards applying to it differed quite markedly, depending on where it took place. Those available *inside* the police station included contemporaneous recording or tape-recording; the ability to read over, verify and sign the notes of the interview as a correct record; notification of the right to legal advice; the option of having legal advice and of having the advisor present and, where appropriate, the presence of an adult. In 'the field', however, it was only necessary to ensure that an accurate record of the interview was made and, where appropriate, an adult was present. In other words, only a minimum level of protection was available, thus creating greater scope for impropriety, including fabrication of confessions, in such circumstances. The arbitrary dividing line thus drawn between those suspects interviewed in or out of the police station was one of the main deficiencies of the original Code C.

A definition of the term 'interview' is now contained in para 11, which reads: 'An interview is the questioning of a person regarding their involvement or suspected involvement in a criminal offence or offences, which, under para 10.1 is required to be carried out under caution.'

Paragraph 10.1 of Code C requires a caution to be given where the answers to questions (or the suspect's failure to answer questions) may be given in evidence to a court in a

---

22 This appreciation of the law relating to 'interviews' shows excellent skills of identification of relevant issues as well as providing a good account of the law.

prosecution.[23] Questioning which is simply to establish a person's identity, or the ownership of a vehicle, or to assist in the conduct of a search of a person or property, will not, therefore, constitute an 'interview'. Questioning a person at port and border controls under the **Terrorism Act 2000** is also excluded.

The hallmark of an interview is 'questioning', so if the conversation is instigated by the suspect, this may not be an interview (*Menard* (1995)). The current definition is in line with the approach taken in *Absolam* (1989), where an interview was defined as questions directed by the police to a suspect.

Once an exchange can be designated an interview, it will be of significance whether it takes place inside or outside the police station. The significance is not as great as it used to be. Paragraph 11 contains provisions for giving the suspect the record of the interview to verify and sign and unlike the situation prior to 1995, applies to all interviews, not just those that took place in the police station, requires a record to be made of all interviews, wherever they take place. Further, under para 11.7(c), the interview must be recorded contemporaneously wherever it takes place unless, in the investigating officer's view, this would not be practicable or would interfere with its conduct. However, there is no change as far as notification of the right to legal advice is concerned. It is also, at present, unlikely that the interview would be recorded: neither Code E on audio recording nor Code F on visual recording envisage recording taking place anywhere but inside the police station, though the latter is not explicit on the point. Thus, an unsatisfactory distinction between suspects interviewed in or out of the police station is still preserved.

Since 1995, the problem has been addressed in a radical way by means of a prohibition under para 11.1 on interviewing outside the police station except in exceptional circumstances. It is, of course, only 'interviews' which must not occur outside the police station; other exchanges can take place because, in general, the need for them to be subject to the level of protection available inside it will not be so pressing. Any comments made relevant to an offence would need to be recorded and acknowledged by the suspect under para 11.13. However, courts have interpreted any questioning designed to incriminate the suspect as an 'interview': see *Bailey v DPP* (1998).

Under para 11.1(a), (b) and (c), interviewing can occur outside the station in order to avert certain specified risks. The first exception under para 11.1(a), allowing interviewing to take place at once where delay might lead to interference with evidence, could be interpreted very broadly and could apply whenever there was some likelihood that evidence connected with any offence, but not immediately obtainable, was in existence.

23 The continual references to passages of the Codes and sections of **PACE** show how to effectively refer to law without just copying out passages from a statute book.

Wide but uncertain scope for interviewing outside the police station still remains.[24] Thus, things stand as they did under the original Code: in order to bring certain safeguards into play, it must first be found that an exchange constitutes an interview and then that it took place within the police station. Taking access to legal advice, tape-recording and the provision for interviews under paras 11 and 12 as the main safeguards, it becomes apparent that there are three levels of protection available, which depend on the category into which the exchange falls.

Inside the police station, if the person in question is an arrestee or a volunteer under caution and the exchange is an interview, all the available safeguards will apply. If an interview takes place outside the police station, but falls outside the para 11.1 prohibition, the same verifying and recording provisions will apply, with the proviso that contemporaneous recording, tape-recording and, for the future, video-recording are likely to be impracticable. The most important difference is that no notification of the right to legal advice need be given.

If the person is suspected of involvement in an offence, but the level of suspicion is below that which would warrant a caution or *a fortiori* an arrest and the interview takes place in the police station, the lower level of protection described above will apply, but the person also has the right to have legal advice and, possibly, due to the provision of para 11.2, to be told of this right. The paragraph requires a reminder to be given of the entitlement to free legal advice before any interview in a police station. This provision may apply to the situation envisaged, although the use of the word 'remind' suggests that that was not the intention behind it, because the person in question will not already be aware of the right. Utterances relevant to the offence, outside the context of an interview, made by a suspected person (who could obviously be an arrestee or a volunteer under caution) are subject only to the basic level of protection, which obtains under para 11.13, though under para 11.4, 'significant statements' or silences made prior to the interview should, at the beginning of the interview, be put to the suspect for confirmation or denial.

The main objection to this scheme is that an arbitrary dividing line is still being drawn between suspects interviewed inside or outside the police station, although admittedly, interviewing outside it should now occur less frequently. Further, even where, formally speaking, all the safeguards should be in place, there may still be methods of evading them. As research conducted by Sanders in 1989 showed, the police have developed a number of means of subverting the legal advice scheme, with a view to discouraging suspects from obtaining access to legal advice. The 2006 and 2008 revisions of Code C, in para 6 emphasise the importance of legal advice.

....

24 This identification of remaining issues in relation to interviewing shows a good ability to understand and interpret the law.

Disputes over the admissibility of confessions under **s 78** continue, because it is necessary to put exchanges between suspect and police into the categories mentioned above; having done so, if one of the safeguards applicable to that category has not been made available, the confession may be inadmissible (*Samuel* (1988)). Moreover, the scheme is unlikely to prevent miscarriages of justice, because it leaves open scope for evading certain of the key safeguards including tape recording and access to legal advice. Confessions obtained without such safeguards will only be subject to the **s 78** test if the suspect pleads not guilty. Further, evasion of the rules must usually be characterised as a breach of the scheme in order to trigger the use of **s 78**. However, it may not appear that a breach has occurred, again leaving open the possibility that a potential miscarriage of justice will go unrecognised.

In conclusion, it is suggested that, whilst to say that the interviewing scheme in **PACE** and Code C is 'wholly inadequate' to prevent miscarriages of justice may be an exaggeration, the amendments to the Code still do not prevent, as securely as they should, the questioning of suspects away from police stations and the safeguards therein, and this, given the pressures on the police, can increase the possibility of miscarriages of justice. What of the **Convention** as received into domestic law under the **HRA**? **Article 6** applies to pre-trial behaviour, including by the police (*Teixeira v Portugal* (1998)). The extent of its influence in providing protection from police abuses is hard to judge. Undoubtedly, it shifts attention away from the detailed classification of police actions towards an evaluation of the overall fairness of the process. Nevertheless, the UK courts have also recognised and utilised the fact that **Art 6** rights are flexible and context-dependent and appear to have accepted, subject to the access to legal advice provisions mentioned above, that the interviewing scheme in Code C is compatible with **Art 6**. Other potential causes of miscarriages of justice, such as those flowing from inadequate disclosures of evidence to the defence, or from the continued use of public interest immunity, are, perhaps, more likely to change as a consequence of **Art 6**.

Prisoners' Rights and Discrimination of Vulnerable Groups

INTRODUCTION

The topic of discrimination is vast and can cover a multitude of different areas. The topic is likely to be covered in different ways in different institutions: sometimes discrimination is taught as a topic in itself; alternatively, different groups of vulnerable people can be looked at separately. The main focus of this chapter is upon a particularly topical and increasingly taught area of one class of vulnerable people; prisoners. However, the chapter also concludes by looking at discrimination more generally.

In relation to questions about the law relating to prisoners, examiners tend to set both problem and essay questions in this area. Problem questions often concern the use of judicial review by prisoners to challenge disciplinary hearings which appear to have fallen below the standards demanded by natural justice. Essay questions often concern the use of judicial review and **Arts 6** and **8** of the **European Convention on Human Rights (ECHR)** to uphold prisoners' rights.

In relation to discrimination law more generally, the law in this area has been changed substantially by the **Equality Act 2010** since the last edition of this book. The Act brings all anti-discrimination provisions (over 100 pieces of separate legislation) together in one statute and attempts to create a single equality law framework. Rather than changing the law in a radically different way, the main focus of the legislation was consolidation of the law.

Examiners tend to set essays in this area which focus not only on the provisions of the domestic non-discrimination legislation, but also on the relevant European Union (EU) provisions. As well as the **Equality Act 2010**, another significant piece of legislation is the **Equality Act 2006** which made extensive amendments to the anti-discrimination statutes that were in force prior to it, and pushed the boundaries of equality law much further than previous legislation. The **2010 Act** repealed and replaced some of the **2006 Act** but many of the 2006 provisions remain in force. The drive behind the **2006 Act** was partly a result of the need to implement EU Directives and respond to human rights decisions and partly to do with a new domestic drive towards a more holistic view of equality principles. Discrimination law can no longer be viewed as an aspect of employment law but covers a vast and ever expanding field of human activity. A parallel development has been the expansion of the protected characteristics from the original areas of race and sex to disability, gender reassignment and more recently religion, age and sexual orientation.

There are, however, other Acts that need to be taken into account. The **Civil Partnership Act 2004** granted gay and lesbian couples similar rights and obligations to married couples if they entered into a civil partnership. The **Gender Recognition Act 2004**, passed in response to the cases of *Goodwin v UK* (2002) and *Bellinger v Bellinger* (2003), now provides a legal framework for recognising changed sex and supplements earlier changes to the **Sex Discrimination Act** to protect transgendered persons.

Alongside these developments examiners will expect some appreciation of the impact of the **Convention** rights in **Sched 1** to the **Human Rights Act** as they affect the concept of equality, although it should be noted that the UK has not yet signed up to the **Protocol 12** freestanding non-discrimination right so any allegation of discrimination under **Art 14** must be pegged to the protection of other **Convention** rights.

Monitoring, enforcing and awareness-raising of the new equality framework is partly the responsibility of the Equality and Human Rights Commission which combines the activities of the existing commissions and adds the new equality areas plus human rights protection within its remit. This mega-Commission leads the development of the equality agenda and works towards consolidating and modernising equality law in the future, hence its importance.

It is clear, then, that at the present time, discrimination on grounds of sex, race and disability is now only part of the picture, albeit still a hugely important part. Questions will increasingly require awareness of broader equality issues and recognition of the expanded reach of the law.

Checklist ✔

Students should be familiar with the following areas:

- **Arts 6** and **8** of the **ECHR**;
- key decisions of the European Court of Human Rights (EctHR) on privacy, access to a court and standards in disciplinary hearings;
- recent decisions of the ECtHR on **Art 3** and the treatment of, in particular, ill, disabled and mentally ill prisoners;
- use of judicial review in this area, particularly the application of the principles of natural justice;

- key provisions of the **Prison Rules 1999** (consolidated 2002);
- the Woolf proposals and Ramsbottom reports;
- influence of private law remedies;
- key decisions of the domestic courts post-**HRA**;
- proposals for prison reform;
- the **Equality Act 2006** provisions for the creation of the Commission for Equality and Human Rights;
- The **Equality Act 2010**

QUESTION 30

'The measures available to deal with suspected terrorists in the **Terrorism Prevention and Investigation Measures Act 2011** have the same crippling effects upon a suspect's human rights as the previous regimes did'.

◗ **Discuss.**

How to Answer this Question

- ❖ background to the Control Order scheme – detention under the **Anti-Terrorism Crime and Security Act 2001**;
- ❖ the *A* case – why detention without trial violated the **ECHR**;
- ❖ Control Orders under the **Prevention of Terrorism Act 2005**;
- ❖ derogating and non-derogating Control Orders;
- ❖ impact on suspects' human rights;
- ❖ challenges to Control Orders;
- ❖ **TPIM** regime under the **Terrorism Prevention and Investigation Measures Act 2011**;
- ❖ comparison between **TPIM** regime and previous regimes and their impact upon human rights.

Answer Structure

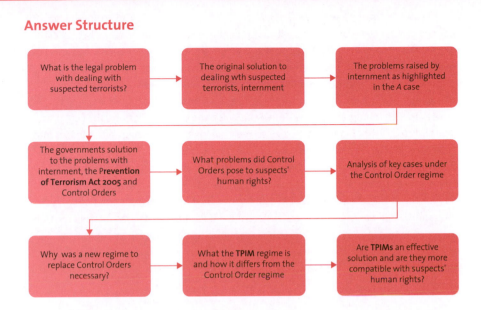

| What is the legal problem with dealing with suspected terrorists? | → | The original solution to dealing wth suspected terrorists, internment | → | The problems raised by internment as highlighted in the *A* case |

| The governments solution to the problems with internment, the **Prevention of Terrorism Act 2005** and Control Orders | → | What problems did Control Orders pose to suspects' human rights? | → | Analysis of key cases under the Control Order regime |

| Why was a new regime to replace Control Orders necessary? | → | What the **TPIM** regime is and how it differs from the Control Order regime | → | Are **TPIMs** an effective solution and are they more compatible with suspects' human rights? |

Aim Higher ★

Examiners will give credit to attempts by students to critically consider the **TPIM** regime and to actively make comparisons between the **TPIM** regime and the Control Order regime which will require personal judgment calls by the student on the evidence that they present.

Common Pitfalls ✗

Students who would not perform well in this question are those that would merely describe the Control Order regime and the **TPIM** regime.

ANSWER

The statement argues that the latest tool to try and deal with the threat posed by suspected terrorists breaches suspects' human rights as much as the previous regimes. Whilst there is abundant evidence that the previous regimes often did not respect suspects' human rights, it will be argued that the **TPIM** regime does offer an improvement on its predecessors, but that these improvements are slight, and there are still concerns about their compatibility with suspects' rights.

Control Orders were introduced by the **Prevention of Terrorism Act 2005**. They were aimed at reducing the perceived risk from suspected terrorists following the attack on the

World Trade Centre in New York in 2001. Prior to Control Orders the Government had detained foreign terrorist suspects without trial at Belmarsh prison under **s 23** of the **Anti-Terrorism Crime and Security Act 2001**. The problem the Government then faced was that certain foreign terror suspects could not be prosecuted due to lack of admissible evidence but the Government could not deport them due to its human rights obligations (following the ruling in *Chahal v UK* (1996)). The solution was to detain the suspects under amended immigration rules. They were given the option of leaving the UK voluntarily but if they did not do so they were detained at a high security prison in a form of internment. The Government issued a derogation order relating to the right to liberty under **Art 5** of the **Convention** on the basis that the detention was a strictly necessary response to a public emergency. The decision of the House of Lords in *A v Secretary of State for the Home Department* (2005) dealt a body blow to the internment policy. The derogation order was quashed and a declaration of incompatibility was made in relation to the power to detain. This decision led to a problem for the government of the day. The detainees would have to be released soon and the Government had no alternative power to deal with them. The **2005 Act,** which introduced the Control Order regime, was rushed through Parliament.[1]

Control Orders were described as a kind of 'super-ASBO' aimed at suspected terrorists. They attempted to control the location, activities and associates of suspects with a view to reducing the risk of terrorist action. There were two types of Control Order: derogating and non-derogating. The former breached **Art 5** of the **Convention** and had to be accompanied by a valid derogation under **Art 15**. No derogating Control Orders were ever made. Non-derogating Control Orders purportedly did not deprive the suspect of their liberty and thus did not engage **Art 5**. However, the terms of such Control Orders were on occasion found to amount to a deprivation of liberty and thus violate **Art 5** of the **Convention**.

The Secretary of State could make a non-derogating Control Order if he had reasonable grounds for suspecting that the individual was or had been involved in terrorism-related activities and considered it necessary to impose the order to protect the public from the risk of terrorism. 'Terrorism-related activities' was very broadly defined to include not just commission, preparation and instigation of acts of terrorism but also encouragement, support or assistance. Conditions imposed can be any that the Secretary of State considers necessary.

The restrictions that could be imposed in a Control Order were extensive. They included: residence, curfew, electronic tag, geographical movement, search, work and association. The independent monitor, Lord Carlile, cautioned in his 2006 report that each order had

----

1   This paragraph summarises the legal reaction to the problem of dealing with suspected terrorists in a succinct yet detailed way. Try and be as concise as possible when detailing large amounts of law.

to be tailored to meet the circumstances of each individual suspect and must not have been over-generalised. The Government subsequently established a review group to keep each order under quarterly review.

One major problem with Control Orders and their impact upon suspects' human rights was that the information which led to the order was normally considered in secret. Thus the court could hold secret hearings and was prevented from disclosing any information which may damage the public interest. In *Secretary of State for the Home Department v F* (2009) the House of Lords, in reliance on the European Court decision in *A v United Kingdom* (2009) altered its previous view and held that controllees could not be kept in ignorance of the case against them so that where the open material was purely general assertions the trial would not be fair. The ability to withhold information from suspects remained though and it is important to note that this is still the case with the new **TPIM** regime.

Non-derogating Control Orders were not lawful if they breached the **Art 5** right to liberty. A difficult issue was the extent to which curfews and other restrictions impinge on the right to liberty. In *JJ* (2006), the Court of Appeal held that curfews of 18 hours per day violated **Art 5** when considered in conjunction with additional restrictions applicable when the suspect was permitted to leave his home. The Control Order was thus quashed. However, in *E* (2007), the Court of Appeal held that a 12-hour curfew monitored by electronic tagging and reporting together with restrictions was far from a deprivation of liberty under **Art 5**. The authorities nevertheless did establish that it is possible for **Art 5** to be breached despite the suspect living in his own home. A lot appeared to rest on the duration of any curfew and the suspect's ability to lead a normal life. In this sense the interference with other **Convention** rights such as respect for privacy, association etc. has a direct relevance to whether **Art 5** has been breached. In *R (AP) v Secretary of State for the Home Department* (2010) the Supreme Court found in a 16-hour curfew case that although interference with family life (AP was required to live over a hundred miles away from his family) was proportionate, this tipped the situation into a deprivation of liberty case.

It is clear that Control Orders did have the ability to impinge significantly on qualified rights in the **Convention** such as the right to respect for private and family life, manifestation of religion, freedom of expression and freedom of assembly and association. Given the criticism of the Control Order regime from all quarters, but bearing in mind the need for the government to have measures in place to try and deal with suspected terrorists, the **Prevention of Terrorism Act 2005** and the Control Order regime was abolished by the **Terrorism Prevention and Investigation Measures Act 2011 (TPIM Act)**.

Under the **TPIM Act** the Home Secretary may issue a '**TPIM Notice**' (**Notice**) courtesy of **s 2**. **Schedule 1** lists all the measures that can be imposed under a **Notice**. These include: overnight residence measures; travel measures; exclusion measures; movement directions measures; electronic communication device measures; association measures, amongst others.

A Notice including such measures can be made by the Home Secretary if he possesses a reasonable belief that the individual is, or has been, involved in terrorism-related activity (s 3). Section 4 of the Act sets out the definition of 'terrorism-related activity' and it is very wide and essentially the same definition as was given in the Prevention of Terrorism Act 2005. The Home Secretary must apply to the court for permission to impose a Notice, or he can impose one without such initial permission if he considers it a matter of urgency, although the court must still review such decisions after the event. The role of the court is essentially the same as it was in relation to Control Orders. They are limited to interfering and refusing/quashing Notices, only if they hold that the Home Secretary's decision was 'obviously flawed', which is quite a high threshold to satisfy. There is therefore no real change insofar as the Home Secretary has the power to impose a Notice in the same way as he could impose a Control Order, with scant powers of review by the courts.[2]

There is a slight difference to the standard of proof that is required in order to impose a Notice as compared to Control Orders. The Home Secretary needs reasonable grounds to 'believe' rather than reasonable grounds to 'suspect' that the individual is involved in terrorism-related activity. The significance of this is that belief is a higher threshold to meet than suspicion, although the practical significance of this is likely to be negligible at best.

Another key difference between Control Orders and TPIMs is their duration. Control Orders had a 12 month time limit but they could be renewed with no limits on how many times they could be renewed. TPIMs have a 2 year time-limit. It should be noted that this is subject to the caveat that if the individual is believed to have been involved in a new act of terrorism, then a new TPIM Notice can be issued in relation to that new evidence.

There are still concerns over the measures available under TPIMs. Whilst they were described by the government as being much less restrictive upon individuals, there is not a great deal of evidence that this is the case. For example, one of the major impositions upon individuals' human rights was the curfew measures, extreme examples of which were successfully challenged a number of times (such as the *JJ* and *(R) AP* cases mentioned above). Measures available under the TPIM regime include an overnight residence order. Whilst this appears to be offer less scope for lengthy curfews, this is still a major imposition upon the liberty and freedom of movement of an individual, as requirements can be imposed as to where the individual resides and that they have to remain within such premises overnight between certain hours required by the Home Secretary. It is therefore difficult to say that there have been major changes or improvements in this area.[3]

There are some changes in other areas however that it is worthy to note. Under Control Orders individuals could be subject to significant limitations upon their freedom of

----

2   This brief analytical comment shows how easy it is to incorporate analysis as you go along.

3   Some good comparative analysis of the Control Order and TPIM regime takes place here.

movement, even taking the form of relocating individuals to completely new areas of the country where they had no prior connection (see *R(AP)* case above). The **TPIM** measures seek to prevent this type of activity. If, however, the individual does not have a residence in a particular area and they cannot show a connection to an area then they can be required to reside in any area in the UK that the Home Secretary considers appropriate. In addition there are still restrictions available to an individual's freedom of movement in the form of restrictions upon certain locations and restrictions on foreign travel.

In January 2011, Liberty called the new **TPIM** regime 'Control Orders lite' and it is easy to see why.[4] Whilst the potential interferences upon individuals are scaled back, they are not a completely radical and new solution to the problem of dealing with suspected terrorists. The measures are in the same vein as those contained in the Control Order regime, and there are still concerns about their potential compatibility with human rights. For example, if the overnight residence order is used in a heavy-handed way, in conjunction with other measures such as restrictions on movement, access to communication devices and contact with other people, there are legitimate questions to ask about the compatibility of these measures with **Convention** rights, such as **Art 5** and **8** rights in particular. In addition, the ability to withhold information from suspects and the use of Special Advocates that was created with Control Orders remains. So whilst **TPIMs** may not appear on paper to be as crippling upon individual's rights as their predecessors, they do still have the possibility to seriously impact upon individuals' **Convention** rights. It is a matter of time before the measures will be tested before the courts, but if the measures are used in a heavy-handed way, for which the possibility remains a reality, then it will be interesting to see what the courts have to say about the measures.

QUESTION 31

'Enjoyment of civil liberties no longer stops at the prison gates. Nevertheless, despite the influence of the **European Convention on Human Rights**, prisoners' rights are still in their infancy.'

▶ **Discuss.**

How to Answer this Question

It is necessary to identify the areas in which improvement has occurred and to consider how far the **Convention** has influenced those areas. Good answers will assess how far domestic decisions have developed prison law and where there is scope for further development. Essentially, the following matters should be considered:

❖ key decisions of the ECtHR on privacy, access to a court and standards in disciplinary hearings;

---

4   This quote from Liberty shows the examiner that you have undertaken wide reading and research in the area.

❖ use of judicial review in this area, particularly the application of the principles
   of natural justice: general influence of the ECtHR;
❖ influence of the **HRA**;
❖ limitations of the **ECHR**, particularly in relation to improving basic living
   standards in UK prisons.

Answer Structure

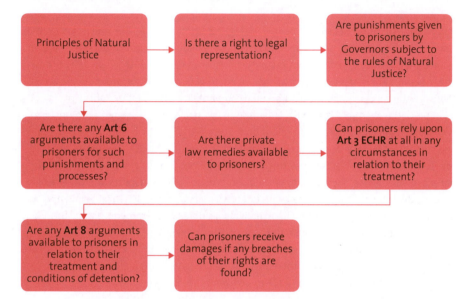

Common Pitfalls ✗

Take care with how much time and space you devote to recitation of the
facts of cases. Although the facts of decided cases may often be relevant
to your answer you need to use them sparingly or you will have no time
to develop your narrative and analysis. There is sometimes a tendency for
students to allow the facts of cases to dominate an answer. Long rehearsal
of the facts rarely works effectively. Try to be concise in your explanation of
facts and where possible integrate the factual account with your analysis of
the case so as to develop your essay. See for example the very sparse use of
facts in relation to the case of *Ezeh v UK* (2002) in the answer below.

ANSWER

The law on fair procedures relating to disciplinary action against prisoners has gone
through major changes in recent times, largely required by the impact of **Art 6** of the

ECHR. Under the old system, serious disciplinary offences were heard by the Boards of Prison Visitors. The rules of natural justice were applied to these hearings. In *Board of Visitors of Hull Prison ex p St Germain (No 1)* (1979), certain prisoners complained that the disciplinary proceedings which followed the Hull prison riots were not conducted in accordance with the principles of natural justice. The Court of Appeal held that prisoners only lose those liberties expressly denied them by Parliament – otherwise, they retain their rights under the law. There was nothing in the **Prison Act 1952** or the **Prison Rules** made under it to take away the jurisdiction of the courts, and the Board of Visitors was discharging a quasi-judicial function. Thus, it was found that the decision in question must be open to review and that Boards of Visitors must act in accordance with the rules of natural justice.[5]

An important issue was whether, given the application of the rules of natural justice, prisoners were always entitled to legal representation. The House of Lords refused, in *Secretary of State for the Home Department ex p Tarrant* (1985), to hold that legal representation was mandatory for Boards of Prison Visitors. In *Campbell and Fell v UK* (1984), the ECtHR found that **Art 6** of the **ECHR** had been breached by a failure to allow legal representation to a prisoner in a disciplinary hearing. Breaches were found of **Art 6(3)(b)** and **(c)** concerning time and facilities to prepare a defence and availability of legal assistance; the applicants had had no assistance before the hearing or representation at it. It became increasingly difficult to be satisfied that the disciplinary function of the Board of Prison Visitors could be exercised compatibly with the **ECHR** and the function was abolished by the **Criminal Justice Act 1991**. Now serious disciplinary offences are dealt with as criminal offences by the ordinary courts, before which a prisoner has full rights of representation.

The less serious offences, called offences against prison discipline, are still dealt with within the prison service. Traditionally, the governor would determine such cases and had the power to punish in various ways including the imposition of up to 42 'additional days' imprisonment. The question that arose after the introduction of the **HRA** was whether the procedural requirements for a fair trial applied to governors' hearings and, if they did, whether the application of natural justice was sufficient to satisfy **Art 6**. In *Ezeh v UK* (2002), a more direct impact of the **ECHR** was found. Two prisoners had been found guilty in disciplinary hearings in which neither was represented. The ECtHR decided that the seriousness of the charges and the severity of punishments open to the governor meant that disciplinary proceedings involved the determination of a criminal charge and thus the standard of a fair trial was set by **Art 6** with the consequent due process rights. Failure to permit legal representation in these circumstances violated **Arts 6(1)** and **6(3)(c)**. In a subsequent House of Lords case the Home Secretary conceded that the procedure did

---

5   This is a very useful introduction as it sets out the background to the complex area of law relating to prisoners, which helps to give clarity to the answer.

violate **Art 6** so that the only question remaining was whether damages were available for the breach (*R (Greenfield) v Secretary of State for the Home Department* (2005)). Following *Ezeh*, the **Prison Rules** were amended (see **rr 51–61**) so that an independent adjudicator who is a District Judge (Criminal) must adjudicate additional day cases with attendance due process guarantees.

In a succession of cases (for example, *Raymond v Honey* (1983) and *R v Secretary of State for the Home Department ex p O'Brien and Simms* (1999)), the courts have accepted that imprisonment does not mean that prisoners lose their fundamental rights. Unless fundamental rights are taken away expressly or by necessary implication of the fact of imprisonment, they are retained. There have been a number of significant improvements relating to prisoners' rights to privacy (e.g. *Silver v UK* (1983) regarding prisoner correspondence and *Golder v UK* (1975) regarding access to a court). The position was strengthened by later cases which emphasised rights of legal privilege and unimpeded access to legal advisors. Such principles are of such fundamental and constitutional importance that they can only be taken away by clear and express words in primary legislation. These principles continue to be asserted and strengthened by the courts, particularly in the light of the **HRA**. In *R (Daly) v Secretary of State for the Home Department* (2001), the House of Lords held that a blanket rule requiring prisoners to be removed from their cells during examinations of correspondence was a disproportionate interference with their right of privileged access to legal advisors.[6]

These improvements may be contrasted with the failure of prisoners to successfully use the courts to challenge alleged inhuman or degrading treatment in prisons. Once a prisoner is inside a prison, he or she may be subject to various punishments such as solitary confinement or withdrawal of privileges. Where formal punishment is not ordered, a decision may nevertheless be taken which subjects a prisoner to unpleasant conditions or even to violence from other prisoners. However, the courts have not shown much willingness to provide remedies where prisoners complain of punishment or of conditions in prison.

Prisoners have explored private law remedies to challenge the use of certain punishments, but with limited success. If a punishment is imposed in a manner that is in breach of the **Prison Rules**, it would be unlawful, but in cases such as *Williams v Home Office (No 2)* (1982), the courts have refused to interpret the **Prison Rules** as conferring a right of action for damages on an individual prisoner.

In *Deputy Governor of Parkhurst Prison ex p Hague; Weldon v Home Office* (1991), the House of Lords found that **r 43** had not been complied with in determining segregation

---

6   This passage exploring cases in relation to various aspects of law relating to prisoners is a good illustration of how to effectively use authority and how to structure such use.

but refused to give damages for breach of statutory duty. Moreover, a claim for false imprisonment failed because the prisoner was lawfully restrained by the fact of imprisonment; segregation was merely the substitution of one form of restraint for another.

Hague and Weldon confines private law remedies to assault, negligence and misfeasance in public office and may be contrasted with the development in public law relating to fair procedure, considered above. In *Watkins v Home Office* (2006) the House of Lords confirmed the limited value of private law remedies when it held that the tort of misfeasance in a public office was not actionable *per se* so that a prisoner whose legal correspondence had been unlawfully interfered with would have no right of action unless he could prove material damage.

Recent Strasbourg decisions suggest that **Art 3** has increasing relevance especially as regards the treatment of prisoners who are mentally or physically ill or disabled. In *McGlinchey v UK* (2003), for example, the treatment of a prisoner who was both a heroin addict and asthmatic was held to violate **Art 3**. In *Keenan v UK* (2001) the failure of the prison authorities to take account of a suicidal prisoner's vulnerable mental state and failings in the disciplinary process violated **Art 3**. In *Price v UK* (2002) institutional failings to cater for the needs of a disabled prisoner violated **Art 3**, despite there being no intention to humiliate or debase the victim. **Article 3**, therefore, is likely to be of increasing significance in the development of the law on prison conditions.[7]

Other **Convention** rights are having a significant impact on the law relating to prison conditions, especially through the application of 'proportionality'. In *R v Secretary of State for the Home Department ex p Simms* (2000), the House of Lords insisted that restrictions on contacts with the media should not be allowed to prevent prisoners being able to pursue and publicise their claims of innocence, and in *Hirst v Secretary of State for the Home Department* (2002), the High Court allowed regulated contributions to radio programmes on prison conditions. Nevertheless there are clearly limits. In *Nilsen v Governor HMP Full Sutton* (2005) the prison authorities could prevent the claimant, a notorious murderer, from receiving a draft of his autobiography from his publishers. The Court of Appeal held that Strasbourg decisions recognised it was proportionate for imprisonment to carry with it some restrictions on freedom of expression and to have regard to the effect of that freedom in the outside world.

Of somewhat less significance so far has been **Art 8** in respect of developing private or family rights. See for example, the refusal of the courts to accept a challenge to the extremely restrictive policy on access to artificial insemination services

---

7   These references to ECtHR cases show a very good understanding of the area and that you have undertaken wider research into the area.

(*R (Mellor) v Secretary of State for the Home Department* (2001)). Although the blanket ban on prisoners voting was held in *Hirst v United Kingdom* (2005) to violate **Art 3** of the first Protocol the UK has still not rectified the position in domestic law.

An important question when considering the extent of prisoners rights is the availability of damages. We have noted the limited applicability of private law remedies for prisoners claiming violation of prison regulations. Clearly damages are available for breach of **Convention** rights under **s 8** of the **HRA**. However, the House of Lords has made clear in *R (Greenfield) v Secretary of State for the Home Department* (2005) that damages in **HRA** claims were likely to be rare and, where awarded, modest, certainly not equivalent to tortious claims. Normally a finding of a violation alone would amount to just satisfaction. In two recent first instance decisions, *Woodin v Home Office* (2006) and *Francis v Home Office* (2006) the High Court held that where there was a breach of the rules relating to the handling of legal correspondence with no evidence of additional harm or damage to the claimant, an apology was sufficient to remedy the **Art 8** situation so that the prisoner was not a victim for the purposes of the **Convention**. This is a narrow view of the concept of victim status under the **HRA** and if it survives it is likely to stifle many challenges by prisoners under the Act.

Serious problems involving prisoners' rights remain, even accounting for the influence of the **ECHR**. However, there have been significant developments and it is misleading to say that such rights are still in their infancy. Under the common law, there were significant developments regarding disciplinary procedures. Now we can see that the **HRA** is beginning to have considerable influence over a range of matters. This is not only because UK courts must take the **Convention** into account, but also because the ECtHR is interpreting the **ECHR** in a way that gives greater recognition to the position of prisoners even as regards questions of their treatment.[8]

QUESTION 32

Prisoners at Burham prison occupy the roof in an attempt to air their grievances. After the disturbance has been brought under control, Abel and Bert, two of the prisoners, are charged with various offences against discipline as laid down in the **Prison Rules 1999**. Abel is charged with attempting to assault an officer by throwing a slate from the prison roof. On an initial consideration of the evidence, the governor takes the view that 20 'additional days' would be the appropriate punishment if the allegation is proved. Bert is charged with intentionally obstructing an officer in the execution of his duty. He is dealt with by the governor, who imposes a punishment of 14 days' forfeiture of privileges and 28 days' stoppage of earnings.

---

8   This shows how to effectively conclude an answer by bringing together all the issues surrounding prisoner's rights and answering the set question.

Both Abel and Bert are allowed to appear in person at their respective hearings, but both are refused legal representation on the ground that the hearings must be dealt with swiftly. Abel is permitted to call one witness in his defence, but two others are refused on the ground that they have been dispersed to other prisons. Bert's request to call a witness is refused. Abel is allowed to remain present during his hearing while a prison officer gives evidence against him, but is refused permission to cross-examine him. The governor gives Bert a summary of the allegations made against him by a prison officer, but refuses to allow him to see the full statement. Bert is surprised by the content of the allegations, which appear to be more extensive than those appearing in the statement of charges given to him prior to the hearing. Despite this, the governor refuses to give him time to consider them.

▶ **Advise Abel and Bert as to any redress they might have.**

How to Answer this Question

This is a straightforward question on the operation of the **Prison Rules**, the principles of natural justice and the impact of **Art 6, Sched 1** to the **HRA 1998**. Answers must take into account changes to the **Prison Rules** required following decisions of the European Court of Human Rights (ECtHR) in Strasbourg and the need to ensure that the **Prison Rules** and practices are compatible with **European Convention** rights. It is very important to bear in mind that what is meant by a fair hearing will vary from hearing to hearing, and that the more serious the penalty, the higher should be the standards observed. Thus, it is probably a good idea to deal with both hearings separately. It must first be shown that the courts are prepared to review the decision in question on the ground of want of natural justice and, secondly, in relation to each hearing separately, that a breach (or breaches) of natural justice have taken place. Although one serious breach might lead to the quashing of the decision, you should strengthen your argument by considering as many as possible.

Essentially, the following matters should be discussed:

- ❖ the courts are prepared to review prison disciplinary decisions on the ground of want of natural justice (*St Germain* (1979));
- ❖ the courts are prepared to review decisions of governors in prison disciplinary hearings on the ground of want of natural justice (*Leech v Deputy Governor of Parkhurst Prison; Prevot v Deputy Governor of Long Lartin Prison* (1988));
- ❖ the new system for imposing the punishment of 'additional days', introduced following *Ezeh v UK* (2002) and incorporated into the **Prison Rules**;
- ❖ the discretion to allow the calling of witnesses;
- ❖ the discretion to allow cross-examination;
- ❖ whether there is a duty or merely a discretion to allow legal representation in the different types of disciplinary hearings;
- ❖ the right of a prisoner to a full opportunity of hearing the allegations against him and to present his case (**r 54**) and **Art 6** of the **ECHR**.

Answer Structure

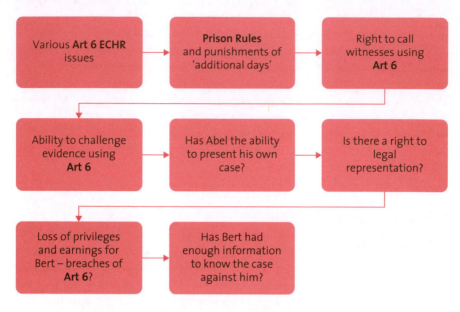

ANSWER

Both Abel and Bert will wish to show that these decisions were made in breach of the principles of natural justice. First, it must be determined whether the rules of natural justice apply to the process in question. It was determined in *Board of Visitors of Hull Prison ex p St Germain (No 1)* (1979) that hearings in front of a Board of Visitors were subject to the principles of natural justice. This was extended to governors' hearings by

Leech v Deputy Governor of Parkhurst Prison; Prevot v Deputy Governor of Long Lartin Prison (1988).

In Abel's case the impact of **Art 6** has been important.[9] **Article 6** imposes a right to a fair hearing and other ancillary rights in respect of the determination of a 'criminal charge'. Whether or not a criminal charge is being determined is a matter of **Convention** jurisprudence and is not conclusively decided by how an issue is described in domestic law. The nature of the charge and the severity of the punishment are important factors. If a hearing can result in additional time in prison, then it is likely to be a hearing determining a 'criminal charge' and the rights in **Art 6(1)–(3)** will apply. In *Ezeh v UK* (2002), the ECtHR held that a governor's hearing which could impose 'additional days' as a punishment was covered by **Art 6**. As a result, the **Prison Rules** have been changed. Where an allegation is made against a prisoner, the governor, on an initial consideration of the evidence, must decide whether, if the facts alleged are proved, 'additional days' would be an appropriate punishment (**r 53A**). If so, the governor must pass the case over to an independent adjudicator to be 'inquired into' and only an adjudicator has the authority to punish by the imposition of additional days. Adjudicators' hearings must comply with the requirements of **Art 6**.[10]

Given that the governor's initial assessment is that 20 additional days would be an appropriate punishment if the allegation against Abel is proved, he ought to have referred the matter to the adjudicator, under **r 53A**. The hearing should therefore be governed by **Art 6**, which will supplement and, where there is conflict, have priority over the rules of natural justice.

The first question in Abel's case is whether a disciplinary hearing requires the calling of all or any of the witnesses requested by the prisoner. **Article 6(3)(d)** gives him the right to call and challenge witnesses. This does not give an absolute right to call any witness he pleases (see, e.g. *Vidal v Belgium* (1992)). Regarding domestic law, it was held in *Board of Visitors of Hull Prison ex p St Germain (No 2)* (1979), that Boards of Visitors must be able to exercise a discretion to refuse a prisoner's request for witnesses if it would subvert the proceedings or was unnecessary. Such a principle is likely to be consistent with **Art 6**. However, mere administrative inconvenience would not support a decision to refuse such a request. Section 10 of the *Prison Discipline Manual* requires the calling of any witness whose evidence is deemed to be relevant. In Abel's case there is no suggestion that the two refused witnesses' evidence was not relevant. If the only reason for the refusal was the inconvenience involved in recalling the witnesses from other prisons this should have been disregarded.

----

9 This reference to, and subsequent application of, **Art 6** could only be made if you know the law in this area well.
10 This discussion about the Governor's duties shows a good understanding of the mechanics of the law.

Furthermore, given the fact that Abel was allegedly merely one of a group of prisoners on the roof, it would seem essential that he should be able to challenge evidence that he was present, that he threw the slate and that, in doing so, he was attempting to assault a prison officer. The failure to allow him to present his defence would violate **Art 6**. If Abel can demonstrate that calling more than one witness was necessary due to the nature of his defence, it would follow that he should have been allowed to call them.

The **Prison Rules** give Abel the right to present his own case but do not specify that he has a right to cross-examine witnesses. However, para 10.12 of the *Prison Discipline Manual* does state that the prisoner should be asked whether he wishes to question the reporting officer[11]. Although, under both the rules of natural justice and **Art 6(3)(d)**, the right to cross-examine is not absolute if the effect of cross-examination can be met in other ways (as in *R v Governor of HM Prison Swaleside ex p Wynter* (1998), for example). In the present case, a fair trial requires that Abel be able to challenge the main prosecution evidence and, it is submitted, the failure to allow cross-examination is a breach of both **Art 6** and natural justice.

In relation to the lack of legal representation, in *Secretary of State for the Home Department ex p Tarrant* (1985) the court permitted discretion as to the grant of representation. Factors which could properly be taken into account included: the seriousness of the charge and penalty; the likelihood that points of law might arise; the ability of the prisoner to conduct his own case; and the need for swift adjudication. This situation has now changed following *Ezeh v UK* (2002). The failure to permit representation in respect of a criminal charge violated **Art 6(3)(c)**, which gives a right to a defendant to 'defend himself in person or through legal assistance of his own choosing . . .'. **Prison Rule 54(3)** was amended accordingly. The refusal to allow Abel representation is, therefore, a breach of the **Prison Rules**.

The requirements of a fair hearing in Bert's case will differ from those in Abel's, because the consequences for Bert are less serious than for Abel: he is losing privileges and earnings, rather than having additional days in prison added on. In *Aston University ex p Rothy* (1969), it was held that natural justice would apply, although there was no kind of legal right in question; it was necessary to look at all the circumstances – the expectation of a fair hearing and the serious consequences which would follow from the decision. Possibly, the loss of privileges might not alone be sufficiently serious to warrant the application of the principles of natural justice, but might be so if coupled with the loss of earnings. On this argument, *Leech v Deputy Governor of Parkhurst Prison*; *Prevot v Deputy Governor of Long Lartin Prison* (1988) applies to Bert's hearing so that natural justice principles should apply. The fact that the charges against Bert and the punishments are

....

11   This reference to the *Prison Discipline Manual* shows a good appreciation of the relevant source that can be used in this area.

relatively less serious than for Abel (in particular, they do not involve the loss of liberty) also suggests that these hearings would be accepted as determining disciplinary rather than criminal matters and so it is unlikely that **Art 6** would apply. This view is supported by the High Court decision in *R (Napier) v Secretary of State for the Home Department* (2005) where it was found that *Ezeh v UK* drew a distinction between criminal matters and disciplinary matters and did not apply where there had been no additional days. Bert has four grounds of complaint: he was not allowed to call witnesses; have legal representation; see a full statement of the allegations against him; and it seemed that the allegations had been added to since he saw the statement of charges against him prior to the inquiry.

In relation to legal representation, following the *Tarrant* case the governor should consider: the seriousness of the charge and the potential penalty; whether any points of law are likely to arise; the capacity of Bert to present his own case; whether any procedural difficulties might arise; the need for reasonable speed; the need for fairness between prisoners and between prisoners and prison staff. None of these are obviously applicable to Bert's case but one argument for representation may be the complexity caused by the mismatch between the charge and the allegations made at the hearing.[12]

It can be argued that the governor should have exercised his discretion in favour of allowing Bert to call a witness (and allowing cross-examination of the prison officer whose evidence is presented). **Rule 54** of the **Prison Rules 1999** gives a prisoner a 'full opportunity of hearing what is alleged against him and of presenting his own case'. The administrative inconvenience involved would be minor since the witness is presumably present in the prison. As noted earlier, the *Prison Discipline Manual* suggests that requests to call witnesses and to cross-examine witnesses should be complied with. In *R (Szuluk) v Secretary of State for the Home Department* (2004) the court found a governor's hearing lacked fairness due to mistakes over a previous order he had made for disclosure and also the failure to make available a witness who might have assisted the prisoner show a lack of reasonable suspicion for ordering a urine sample.

In relation to Bert's inability to see a full statement of the allegations, **r 54** of the **Prison Rules** provides that a prisoner shall be informed of the charge as soon as possible and, in any case, before the time when it is inquired into by the governor. It was determined in *Tarrant* that a prisoner should be given sufficient time to understand what is alleged against him and prepare a defence. Clearly, if somebody is unaware of the extent of the charges against him, he will be unable to answer them; the inconvenience involved would have been very minor.

---

12   This passage summarises the law about representation well and then applies it to the facts at the end of the passage. This is an effective way to tackle this.

In general, what is required for a fair hearing will differ as between governors, who hear the more common, less serious offences; the independent adjudicators, who hear the more serious disciplinary offences; and the courts, who deal with serious criminal allegations against prisoners. Although adjudicators and the courts will be expected to adhere to the highest standards, a reasonable standard must be observed in governors' hearings, even though loss of liberty is not in question. It does not appear that such standards have been observed here. Therefore, Bert may be able to show that the *Audi* rule has been breached with regard to all his complaints, apart from the denial of legal representation.

Thus, since both Abel and Bert are able to show breaches of the principles of natural justice, the decisions will be void. (In *Anisminic v FCC* (1969), the House of Lords held that a decision which breached the principles of natural justice would be void, not voidable.) Under the **Civil Procedure Rules**, quashing orders will be issued to quash the decision in each instance. Abel has an additional claim of breach of **Art 6**. Although damages are available for breach of a **Convention** right under **s 8 HRA**, the court must make such assessment in light of the decisions of the European Court principles in respect of just satisfaction. In *R (Greenfield) v Secretary of State for the Home Department* (2005) the House of Lords emphasised that damages for breach of **Art 6** were exceptional and a finding of a breach would normally be sufficient just satisfaction. This is likely to undermine any claim Abel makes for compensation.

QUESTION 33

'Recent developments have made it apparent that prisoners must look to the **European Convention on Human Rights** in order to uphold their basic rights to privacy and to access to a court.'

▶ **Do you agree?**

How to Answer this Question

This is a reasonably straightforward essay question. It should be noted that it is confined to two particular areas of prisoners' rights. Clearly, it is necessary to consider the general influence of the **ECHR**, not merely the decided cases. It is also necessary to ask whether in certain instances the domestic courts have gone further in protecting prisoners' rights than the European Court of Human Rights (ECtHR). Finally, it might be asked whether domestic courts are now taking a more activist stance in these areas.

Essentially, the following areas should be considered:

- ❖ key provisions of the **Prison Rules** relating to correspondence;
- ❖ **Arts 8** and **6** of the **ECHR**;
- ❖ key decisions of the ECtHR on privacy and access to a court;
- ❖ use of judicial review in this area – general influence of the ECtHR.

Answer structure

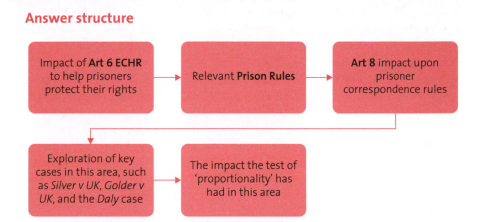

Impact of **Art 6 ECHR** to help prisoners protect their rights → Relevant **Prison Rules** → **Art 8** impact upon prisoner correspondence rules

Exploration of key cases in this area, such as *Silver v UK*, *Golder v UK*, and the *Daly* case → The impact the test of 'proportionality' has had in this area

Aim Higher ★

Highly perceptive answers will often include some attempt to think outside the box or beyond the predictable line of narrative that the examiner may have been expecting. This should be approached with caution – clearly you need to ensure that everything you put into your answer is relevant to the question – but if you are able to point to parallel developments, comparative material, historical lessons, proposals for reform etc. this can help make your answer stand out from the crowd. See for example the way that the *Daly* (2001) case is used in the answer below to make the interesting suggestion that the **Convention** is not the only way of enhancing prisoners' rights: 'Such rulings, it is suggested, represent an example of judicial activism in using the common law and demonstrate that reliance on the **ECHR**, via the **HRA**, is not always necessary.'

ANSWER

It is an inevitable concomitant of imprisonment that certain basic rights, such as freedom of movement, are removed from prisoners, while others are curtailed. Privacy is clearly curtailed, but this does not mean that a prisoner enjoys no privacy, while, on the other hand, the fundamental right of access to a court need not be abrogated at all. Articles 6 and 8 of the ECHR have been used successfully by prisoners to protect these fundamental liberties and recently the domestic courts have, it will be argued, adopted a more activist stance in these areas. Now that the HRA 1998 is in force, domestic opportunities for challenges of the Prison Rules 1999 have become far greater.[13]

13 This overview of the pertinent issues and law relating to prisoners demonstrates why it is essential to have a good introduction to your answers.

Cases brought under **Art 6** of the **ECHR** have led to greater protection for the right of free access to the court. Under **r 34** of the **Prison Rules**, which related to correspondence (now **r 39**), the Home Secretary's permission was required before a prisoner could contact a solicitor. This provision was challenged in *Golder v UK* (1975). Golder alleged that the Home Secretary's refusal to give permission in relation to a potential defamation action against a prison officer was in violation of **Art 8**, which expressly protects correspondence, and of **Art 6**, which governs the right to a fair hearing. Golder's claim that he had been denied the right to a hearing could be considered only if **Art 6** included a substantive right of access to a court, rather than merely providing guarantees of fairness once the hearing was in being. The ECtHR held that **Art 6(1)** could not be narrowed only to include procedural guarantees, because it would not be possible to benefit from such guarantees if access to a court itself could be denied. Thus, it was found that access to a court must be inherent in **Art 6(1)**.

The Court did not rule that prisoners have an absolute right of access to court. It ruled that, in this particular instance, given all the factors in the situation, including the fact that unpleasant consequences had already arisen from the alleged libel, Golder should have been able to go before a court. Thus, a breach of **Art 6** had occurred. In responding to this finding, the Government modified **r 34** of the **Prison Rules**, but in a fairly minimal fashion – only to the extent that prisoners could communicate with their solicitors freely, but complaints about the inner workings of the prison could not be communicated, unless the internal complaints machinery had first been exhausted. This was known as the prior ventilation rule and it was clearly still likely to inhibit access to a court. Not surprisingly, in *Silver v UK* (1983), the prior ventilation rule was found to be an unwarranted curb on correspondence. Prison orders regarding correspondence were again modified so that a solicitor could be contacted with matter relating to a complaint as soon as the complaint had been registered internally. This rule, known as the simultaneous ventilation rule, was itself challenged successfully in the domestic courts in *Secretary of State for Home Department ex p Anderson* (1984). It was found that if prisoners had to register a complaint internally before communicating with a solicitor, this would constitute an impediment to their right of access to the court; an inmate might hesitate to make an internal complaint, because he could lay himself open to a disciplinary charge. The court held that the restriction placed on him by the simultaneous ventilation rule was *ultra vires*, because it conflicted with this fundamental right – a right so fundamental that it could only be taken away by express language.[14]

Anderson is an interesting case, because it provides an instance of a domestic decision going beyond the rights provided by the **Convention**, and the same may be said of *Secretary of State for the Home Department ex p Leech (No 2)* (1993), in which the Court of

---

14   This good exploration of the *Anderson* case shows how to effectively and actively use case law.

Appeal found that it was a principle of great importance that every citizen had an unimpeded right of access to a court, and that this was buttressed by the principle of legal professional privilege. Legal privilege, recognised by common law, could openly be taken away by subordinate legislation only where that was expressly authorised by the enabling legislation (s 47 of the Prison Act 1952). Section 47 might authorise some screening of correspondence, but it must be strictly construed in accordance with the presumption against statutory interference with common law rights. The point was emphasised by the House of Lords in *R (Daly) v Secretary of State for the Home Department* (2001). The Home Secretary imposed a policy that, without exceptions, prisoners should be removed from their cells during searches, even when the searches might involve the scrutiny of legally privileged material. Because of its lack of exceptions, the policy was held to be void and incapable of authorisation under s 47 of the Prison Act 1952; the House of Lords emphasised both the common law protection of legal privilege and the impact of Art 8 of the ECHR. Such rulings, it is suggested, represent an example of judicial activism in using the common law and demonstrate that reliance on the ECHR, via the HRA, is not always necessary.

The area in which the ECtHR, as opposed to the domestic courts, has had a particular influence is that of privacy of correspondence under Art 8. In *Golder v UK*, it was found that prisoners' privacy of correspondence must be upheld; implied limitations on it due to detention were rejected. *Silver* was also concerned with privacy of correspondence generally; certain letters unconcerned with legal proceedings, including communications with journalists, had also been stopped. It was found that such interference with correspondence was in breach of Art 8, and certain changes were therefore made to standing orders in prisons. Prisoners were freer as to the contents of letters; previously, they could not make criticism of persons in public life or make complaints about the prison. They were also allowed greater freedom in their choice of correspondents; they were not confined to relatives or friends, but could correspond with others, including journalists.[15]

However, under the old rules, all letters at non-'open' establishments could be routinely read, except for correspondence relating to legal proceedings to which the inmate was a party. Such correspondence could not be read or stopped unless the governor had reason to suppose that it contained matter not relating to the proceedings. However, other correspondence with a solicitor, including that in respect of proceedings to which the inmate was not already a party, could be read and stopped if objectionable. The latter rule was challenged successfully in *Campbell v UK* (1992) under Art 8, the applicant alleging that correspondence with his solicitor and with the European Commission had been opened without justification. Thus the provisions of r 39 were extended to all such

---

15   This passage highlighting the contrasting issues in UK courts and in the ECtHR shows a good knowledge of the area to the examiner.

correspondence whether or not legal proceedings have been commenced. However, such correspondence may still be opened under **r 39(2)** and **(3)** if the governor has reasonable cause to believe its contents to be illicit, illegal or a threat to security, albeit this will be done in the presence of the prisoner. In *Cannan v Secretary of State for the Home Department* (2003), the Court found that a policy that required advance permission for the passing of any documentation between a legal adviser and a prisoner except in exceptional circumstances would breach **Art 6** of the **ECHR**. The policy did not strike the correct balance between the right of access to legal advice and the legitimate security concerns of the prison.

A major issue for prisoners is whether damages will be secured for improper opening of legal correspondence in breach of **r 39**. In *Watkins v Home Office* (2006) the House of Lords ruled that the tort of misfeasance in a public office was not actionable *per se* so that a prisoner whose legal correspondence had been unlawfully interfered with in bad faith would have no right of action unless he could also prove material damage. However, their Lordships suggested that for post-**HRA** breaches there may be a remedy for breach of **Convention** rights. However, in two first instance decisions, *Woodin v Home Office* (2006) and *Francis v Home Office* (2006), the High Court held that where there was a breach of the rules relating to the handling of legal correspondence with no evidence of additional harm or damage to the claimant, an apology was sufficient to remedy the **Art 8** situation so that the prisoner was not a victim for the purposes of the **ECHR**. If this view prevails, it seems that so long as the prison can show its general approach to correspondence is compatible with **Art 8** and offers an apology, there will be no remedy for individual interference with legal correspondence despite the important constitutional function of the rule. As further evidence of the influence of **Art 8** in *R (Szuluk) v Governor of Full Sutton* (2004), the Court of Appeal held that the refusal to waive, in relation to medical correspondence, the requirement for routine reading, could amount to a violation of **Art 8**, although on the facts of that case it was justified.

The impact of **Art 8** and also **Art 10** has, for example, led the courts to invalidate blanket bans or restrictions on prisoners' contacts with the media. In *R v Secretary of State for the Home Department ex p Simms and Another* (1999), a refusal by the Prison Service to allow prisoners unrestricted access to journalists in order to further claims of wrongful conviction was overturned, and in *R (Hirst) v Secretary of State for the Home Department* (2002), a refusal to allow even conditional access of a prisoner, who was an advocate of prisoners' interests, to live radio shows was also invalidated.[16]

Article 8 is beginning to have an impact in areas of privacy other than communications and correspondence although, from a prisoner point of view, this has not always been

---

16   This passage highlighting the impact **Arts 8** and **10** have had in this area shows the examiner you have a deep understanding of the area.

successful. **Article 8(2)** allows law-based restrictions on private and family life if they are a proportionate way of achieving one of the listed legitimate purposes. Restrictions that are consistent with the overall purposes of prison (incarceration, punishment and deterrence, for example) are, subject to proportionality in individual cases, likely to be upheld. For example, a refusal by the Prison Service to allow a prisoner to conceive a child with his wife by artificial insemination was upheld in *R (Mellor) v Secretary of State for the Home Department* (2001). However, more recently in *Dickson v UK* (2008) the Court of Human Rights ruled that the restrictive UK policy did not permit a balance to be struck between competing public and individual interests and thus violated **Art 8**. The policy of separating prisoner-mothers from their babies at 18 months has been found to be compatible with **Art 8(2)**, although proportionality requires the policy to be responsive to needs in particular cases – *R (P and Q) v Secretary of State for the Home Department* (2001) and *R (CD) v Secretary of State for the Home Department* (2003). Moreover, **Art 8** has imported procedural safeguards into the process of removal of children from mothers (*Claire F v Secretary of State for the Home Department* (2004)).

In conclusion, although the ECtHR has provided the impetus needed to ensure that rights to privacy and access to the court are upheld, improvement has also come about through the application of common law principles including natural justice in judicial review proceedings. It is clear that UK judges have set out to ensure that UK law is at least in conformity with and perhaps better than, the **ECHR**. With the **HRA**, giving effect to the **ECHR** is more straightforward than previously and it is to be hoped that courts will use their post-enactment powers to improve prisoners' human rights to embody and, where necessary, enhance the spirit of the **ECHR**.

QUESTION 34

Frank and Dieter are prisoners at HMP Ackland. Frank is serving a life sentence for murder and Dieter is serving a six-year sentence for drug importation.

Frank is 35 and has discovered that he has testicular cancer. The doctor tells him that he requires radiotherapy to treat the cancer but that the treatment will result in Frank being unable to have any children in the future. Frank makes a request that the prison permit him to have overnight visits from his wife or alternatively permit him to access artificial insemination treatment with a view to his wife becoming pregnant before his cancer treatment. The prison governor refuses Frank's request as it is contrary to prison policy. Frank's wife decides to stand as a candidate in upcoming local council elections to protest at the failure of the prison system to help families. Frank wishes to support his wife but is told that he is ineligible to vote. Frank is also concerned that the prison governor will not permit him to receive visits from his eight-year-old nephew. The reason for this is that Frank has an assault conviction from two years ago for punching a child who had been throwing stones at his window.

Dieter is 25 and has struggled for a long time with his sexual identity. He has now decided that he wishes to live as a woman with a view in due course to seeking gender reassignment treatment. He wishes to wear women's clothes in the prison. Initially Dieter's request is refused for common areas but he is permitted to wear women's clothes in his own cell. However, following a complaint from Dieter's cell-mate, the governor also prohibits Dieter from dressing as a woman in his cell.

Dieter is angry about his treatment and wishes to appear in a television documentary about the lack of sexual rights in prisons. However, the prison governor will not give permission for the television production company to visit Dieter to film an interview. Dieter writes to a solicitor about this refusal with a view to challenging it. He is concerned that a letter from his solicitor about the matter is opened by the prison without Dieter being present. When he complains about this he is told it was an administrative error.

▶ **Advise Frank and Dieter as to whether their rights have been violated by the prison authorities.**

How to Answer this Question

This problem question is relatively straightforward but quite wide ranging. It requires detailed knowledge of some of the **Prison Rules** and case law challenging prison decisions under the **Human Rights Act 1998**. It is important to identify each area of advice required and to be specific when dealing with the legal and factual circumstances.

Essentially the following matters should be addressed:

- ❖ ban on conjugal visits;
- ❖ policy on access to artificial insemination as health care;
- ❖ electoral rights of prisoners;
- ❖ restrictions on family visits;
- ❖ regulation of dress;
- ❖ access to journalists;
- ❖ legally privileged correspondence.

Answer Structure

| Has Frank's **Art 12 ECHR** right been breached or does he not enjoy such rights as a prisoner? | → | Exploration of cases in this area, such as *ELJ and PBH, Mellor, Dickson* | → | Have Frank's **Art 8** rights been breached and does he enjoy such rights as a prisoner? |

| Do prisoners have the right to vote? **Representation of the People Act 1983** and the *Hirst* decision | → | Does Frank have a right to visits from his nephew? Any **Art 8** arguments here? | → | Does Dieter have the ability to rely upon **Art 8** rights as a prisoner to respect for his private life? |

| Does the decision by the Governor to refuse the television interview with Dieter breach his **Art 10** rights? | → | Does Dieter have any rights in relation to his correspondence? |

Aim Higher ★

You should be ready to think across topic areas when answering examination questions. It is often the case that a question will straddle two different areas, e.g. freedom of expression and privacy, or will require some knowledge of another topic in order to be answered fully. One area of knowledge that is likely to be applicable to many if not all questions on the examination paper is the operation of the **Human Rights Act**. Note that although the answer below relates to prisoners' rights it contains references to **ss 2, 3** and **4** of the **HRA** and references to numerous Convention rights. It is very difficult to compartmentalise your knowledge in civil liberties exams and good answers are likely to draw from a wide range of sources.

ANSWER

Frank and Dieter have sought to assert a number of rights that would normally be available to citizens who are at liberty. The advice to be given to them must address the extent to which the fact of detention or their status as prisoners permits a restriction on rights that they would otherwise be at liberty to exercise. As a matter of domestic law the House of Lords in *Raymond v Honey* (1983) confirmed that prisoners retain all civil rights that are not restricted expressly or by the fact of their imprisonment. Of more significance here is the fact that the prison governor is a public authority under the

Human Rights Act 1998 and as such must act compatibly with Frank and Dieter's **Convention** rights.

On the face of it the refusal of the prison governor to permit Frank to have conjugal visits is an interference with his right to found a family under **Art 12** of the **ECHR**. Nevertheless, the absence of conjugal visits may be said to be an inevitable consequence of Frank's imprisonment and as such does not give rise to interference.

Alternatively it may be a justifiable interference as it may be essential to the maintenance of prison security that such visits do not take place. The European Commission of Human Rights in *ELJ and PBH v United Kingdom* (1998) ruled an application challenging the blanket ban on conjugal visits as inadmissible, due to such a ban being within the State's margin of appreciation.[17]

The refusal of artificial insemination treatment is potentially more problematic. Frank's cancer will mean that it is impossible for him to have children following his medical treatment and his life sentence means that he will not be released before his treatment. Unlike conjugal visits there is no security reason why such treatment should not be available. Indeed the Prison Service does have a policy of permitting artificial insemination in exceptional circumstances if the application is approved by the Family Ties Unit of the Prisoner Administration Group. We would need to establish whether Frank's application had been properly considered under the policy.

If Frank were to challenge the refusal he would face some unhelpful decisions such as *R (on the Application of Mellor) v Secretary of State for the Home Department* (2001), where the Court of Appeal upheld the exceptional circumstances policy as lawful. The Court thought that one of the purposes of imprisonment was to punish the criminal by depriving him of certain rights which could be enjoyed while at liberty, including the enjoyment of family life, the exercise of conjugal rights and the right to found a family. Although the decision has been criticised, it has been followed in a number of cases, including *Dickson v Premier Prison Service Ltd* (2004), where the Court of Appeal upheld a decision to deny artificial insemination to a couple where the wife would be 51 by the time her husband was released. It was permissible for the authorities to take into account the implications of effectively creating a single-parent family, and public concern over the punitive and deterrent effect of custodial sentences. However, the Grand Chamber of the **ECHR** in *Dickson v UK* (2008) ruled that the policy did not permit a balance to be struck between competing public and individual interests and this violated **Art 8**. Frank is able to

---

17   This use of the conjugal visits case shows how it is important to back up your arguments with authority, as it adds weight to your arguments.

rely on this case by virtue of **s 2** of the **HRA** and it is likely that domestic courts will follow the approach set out by the Strasbourg Court.[18]

Frank's inability to vote in the election is a consequence of **s 3(1)** of the **Representation of the People Act 1983**. This applies to prohibit all convicted prisoners from voting in elections. This ban was challenged in *Hirst v United Kingdom* (2005). The Grand Chamber of the European Court of Human Rights ruled by a majority that the right to vote in **Art 3** of the first Protocol was not a privilege and there must be a presumption of universal suffrage. Although the right was not absolute, disenfranchisement of prisoners was a severe measure and the principle of proportionality required a discernible and sufficient link between the sanction and the conduct and circumstances of the prisoner. The indiscriminate blanket restriction on all convicted prisoners fell outside any acceptable margin of appreciation.

It follows that the ban in the **1983 Act** is incompatible with Frank's **Convention** rights. It is unlikely that a court will read the provision down under **s 3** of the **Human Rights Act** to be compatible (see *R (Chester) v Secretary of State for Justice* (2010)) so the only remedy he could seek under domestic law is a declaration of incompatibility under **s 4**. Given that a declaration has already been granted in *Smith v Scott* (2007) it is unlikely that a further declaration will be granted.[19]

The refusal to let Frank have visits from his nephew is likely to be a consequence of the 'Safeguarding Children' policy in the *Prison Service Public Protection Manual*. A prisoner who has been convicted of an offence against a child will normally have access limited to their immediate family. Access to any other child will not be permitted unless the governor agrees that such contact would be in the interests of the child and after a full risk assessment has been carried out. In all cases the welfare of the child is paramount. The refusal may amount to an interference with Frank's family life under **Art 8** of the **ECHR**. If so, it will need to be justified by the prison service as a proportionate response to a legitimate aim in **Art 8(2)**. It is essential to check that the Prison Service has addressed Frank's case on an individual basis. In *R (Banks) v The Governor of HMP Wakefield and the Home Secretary* (2001), the Court held that a prisoner's family rights were on the facts not engaged in respect of his six-year-old nephew but even if they were, the decision not to permit access was a proportionate response to the need to protect the rights of children.

Dieter's desire to wear make-up and dress in women's clothes could be seen as an exercise of his **Art 8** right to respect for his private life. This aspect of the article has been

----

18 You will impress the examiner by highlighting criticisms of cases and the difficulties they throw up, such as with the *Mellor* case here.

19 This passage shows some excellent application of **s 3 HRA** to the **1983 Act**, which can only be undertaken with a confident knowledge of the area.

interpreted broadly by the European Court in cases such as *Pretty v United Kingdom* (2002) as implying autonomy and respect for personal identity. In *R v Ashworth Hospital ex p E* (2001) the High Court refused an application for judicial review of a special hospital's refusal to permit a patient to dress and assume the appearance of a woman anywhere but in his own room. It held that the refusal was authorised under the **Mental Health Act 1983** and the admitted interference with his private life was permitted for the purposes of control and security and thus legitimate reasons within **Art 8(2)**. The court highlighted the risk of patients or others absconding by masquerading as women if cross-dressing was allowed. This reasoning would be equally applicable in the context of a prison. Assuming Dieter has credible evidence of gender disphoria, a potential problem could be the refusal of permission to wear such clothing in his own cell. It may not be sufficient simply to refer to the complaints of the cell-mate. Arguably proportionality may require that the prison find a solution such as placing Dieter in a cell on his own or placing him with someone who has no objection to him wearing women's clothes. Such an approach may be a less intrusive way of dealing with prison security concerns while permitting Dieter some autonomy over his private life and continue his treatment towards gender reassignment.

The refusal of the prison governor to permit the television production company to visit Dieter to film an interview could be said to interfere with Dieter's freedom of expression. **Article 10** of the **Convention** extends to the right to receive and impart information and ideas. Clearly the interview falls within this as it is intended to enable Dieter to impart his concerns over sexual rights in the prison system. The question of the extent to which prisoners' rights to free expression have been restricted by the **Prison Rules** or the fact of detention has been analysed on a number of occasions.

In *R v Home Secretary ex p Simms and O'Brien* (1999), the House of Lords held in a pre-**HRA** case that there was a common law right to communicate with journalists with a view to the investigation of a possible miscarriage of justice. The State required lawful authority on the basis of pressing social need to interfere with this right and an almost blanket ban on interviews could not be justified.

In *R (Hirst) v Home Secretary* (2002), the Court recognised that although the right to free expression in **Art 10** was qualified, it was not necessarily removed altogether by the fact of imprisonment. The court thought it was permissible to place restrictions on contact with the media but the decision to impose restrictions must be justified by reference to the legitimate aims in **Art 10(2)**.

In *Nilsen v Governor of HMP Full Sutton* (2004), the Court of Appeal held that the refusal of a prison governor to permit the claimant to receive a copy of his autobiography for editing purposes was within the powers vested in him under the **Prison Act 1952** and did not unjustifiably interfere with his rights under **Art 10**. Arguably the case could be distinguished in that the court was of the view that the claimant did not seek to make any serious comment about the safety of his convictions or the penal system. Dieter's concerns may well be seen as a serious contribution to the debate about prisoners' rights.[20]

The letter from Dieter's solicitor is probably legally privileged, in that it is a communication relating to legal advice or to potential court proceedings. Dieter has a right to receive such communications under **Art 8** (the right to respect of correspondence) and under **Art 6** (the right to a fair trial, which includes access to a lawyer). The extent to which a prison is entitled to interfere with legally privileged correspondence has been considered on numerous occasions and it is now clearly established in cases like *Campbell v United Kingdom* (1992) that routine reading of legal correspondence breached **Art 8**. This led to a revised **Prison Rule 39** which permits prisoners to send and receive legal correspondence without interference except where there is reasonable cause to believe that the correspondence or enclosures are criminal or may endanger prison security. In such cases the prisoner should be permitted to be present. The 'administrative error' in relation to Dieter's letter means that **r 39** has not been complied with. On the face of it, this amounts to an unlawful interference with **Art 8** and Dieter would have a remedy under the **Human Rights Act** against the prison. However, in two cases, *Woodin v Home Office* and *Francis v Home Office* (2006), the High Court held that where there was a simple breach of the rules relating to the handling of legal correspondence, and where there was no evidence of additional harm or damage to the claimant, an apology was sufficient to remedy the situation so that the prisoner was not a victim for the purposes of the **ECHR**. The House of Lords has also held that, absent evidence of material damage, an action for misfeasance in public office will not lie against a prison officer for unlawful interference with correspondence. These decisions mean that Dieter may not have any remedy other than an apology from the prison concerned.

QUESTION 35
‐‐‐

'The Equality and Human Rights Commission provides long overdue coherence and expanded reach for strategic action, monitoring and enforcement of the growing body of anti-discrimination and human rights legislation.'

▶ **Discuss.**

How to Answer this Question

This essay question covers the general topic of discrimination, rather than focussing upon one particular vulnerable group, such as prisoners. It requires you to focus on the development of the various commissions that provide expertise and co-ordinated action in the anti-discrimination field. You need to comment on whether the unified

---

20 This use of the *Nilsen* case shows how you can use and apply cases to the given facts of a problem to serve your own ends.

Commission provides a solution to problems associated with having separate commissions.

Essentially the following areas should be covered:

- ❖ What is the Equality and Human Rights Commission?
- ❖ The history and development of the Equality and Human Rights Commission;
- ❖ the separate commissions: Commission for Racial Equality, Equal Opportunities Commission, Disability Rights Commission;
- ❖ is there a need for more coherence?
- ❖ Is there a need for expanded reach? Developments in human rights law, sexual orientation discrimination, religious discrimination, age discrimination?
- ❖ Possible future developments.

Answer Structure

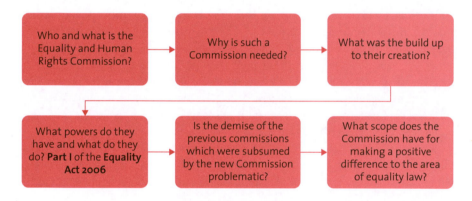

Who and what is the Equality and Human Rights Commission? → Why is such a Commission needed? → What was the build up to their creation?

What powers do they have and what do they do? **Part I of the Equality Act 2006** → Is the demise of the previous commissions which were subsumed by the new Commission problematic? → What scope does the Commission have for making a positive difference to the area of equality law?

Common Pitfalls ✖

Look before you leap: it would be easy in a question like this to jump straight into describing and explaining the powers and functions of the Equalities and Human Rights Commission. If you read the question carefully, however, you will see that its reference to 'long overdue coherence' requires some analysis of the policy behind the new Commission and the perceived deficiencies of the previous commissions. If you fail to spot this you are likely to lose valuable credit.

ANSWER

The Equality and Human Rights Commission (the Commission) was created by the **Equality Act 2006**. The Commission subsumes the functions of the various commissions that have been linked to specific anti-discrimination legislation. In October 2007 the

Commission for Racial Equality, the Equal Opportunities Commission and the Disability Rights Commission were absorbed into the new Commission. The new Commission also assumes responsibility for sexual orientation, religious and age discrimination in addition to general human rights matters.

The Commission was proposed in the 2004 White Paper, *Fairness for all: a New Commission for Equality and Human Rights*.[21] It had earlier been suggested in the Government's 2002 consultation paper on implementing the EU Race and Framework Directives. In the White Paper the Commission was described as a 'strong and authoritative champion for equality and human rights' indicating a desire on the Government's part to enhance the effectiveness of the commission mechanism and to expand its remit. There had been a proliferation of equality laws which provided an impetus for consolidating and expanding the role of the various commissions. Examples from the European Union include the following: the **EU Race Directive 2000** which requires the prohibition of direct and indirect discrimination based on racial or ethnic origin in the fields of employment, social protection, and access to goods and services including housing; and the **EU Framework Directive 2000** which requires the prohibition of discrimination in the field of employment on the basis of religion or belief, disability, age and sexual orientation; and the **Gender Goods and Services Directive** which expands the prohibition on gender discrimination in relation to public and private goods and services.

Domestic equality legislation passed over the previous few years included the **Race Relations (Amendment) Act 2000** (now repealed), which implemented the Stephen Lawrence inquiry recommendation of outlawing discrimination by public authorities in carrying out their functions and imposing a duty on certain such authorities to have regard to the need to eliminate unlawful discrimination and promote good race relations; the **Gender Recognition Act 2004**, which enabled changed gender to be recognised in law; the **Civil Partnerships Act 2004** which permitted gay couples to enter into partnerships with similar rights and obligations as marriage; the **Employment Equality (Age) Regulations 2006** (now revoked) which introduced some protection against age discrimination in relation to employment, albeit with extensive exemptions; and the **Equality Act 2006** itself which contained a raft of provisions intended to implement aspects of the EU Directives. At a late stage, **s 81** was added (now repealed) which permitted wide-ranging secondary legislation to protect against discrimination on the grounds of sexual orientation outside the existing workplace protection. The resulting **Equality Act (Sexual Orientation) Regulations 2007** (now repealed) were far reaching and controversial. The **Equality Act 2006** also contained provisions outlawing discrimination on the basis of religion or belief.[22]

....

21   This reference to the White Paper shows the examiner you have breadth of knowledge in the area.

22   This passage covering the legal developments in equality law is a good demonstration of how to cover lots of law in a short space of time effectively.

This growth of anti-discrimination measures emanating from domestic and European policy development was matched by dramatic development of generic human rights protection. The implementation of the **Human Rights Act 1998** in October 2000 effectively incorporated the **European Convention** rights into United Kingdom law and created a sophisticated domestic enforcement mechanism including enhanced powers for the courts and a Parliamentary Joint Committee. However, despite extensive calls for its creation, the Government declined to create a Human Rights Commission. This was seen as the missing piece of the human rights jigsaw and there were repeated calls from the Joint Committee and others for the creation of a commission to help foster a culture of respect for human rights.

Thus it can be seen that the pressure had been building for some time to establish a commission capable of giving some coherence to the equality and human rights legal and policy frameworks. The Commission created by the **Equality Act** is perhaps an inevitable culmination of the development of a more extensive equality agenda in domestic law.

An obvious consequence of the creation of the unified Commission is the demise of the existing commissions: the Commission for Racial Equality, the Equal Opportunities Commission and the Disability Rights Commission. For many years the existence of separate commissions was inevitable, as equality law developed slowly and with differing emphasis and priority. For 20 years, equality legislation effectively only applied to race and sex, and there were vastly different problems and priorities for these groups. In the 1990s the Government rather grudgingly adopted limited disability discrimination laws, but created a weak National Disability Council. Only in 1999 did the Disability Rights Commission come into being, which more closely matched the powers of the other commissions. The earlier commissions most certainly did lack coherence but for much of their life there was little call for coherence and they worked more effectively as discrete organisations focused on the needs of their stakeholder groups.[23]

Since the turn of the century there has developed a more holistic view of discrimination and a more inclusive notion of equality. A single, strong and authoritative body is likely to enhance understanding of equality and foster a culture of respect for human rights in a way that separate commissions could not achieve. It is also able to cement the obvious and essential link between equality law and human rights law. Thus it is now correct to say that coherence in equality law and policy is essential but it is wrong to say that the Commission is 'long overdue'. Rather, this is an idea whose time has come.

The statement refers to strategic action, monitoring and enforcement of equality and human rights laws. The Commission has powers in relation to all of these areas. Thus, for

23 This passage demonstrates clear and confident analysis of the Commissions, which will impress the examiner.

example, it has overarching duties to seek to achieve respect for the dignity of individuals (**Equality Act s 3**), promote understanding of the importance of equality and diversity, promote equality of opportunity (**s 8**), and promote awareness and understanding of the importance and protection of human rights (**s 9**). These are broad, some may say vague, aspirations. But they establish the breadth of purpose of the Commission and set out the parameters for its strategic objectives.

A novel approach is to require the Commission to promote understanding between different groups and to challenge prejudice, hatred and hostility towards groups. Here the **Equality Act** makes no distinction between the diverse areas it seeks to protect. Groups are defined to include any class of persons who share common attributes in relation to age, disability, gender (and reassignment of gender), race, religion, belief and sexual orientation. Here we can see the vastly extended reach of the new Commission as compared with the earlier strategic bodies. The inclusion of age, disability, religion and sexual orientation in the ambit of equality law has begun the process of creating a comprehensive equality framework. This enables the Commission to work towards understanding not only of isolated groups but towards an appreciation of the value of diversity and the principle of equality across society. This is underlined by a broader power to issue Codes of Practice to encourage compliance with the equality legislation.

It was not sustainable to continue with only three commissions while at the same time legally protecting many more groups. This would have led to ineffective implementation of the laws and justified allegations of tokenistic implementation of the EU Directives. Neither was it realistic to create four or more new commissions with responsibility for the new protected groups and human rights. Such an approach would have been chaotic and ineffective.

Nevertheless, there was a risk that the Commission, by absorbing the existing bodies and expanding to cover the new protected groups, would lose focus so that some issues or groups would be neglected. In the early policy statements the Government appeared to favour a broad-brush, light-touch commission which focused on promotional activity rather than law enforcement. This led to fierce criticism of the White Paper by the existing commissions. The Government appeared to listen, because the Equality Bill was strengthened and ultimately all of the existing commissions signed up to the new Commission.

The Commission has a broad range of powers. To a large extent these reflect the powers of the earlier commissions but in some areas the new Commission's powers are more extensive and, of course, apply to a much broader range of legislation. In additional to formal investigation powers it has a new power under **s 16** of the **Equality Act** to hold general inquiries, for example into the causes of unequal outcomes. Again, due to its broader remit, these inquiries can cut across different equality areas and human rights issues in a way not previously possible. The reports ought to provide a valuable contribution to national discourse about equality and human rights. The Commission can make assessments of public authority compliance with statutory duties; make recommendations to persons or bodies arising from any inquiry, investigation or assessment; and require evidence or documentation from any person as part of its inquisitive functions. It can enter into conciliation and binding agreements and can issue unlawful act notices requiring persons or bodies to desist from discriminatory practices. An important function will be monitoring the growing duties on public authorities to achieve equality objectives and tackle institutional discrimination in the exercise of powers or functions. This is more pervasive than enforcing individual legal rights but rather seeks to create a culture of respect for diversity and equality within the public services.

The Commission also has the power to issue legal proceedings in its own name or provide assistance to others (assistance may only be in relation to those who claim discrimination etc under the equality legislation). In this respect its powers are similar to the earlier commissions. However, again the expanded reach of the new Commission is important in that the litigation powers of the Commission extend to the whole gamut of equality legislation. Furthermore, and of real significance, the Commission can issue or intervene in proceedings relating to **Convention** rights even outside the field of discrimination (**Equality Act s 30**). It may thus challenge unlawful acts by public authorities under **s 6** of the **Human Rights Act** in judicial review or other proceedings. It does not need to be a victim but there must be one or more victims of such an act. This has the potential to be a valuable source of test cases and could make the **Human Rights Act** much more effective than relying wholly on victim-inspired litigation.

Overall, the new Commission certainly provides much needed coherence and expanded reach over the earlier commissions. This is not long overdue but it is now required in order to cement the foundations of a legal and social structure that values diversity and demands equality. The Government also established a Discrimination Law Review and an Equalities Review to consider the causes of persistent discrimination and inequality in Britain. This work, together with the efforts of the new Commission, culminated in the passage of the **Equalities Act 2010** which consolidated existing equality law and provides a coherent and comprehensive legal and enforcement framework.[24]

---

24 This is a confident and assured conclusion about the Commission.

Freedom of Movement

INTRODUCTION

Freedom of movement is often viewed on civil liberty syllabuses as an issue relating primarily to immigration and asylum (i.e. freedom of movement between nations). However, internal freedom of movement was formerly a significant aspect of this area until the power to make Exclusion Orders banning UK citizens from Northern Ireland or Great Britain lapsed in 1998 and was abolished by the **Terrorism Act 2000**. The advent of Control Orders under the **Prevention of Terrorism Act 2005** once again raised the profile of internal restrictions on freedom of movement. These have now been abolished and replaced with TPIM Notices under the **Terrorism Prevention and Investigation Measures Act 2011** (which have been described by many as a slightly watered down version of Control Orders).

There are persistent problems in using the **ECHR** to analyse freedom of movement issues. First, there is no right to immigration in the **ECHR** and immigration rights have always been viewed as an administrative rather than civil in nature. Secondly, the **ECHR** itself confers no right of freedom of movement within borders. **Protocol 4**, which does contain basic free movement guarantees and **Protocol 7** regarding the right of aliens not to be expelled, have not been ratified by the UK Government and thus do not form part of its international obligations or the **Convention** rights in **Sched 1** to the **Human Rights Act**. Nevertheless, the **Geneva Convention** is of clear significance and the courts have been willing to interpret existing **ECHR** rights as impacting to some extent on immigration decisions.

Examiners usually set essay questions in this area, although a problem question on the effect of the European Court of Human Rights (ECtHR) on asylum and immigration law is becoming more common. The emphasis is usually on the degree to which a balance is struck between the interest of the State in national security and the individual's basic freedom to enter, move about within and leave the UK. Students should be aware that this is an area in which there have been repeated and relatively major changes recently; in addition to the anti-terrorism provisions noted above there have been wide-reaching changes to the asylum process, including to rights of appeal, in the **Nationality, Immigration and Asylum Act (NIAA) 2002**, the **Asylum and Immigration (Treatment of Claimants (etc.) Act 2004**, the **Immigration, Asylum and Nationality Act (IANA) 2006** and the **UK Borders Act 2007**.

Checklist ✔

Students should be familiar with the following areas:

- relevant provisions of the **ECHR**;
- deportation and administrative removal provisions under the **Immigration Act 1971**, as amended, and the **Immigration and Asylum Act (IAA) 1999**;
- the **Geneva Convention of 1951** as amended by the **1967 Protocol**;
- key provisions and effects of the **IAA 1999**, the **NIAA 2002** and the **IANA 2006** relating to asylum seekers;
- the appeals procedure under **Pt IV** of the **NIAA 2002**.

QUESTION 36

'The law governing deportation is in need of further reform in order to create a fairer balance between individual civil liberties and the right of a sovereign State to determine who should come within its boundaries.'

▶ **To what extent do you agree with this statement?**

How to Answer this Question

In answering this question, it will be necessary not only to identify substantive and procedural aspects of the deportation procedure which may have an adverse impact on civil liberties, but also to suggest what might be meant by a 'fairer' balance.

Essentially, the following matters should be discussed:

- ❖ deportation and administrative removal provisions under the **immigration Act 1971**, as amended, and the **Nationality, Immigration and Asylum Act (NIAA) 2002**;
- ❖ the relevant provisions under the **Immigration Rules 2003**;
- ❖ procedure followed in making the decision to deport/remove;
- ❖ the impact on terrorism;
- ❖ infringement of civil liberties;
- ❖ the relevance of the European Court of Human Rights (ECtHR).

Answer Structure

When can someone be deported from the UK?

↓

Examination of **s 3 Immigration Act 1971**

↓

Consideration of the relevant parts of the **Immigration Rules**

↓

Deportation for committing a criminal offence – when can it happen?

↓

When will deportation be 'conducive to the public good'?

↓

How does deportation relate to extradition?

↓

Are there any appeals mechanisms in place against deportation orders?

Aim Higher ★

Even within the limitations imposed by the pressurised circumstances and time constraints of an examination you should try to display your ability to conduct effective analysis of case authority. Often you will use cases simply to provide support for propositions of law but you should also try to show that you have read and understood significant cases by exploring them in more detail, ideally in a way that advances the themes of your essay. This will impress the examiner that you have fully understood your sources. See the concise but effective analysis of the *Samaroo* (2001) case in the answer below.

ANSWER

Deportation and its close relative 'administrative removal' represent the clearest infringement of freedom of movement and therefore should be used only where there is clear justification and where there are mechanisms allowing careful scrutiny of the decision to deport. Broadly speaking, a person who is not a UK citizen with rights of residence is liable to deportation only if the Secretary of State deems that person's removal to be conducive to the common good, or where a court has recommended it after a conviction for a criminal offence, or for national security reasons, or where the person is a relative of someone deported on one of those grounds. European Economic Area nationals may only be deported on grounds that their presence is a threat to public policy, public safety or public health. However, the **Immigration and Asylum Act (IAA) 1999** also allows 'administrative removal' of a person who did originally have leave to enter or remain, but has failed to observe the conditions attached to his leave, overstayed or obtained leave by deception.[1]

Section 3(5) of the **1971 Act** states that deportation may be ordered if the Secretary of State deems the deportation to be conducive to the public good or if s/he belongs to the family of another person who has been ordered to be deported. The deportation of family members of a deportee has caused concern, since the practice seems indirectly discriminatory: a wife will often find it harder to meet the criteria for not being deported than a husband. The wife will not, however, automatically be deported; various circumstances should be taken into account, including representations she makes and her ability to maintain herself. Any bland assumption that all husbands, whatever their actual circumstances, can be treated differently from all wives is unjustifiable, particularly after ECtHR cases such as *Abdulaziz* (1985).

In considering the decision to deport or administratively remove, **r 364** of the **Immigration Rules** suggests that although each case is considered individually the presumption is that it is in the public interest to deport those liable to deportation. The stated aim of the rules is to achieve consistency and fairness, although one case will rarely be identical with another.

Deportation following conviction of a criminal offence can occur in three ways. First, it is mandatory (subject to certain exceptions) for the Secretary of State to make a deportation order when a person is sentenced to 12 months' imprisonment or of certain specified offences irrespective of term of imprisonment (**UK Borders Act 2007 s 32**). The range of offences is extraordinarily wide and includes relatively minor offences such as theft and criminal damage. Secondly, it can follow a recommendation by a criminal court when sentencing an offender. Finally, it can be ordered under the general 'public good' power irrespective of whether a recommendation has been made. Criminal courts have the power to recommend deportation following conviction for any offence which is punishable with imprisonment. The Home Secretary is not bound to follow such recommendations and can

---

1   This concise overview of the relevant law relating to deportation shows the examiner that you have mastery over the area and provides a useful introduction.

order deportation without such a recommendation. The Court of Appeal held in *Nazari* (1980) (building on *Caird* (1970)), no court should 'make an order recommending deportation without full inquiry into all the circumstances. It should not be done . . . as if by an afterthought at the end of observations about any sentence of imprisonment.' Factors to be considered were: the accused's criminal record; the seriousness and circumstances of the offence; the effect of an order in terms of hardship and breaking up of families.[2]

In *Serry* (1980), a single offence of shoplifting was found insufficiently serious, presumably because there were no particular aggravating circumstances (although see now the automatic provisions, above). An important circumstance will be the likelihood of the repetition of the offence; where this factor is present, it may aggravate an otherwise trivial offence; where it is absent, it may have a mitigating effect on a serious offence. Under the **HRA**, the proportionality test must be applied and this requires greater regard to all the individual circumstances of the case. In *Aramide v Secretary of State for the Home Department* (2000), the Court of Appeal held that the seriousness of the criminal offence (to be judged by the sentence actually given, not in a general manner) must be carefully balanced against the applicant's family ties.

In 'conducive to the public good' deportations the majority of orders are made in respect of criminal offences where the court has not made a recommendation. As indicated above, there is no requirement for a recommendation to be made before the Home Secretary can make a deportation order. The Home Office takes into account issues such as the seriousness of the trigger offence, the person's criminal record, the risk of reoffending and deterrence.

Other 'public good' grounds for deportation include deception to secure advantage in immigration matters such as leave to remain (now replaced by administrative removal) and, for political reasons (interests of national security or relations with other countries). The use of this power to exclude people on political rather than criminal grounds has attracted extensive criticism. The journalists Agee and Hosenball were deported on national security grounds, Agee presumably due to the damage he might have done to the CIA in writing books exposing certain of their activities (*Secretary of State for the Home Department ex p Hosenball* (1977)). Rather flimsy grounds were also, it seems, relied upon in making the decision to deport a number of Iraqi or Kuwaiti residents during the Gulf War in 1991 (see *Chahal v UK* (1997)), a policy apparently not followed during the Iraq War of 2003.[3]

An aspect of the controversial nature of this power is that it seems that it can be used as an alternative to extradition, where, for example, there is no power to extradite or to avoid the protections, such as they are, in the extradition process. In *Brixton Prison*

----

2   This passage about the law relating to deportation following a criminal offence shows how to effectively set the law out and how to incorporate authority to help do so.

3   This passage contains very good analysis and critique of some deportation issues and uses examples well to assist the process.

Governor ex p Soblen (1963), a deportation order was challenged on the grounds that the Secretary of State had acted for an improper purpose – allegedly in order to comply with a request from the United States for Soblen's return (there was no extradition arrangement for the offence of conspiracy to commit espionage). The Court of Appeal upheld the deportation order on the basis that the Secretary of State could act for a plurality of purposes. It did not matter if the Government's main motive for acting might have been to comply with the request from the US. The danger in this approach is clearly that the individual circumstances of the person in question may become much less significant than the political expediency of falling in with the wishes of particular governments.

However, there have been indications that such an approach is no longer justifiable, especially since **ECHR** rights (particularly **Arts 8, 3** and **5**) must always be considered in relation to any proposed deportation. Any deportation decision must now meet the **Convention** test of proportionality.[4] There is some uncertainty regarding the extent to which the court must make its own judgment on what proportionality demands in any particular case. In *B v Secretary of State for the Home Department* (2000), the Court of Appeal decided that the applicant had a right both to freedom of movement (he was an EU national) and to family life under the **ECHR**, and that, in the particular circumstances, these rights outweighed any pressing need for deportation. In *R (Samaroo) v Secretary of State for the Home Department* (2001), on the other hand, the Court rejected **Convention** right arguments regarding deportation for drug trafficking offences. Despite undisputed evidence that the appellant was unlikely to reoffend and had a settled family life, the Court upheld a deportation order due to the seriousness of the drug offending and the ability of the Home Secretary to have a policy of using deportation to deter other potential offenders. Whilst reserving ultimate authority to itself, the Court seemed most concerned to ensure that the Home Secretary had made a reasonable decision on proportionality; one that was fully aware and compliant with the range of human rights issues; arguably it focused more on the procedure by which the decision was taken than on the outcome.

The 'public good' head of deportation can cover a number of widely different factors, but it seems reasonably clear that the decision to deport should be based on all the circumstances relevant to the particular evil in question and the likely consequences flowing from any deportation. Thus, in *IAT ex p (Mahmud) Khan* (1983), the applicant in a sham marriage case successfully challenged his deportation, on the ground that the appeal tribunal failed to properly consider whether the couple did intend to live as man and wife. Similarly, it is not enough to show that a person has behaved in an anti-social manner in the past; it must be considered whether future wrongdoing is likely (*IAT ex p Ullah* (1983)).

Appeal rights against deportation decisions have been developed over the years, but there have been major changes to the appeal system, introduced by the **NIAA 2002**, which may

4   An awareness of the impact the **ECHR** has had in this area is essential.

make appeals harder for some applicants. Under s 82, most deportation decisions can be appealed against to an adjudicator and then, if there are grounds, to a tribunal. An important change made by the 2002 Act is to increase the number of appeals that can only be made from outside the UK, which considerably increases the burden on applicants. Human rights violations are amongst the grounds for appeal (s 84(1)(c)) and so Arts 3, 5 and particularly 8 of Sched 1 to the HRA are likely to figure in future appeals. Human rights appeals can still be made from within the UK unless the Home Secretary certifies that the grounds are without foundation. There is no right to appeal against the issuing of removal directions (as opposed to the removal decision itself). The actual removal may be years after the order and it may be argued that circumstances have altered. In *Kariharan v Secretary of State for the Home Department* (2002), the Court of Appeal held that human rights appeals should be allowed against removal directions, but the 2002 Act reversed this decision.

A person to be removed on public good grounds enjoys the right of appeal unless the decision was made by the Home Secretary on 'national security' grounds or on reliance on information which ought not to be disclosed in court. In those circumstances, there is a right of appeal to the SIAC before which the applicant has only the most limited rights. It can, for example, decide a case on the basis of evidence not disclosed to the applicant. Moreover, such appeals must now normally be made from outside the UK.

The law on deportation has undergone significant change in recent years. The law and the administrative and appeal procedures are designed expressly to take account of the Convention rights (both refugee and ECHR) of potential deportees and in that respect it can be said that individuals are potentially treated fairly. It is clear, however, that overall the balance between the individual and the State remains firmly weighted in favour of the latter – a matter which is most clearly illustrated where national security issues are involved. It is difficult to speak of a fairer balance without calling into question the whole notion of immigration controls but the human cost of deportation must be borne in mind by decision makers and arguably the current provisions do not encourage careful analysis of these matters.

QUESTION 37

'The current arrangements for considering the claims of asylum seekers suggest that the UK respects the letter of the Geneva Convention, but not its spirit.'

◗ **Do you agree?**

How to Answer this Question

This essay question potentially covers a wide range of material so you need to be selective. There has been a great deal of recent statutory reform and case law on the subject in response to the rapid growth of asylum seekers in the latter half of the 1990s and early 2000s. There has since been a rapid decline, partly due to the increasingly restrictive laws introduced.

Essentially, the following matters may be discussed:

- ❖ the **Geneva Convention of 1951**, as amended by the **1967 Protocol**;
- ❖ key provisions of the **Immigration and Asylum Act (IAA) 1999**, the **Nationality, Immigration and Asylum Act (NIAA) 2002**, the **Asylum and Immigration (Treatment of Claimants etc) Act (AITC) 2004**, the **Immigration, Asylum and Nationality Act (IANA) 2006** and the **Immigration Rules** relating to asylum seekers;
- ❖ the appeals procedure under the **NIAA, AITC** and **Immigration Rules**.

Answer Structure

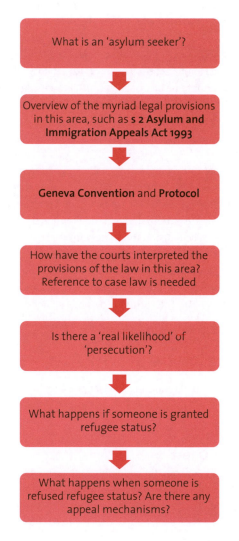

What is an 'asylum seeker'?

Overview of the myriad legal provisions in this area, such as **s 2 Asylum and Immigration Appeals Act 1993**

Geneva Convention and **Protocol**

How have the courts interpreted the provisions of the law in this area? Reference to case law is needed

Is there a 'real likelihood' of 'persecution'?

What happens if someone is granted refugee status?

What happens when someone is refused refugee status? Are there any appeal mechanisms?

ANSWER

The UK accepts certain international obligations in respect of asylum seekers under the **Geneva Convention of 1951**, as amended by the **1967 Protocol** relating to the Status of Refugees. **Rule 334** of the **Immigration Rules** provides that a person will be granted asylum if the Secretary of State is satisfied s/he is a refugee as defined by the **Refugee or Person in Need of International Protection (Qualification) Regulations 2006** and, *inter alia*:

> '. . . refusing his application would result in his being required to go . . . in breach of the Convention and Protocol, to a country in which his life or freedom would threatened on account of his race, religion, nationality, political opinion or membership of a particular social group.'[5]

Section 2 of the **Asylum and Immigration Appeals Act 1993** states that nothing shall be laid down in the immigration rules which would be contrary to the **Geneva Convention**. This is supplemented by the **Immigration Rules para 328** which states that all asylum applications will be dealt with in accordance with the **Geneva Convention**.

The **Convention** and **Protocol** are concerned only with political asylum seekers and this is reflected in the ambit of **r 334**, so that those fleeing from famine or disaster are not covered. Sometimes, it may be hard to make this distinction when a person leaves a country which is in the middle of a civil war.[6] A refugee is defined in **Art 1A(2)** of the **Convention** as a person who has a 'well founded fear of persecution' based on 'race, religion, nationality membership of a particular social group or political opinion' and who is outside his country of nationality and unable or, owing to his fear, unwilling to avail

---

5   It is fine to quote material such as this if it is relevant to do so and you cannot really summarise it effectively in your own words.
6   Try and get analysis in as much as you can, as this answer does here in relation to the difficulties applying the law in relation to who is a political asylum seeker.

himself of the protection of that country. Clearly the fear must be both subjective and objective (well founded). The issue of the burden of proof placed on the applicant to show that the fear would materialise was considered in *R v Secretary of State for the Home Department ex p Sivakumaran* (1988). The House of Lords said that once it appears that the applicant genuinely fears persecution, the Secretary of State is required to ask himself, on the basis of all the available information, whether there has been demonstrated a 'real likelihood' or, as in *Fernandez v Government of Singapore* (1971), a 'reasonable chance' of persecution.

The emphasis of this test differs from that put forward by the High Commissioner, which involves asking whether, subjectively, a real fear of persecution is present and then considering whether it is a fear no one would reasonably hold. The test put forward by the House of Lords therefore provided less protection for refugees and, moreover, the imprecise nature of expressions such as 'real likelihood' leaves considerable latitude for differences of opinion as to the severity of the risk of persecution.

Courts have stressed the importance of adjudicators making an all-round consideration of the facts rather than accepting a narrow, formalistic, interpretation of the rules. In *R (Sivakumar) v Secretary of State for the Home Department* (2003), for example, the evidence was that the applicant, a Tamil, had been horribly tortured by the Sri Lankan authorities as part of an investigation into terrorist acts.[7] The Home Secretary contended that torture in furtherance of a terrorist investigation fell outside the protection of the **Convention**. This was rejected by the House of Lords, which held that the issue was whether, on a full view of the facts, the persecution might, in reality, be on **Convention** grounds such as race or membership of a social group.

Persecution is not defined but is a flexible concept that will depend on the circumstances of each case. The feared persecution must have a causal link with the listed **Convention** reasons: race, religion, nationality, social group or political opinion. In *Islam v Secretary of State for the Home Department* (1999), the House of Lords found that a group of Pakistani women who had been falsely accused of adultery could claim refugee status under the **Geneva Convention**, since they were a group of people unprotected by their own State; there is no requirement of cohesiveness or indeed of minority status for persons to constitute a 'group'. In *Adan (Lul Omar) v Secretary of State for the Home Department* (2000), the House of Lords stated that, on a correct interpretation of the **Convention**, a well-founded fear of persecution could be based on the activities of non-State groups where the State was unable or unwilling to give adequate protection.

Refugee status will not be granted to applicants who are considered on serious grounds to be serious violators of human rights. **Article 33(2)** also permits the denial of asylum if

---

7   Always try to use examples to back up your points, as this use of the *Sivakumar* case does here.

they are deemed a security danger to the country or a danger due to their conviction for a particularly serious crime. Rules in the **NIAA 2002** alarmingly remove the requirement to make a judgment about the danger to the community, by creating a presumption of danger if a person is sentenced to at least two years' imprisonment. It was criticised by the Joint Committee on Human Rights on the basis that it undermined the case-by-case basis for refugee determination, denigrated the proportionality test and reversed the burden of proof. Furthermore the Government specified a huge range of offences including some relatively minor offences such as theft and criminal damage which are not dependent on the length of imprisonment. Again the Joint Committee was concerned that this list included offences that were clearly not particularly serious as required by **Art 33(2)**. It is argued that this is an example of the domestic law violating the spirit and probably the letter of the **Convention** too.

A recent initiative has been the development of 'fast track' procedures for dealing with asylum claims while detaining or otherwise restricting the freedom of asylum seekers. There are a number of detention centres into which are funnelled cases which it is deemed can be dealt with quickly and special provisions apply to them. These relate to cases where the applicants come from countries designated safe by statute or regulations. The vast majority of such applications are refused and there is no in-country appeal against the decision. Another centre deals with applications from countries which are deemed to be capable of quick resolution. Claims are decided within days with very limited appeal rights. The fast track process was unsuccessfully challenged in *R (Refugee Legal Centre) v Secretary of State for the Home Department* (2004). The Court of Appeal considered that despite significant defects that required addressing, the rules were not *inherently* unfair and could be made to work fairly.

Traditionally those granted refugee status would be given leave to remain in the UK indefinitely. However, the **NIAA 2006** provides for only five-year leave to be granted to refugees. Asylum Policy Instructions explain that asylum cases may be reviewed on grounds including where there has been a significant and non-temporary change in the origin country. This is in line with a European-wide trend to permit short-term asylum grants.

Rights of appeal for asylum seekers have been revised, in a restrictive manner. Appeal is to the Asylum and Immigration Tribunal with a further appeal only on points of law to the Court of Appeal. Grounds of appeal can include that the **Geneva Convention** has not been followed or that the immigration decision was taken in violation of the applicant's human rights.

Section 92 of the **2002 Act** reduced the range of appeals that can be heard in the UK. Some asylum seekers, in any case, have been removed to 'safe countries'. Under the **IAA 1999** and the **AITC 2004** asylum seekers can be removed to Member States of the European Union (EU) and European Economic Area, all of which are deemed to be 'safe'.

This runs counter to the decisions in *Besnik Gashi* (1999), *Lul Omar Adan* (1999) and *Aitseguer* (2000) that France and Germany were not 'safe' because they were not applying the **Convention** appropriately.[8]

Outside the safe country provisions **s 92** permits an appeal to be made on human rights grounds from inside the UK. Even here, however, the Secretary of State may certify that a claim is 'clearly unfounded', and again the applicant can only appeal from outside the UK. Since appeals from outside the UK are hard to mount, there may be an argument that an asylum seeker's rights under **Art 13** of the **ECHR** (not a scheduled **Convention** right in the **HRA**) are violated. Rights of appeal from within the UK are also restricted where the Home Secretary certifies that the appeal issue has already been settled or that its real purpose is delay (**s 96**).

Clearly, much depends on the certificates made by the Home Secretary, and it should be noted that these are not subject to appeal, though they are subject to judicial review. The thrust of reforms over the past few years appear to limit the application of the **Refugee Convention** in ways that seek to reduce the potential for findings of refugee status and to streamline the process of determination to the point where often individual circumstances are not really considered.

There have been a number of other important developments in the law and administrative practice, which arguably increase the difficulties faced by people wishing to pursue asylum claims in the UK. For example under the **NIAA 2002**, asylum seekers can be required to reside at 'accommodation centres' in return for welfare support. A similarly infamous provision of the **2004 Act** was **s 9**, which enabled welfare support and accommodation to be withdrawn from failed applicants with young families. The consequence is that children have to be taken into care. The Joint Committee argued strongly that it is difficult to implement **s 9** without violating **Arts 8** and **3**.

The **2002 Act s 55** also reintroduced measures by which even minimal welfare support from the Government could be denied to asylum seekers who did not make their claim as soon as reasonably possible on arriving in the UK. Ultimately the House of Lords established that actual or imminent destitution would amount to a breach of **Art 3** (*R v Secretary of State for the Home Department ex p Adam, Limbuela and Tesema* (2005)). Government policy seems to be reflecting a degree of antipathy towards asylum seekers. Disproportionate measures in this direction could be incompatible with both the **Refugee Convention** and the **ECHR**. The Joint Committee argued that, despite the successful challenges, **s 55** was very likely to breach basic economic social and cultural human rights norms.

....

8   This passage about **s 92** of the Act contains a good account of the law and some critique which is backed up with authority.

It can be suggested, therefore, that, in formal terms, UK law respects the letter of the Geneva Convention. In particular, Convention rights can be argued on appeal. Nevertheless, there is clear evidence that aspects of asylum law and administrative practice, such as those relating to detention, rights of appeal and welfare, seem to have the effect of making asylum claims harder to make and pursue. In this respect, it may be said that the spirit of the Geneva Convention is being ignored.

QUESTION 38

Miss Shia is a trained specialist gynaecological nurse. In the past, she resided and worked in Entriastan (a non-EU State), where she assisted in the carrying out of abortions. Whilst she was resident there, she was under repeated threats from religious fundamentalists opposed to abortion. When the fundamentalists came to power in a coup, she fled to France. From France, she entered the UK illegally, but is seeking political asylum. Her brother is a student at a UK university and intends to begin a PhD after he has completed his undergraduate studies. Miss Shia is under threat of being sent back to France, but is terrified that other fundamentalist groups unconnected with the Entriastan Government may threaten her there. She is also worried that threatened health care cuts in Entriastan would not only cost her a job, but would limit her access to drugs which control her serious asthma.

▶ **Advise Miss Shia of her chances of being allowed to remain in the UK.**

How to Answer this Question

This problem question deals with a variety of issues relating to the grant of political asylum. Students must be aware of not only the relevant domestic law and practice, but also the Geneva Convention, as amended, and a number of key decisions of the European Court of Human Rights (ECtHR).

Essentially, students should discuss the following issues:

❖ Is Miss Shia a political refugee entitled to asylum under the Geneva Convention 1951?
❖ Is she a member of a 'particular social group' (*Ouanes* (1998); *Islam* (1999))?
❖ Is France a 'safe third country' under the Dublin Convention 1990?
❖ Will ECtHR decisions as to Arts 8 and 3 give her a better chance of asylum or a right to remain in the UK?

Answer Structure

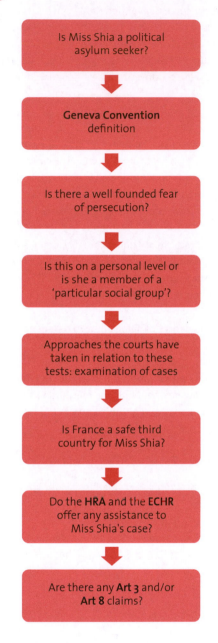

Is Miss Shia a political asylum seeker?

↓

Geneva Convention definition

↓

Is there a well founded fear of persecution?

↓

Is this on a personal level or is she a member of a 'particular social group'?

↓

Approaches the courts have taken in relation to these tests: examination of cases

↓

Is France a safe third country for Miss Shia?

↓

Do the **HRA** and the **ECHR** offer any assistance to Miss Shia's case?

↓

Are there any **Art 3** and/or **Art 8** claims?

ANSWER

The first question which must be answered is whether Miss Shia is in fact a political asylum seeker. In order to assess this, we must look to the definitions given in the **Geneva Convention 1951**, which is adopted into domestic law by the **Immigration and Asylum Act (IAA) 1999**. The **Convention** provides that a person is an asylum seeker when he:

> '. . . owing to a well founded fear of being persecuted for reasons of race, religion, nationality, membership of a particular social group or political opinion, is outside the country of his nationality and is unable or, owing to such fear, is unwilling to avail himself of that protection of that country; or who, not having a nationality and being outside the country of his former habitual residence or as a result of such events, is unable or, owing to such fear, is unwilling to return to it.'

Hence, the key relevant elements of the test are a well-founded fear of persecution, and that the persecution feared must be on relevant grounds. There must be a causal connection between the fear of persecution and the relevant ground. Miss Shia may try to argue that she has a well-founded fear of persecution, either on a personal level due to any acts from which she had already suffered before she left Entriastan, or as a member of a 'particular social group'. In relation to the former, she is unlikely to succeed, particularly if Entriastan is now a violent country where human rights violations are likely to occur: see *Ward v Secretary of State for the Home Department* (1997), where an individual's torture was found to be 'nothing more than the sort of random difficulties faced by many thousands of people in Peru'. Further, 'solitary individuals do not exhibit cohesiveness, co-operation or interdependence', which were seen to be the requirements for a social group by Lord Justice Staughton in *Islam* (1998). But the fact that the threats which she suffered came from anti-abortion fundamentalists is not in itself a problem, since the persecution need not come from a State source: *R v Secretary of State for the Home Department ex p Bouheraoua and Kerkeb* (2000); the **Convention** provides protection from persecution by non-State agents, but only if the authorities of the State in question are unwilling or unable to give effective protection (see *Horvath v Secretary of State for the Home Department* (2001)). Thus, Miss Shia has an arguable claim of fear of persecution if she can show that Entriastan fails to offer her a reasonable level of protection. She may argue that she is a 'member of a particular social group' and fears persecution on that basis.[9]

There is some debate as to the correct approach on which to determine this issue. In *Ouanes v Secretary of State for the Home Department* (1998), the claimant was an Algerian citizen who worked as a midwife for the Ministry of Health. Her job included providing contraceptive advice. She had received threats for not wearing a veil in public, and there

---

9 Problem questions are all about application of law to facts. This passage effectively sets the law out about asylum and applies it to Miss Shia as it goes along.

had been incidents where other midwives similarly employed had been killed by fundamentalists. The Court of Appeal found that 'Government-employed midwives' lacked the degree of cohesiveness required in the earlier case of *Shah* (1997), and that the expression 'particular social group' does not ordinarily cover a body of people linked only by the work that they do. The characteristic which defines a 'particular social group' must be one which members should not be required to change, since it is fundamental to their 'individual identities or conscience'. So, if *Ouanes* is followed, Miss Shia would have great trouble in showing that she is a member of a 'particular social group'. However, there is also the rival approach adopted by the House of Lords in *Islam v Secretary of State for the Home Department* (1999), where Pakistani women were found to be a 'particular social group' within the meaning of **Art 1A(2)** of the **Geneva Convention**. The women claimants had both been falsely accused of adultery in Pakistan and feared that if they were returned, they would face criminal proceedings for sexual immorality and could be sentenced to either flogging or stoning to death. The House of Lords found that, although the general low status of women in Pakistan and the high level of violence against women in that society would not, in themselves, give rise to a claim to refugee status, the fact that the State tolerated and partly sanctioned discrimination against women, coupled with the fact that they were not granted the same rights as men, meant that they were a particular social group and so the claimants could satisfy the **Geneva Convention** test. There was not found to be any requirement of cohesiveness of a 'particular social group'. It is not clear whether a court would find Miss Shia's case sufficiently similar to the facts in *Islam* (1999) for the House of Lords case to be followed in preference to *Ouanes*.[10]

Assuming that she is found to be a member of a relevant particular social group, the next issue to be determined is whether there is a 'safe third country' to which she may be returned under the **Dublin II Regulation 2003** which replaced the **Dublin Convention** in September 2003. This provides that the European country in which an asylum seeker first lodged an application should be the country to determine his application unless, under the **1951 Geneva Convention**, that country would not be considered to be a safe third country. There are exceptions to this, such as where the asylum seeker has a family member lawfully in another country who is an asylum seeker or has been granted refugee status. In Ms Shia's case she has a brother in the UK but he is on a student visa. In addition, **Art 15** permits Member States to bring together family members on humanitarian grounds, although in *R (G) v Secretary of State for the Home Department* (2005) it was held that this did not create any rights for asylum seekers but rather was designed to regulate the relationship between Member States.

It follows that since Miss Shia travelled to the UK via France, we need to decide whether France could be considered to be a safe third country. In *Secretary of State ex p Aitseguer* (2000), the House of Lords held that France could not automatically be treated as 'safe'

---

10 The law is often unclear and can be difficult to apply, so do not be afraid to say so, as the answer does here about Miss Shia's case.

because it was not interpreting the **1951 Convention** properly. In particular, it did not recognise that the threat of persecution could come from a source other than the State itself. However, **AITC 2004 Sched 3** conclusively deems all countries in the European Economic Area as safe countries in respect of persecution in that country, sending back to a country where there was a risk of persecution and sending back to a country where there is a risk of human rights violations. The courts, in cases such as *R (Benda) v Secretary of State for the Home Department (No 1)* (2002), treated an earlier version of this provision as authority whose effect is to overrule *Aitseguer*.

The only possibility of assistance to Miss Shia in this situation, therefore, comes from the **ECHR** and the **HRA**. Although there is no direct or implied right of asylum in either the **Convention** or the Act, a number of other articles of the **Convention** have been employed in certain situations where the removal of an asylum seeker from the jurisdiction would cause exceptional hardship in his or her personal circumstances, or would show a lack of respect for his or her family or private life, or would risk him or her being tortured or otherwise ill-treated on return to his or her home country or to a 'safe' third country. Miss Shia has potential arguments based on each of these lines. First, she might argue under **Art 3** that to return her to her home country or to France would risk torture, inhuman or degrading treatment or punishment contrary to **Art 3**. Cases such as *Chahal v UK* (1997) and *Hatami v Sweden* (1998) have shown that, where there are substantial grounds for believing that there is a real risk that the asylum seeker will be subjected to torture or inhuman or degrading treatment or punishment in the receiving country, then the State which currently has the asylum seeker within its jurisdiction falls under a positive obligation not to expel that person.[11]

Secondly, under **Art 8**, there must be respect for the claimant's right to a private and family life. Since Miss Shia has a brother at university in the UK who intends to be there for an extended period as a postgraduate student, it is arguable that she may have strong family ties within the UK which might be upheld under **Art 8**. The argument failed in *Ahmut v The Netherlands* (1996), but succeeded in *C v Belgium* (1996). The domestic courts' approach towards family life has been dominated by the early **HRA** decision of *R (Mahmoud) v Secretary of State for the Home Department* (2001) in which the Court of Appeal adopted a deferential approach to decisions of the Home Office regarding the impact on family life and emphasised that where there were no insurmountable obstacles to the family remaining together in the destination State there was less likelihood that removal would adversely affect family life. On this basis it is unlikely that an **Art 8** claim would succeed as there is no extreme difficulty for her brother to accompany Miss Shia back to Entriastan.[12]

....

11   A good understanding of the **ECHR** and the **HRA** is essential to this question and this passage demonstrates this understanding to the examiner.

12   This passage explores the **Art 8** issues well and then concludes well with very clear application of the law to Miss Shia's case.

Miss Shia's health *could* be in issue. Lack of medical treatment in her home country might lead to a violation of **Art 3** if she was removed, though the threshold of severity is high (see *D v UK* (1997)). The case of *N v Secretary of State for the Home Department* (2005) illustrates the really difficult position Miss Shia is in legally. N was an AIDS sufferer who was receiving appropriate medical care in the UK and her condition had stabilised. Her return to Uganda, it was acknowledged, would lead to her death within around a year as there was no prospect of her receiving the same anti-retroviral drugs in that country. Nevertheless, the House of Lords distinguished *D v UK* on the basis that the latter case was one of imminent death in distressing circumstances. It did not apply so as to require a positive obligation on Member States to provide medical care for people from countries with poorer health care systems. In *Bensaid v UK* (2001), **Art 8** was considered in circumstances where continued bad health would undermine private and family life. Again, the threshold was found to be high and the ECtHR accepted that immigration control was a valid reason for restrictions under **Art 8(2)**. Neither argument would be effective if Miss Shia was to be returned to France, a country with adequate treatment for asthma. In any event The **AITC 2004** provisions on safe third countries also require the Secretary of State to certify that a human rights appeal would be unfounded in respect of those countries unless she is satisfied that it would not be. In other words, there is a presumption that France will deal adequately with the human rights arguments Miss Shia may wish to raise in her application not to be returned to Entriastan.

The situation seems relatively clear insofar as Miss Shia is concerned. Her claim to asylum on the basis of her membership of a social group appears to be fairly flimsy. It seems almost certain that she is liable under domestic law to be returned to France to process her application and if so, her human rights claims are likely to be certified as unfounded. She would have no right of appeal against the decision to send her to France, and any human rights appeal would have to be made from France.

QUESTION 39

'A political asylum seeker has a greater chance of success in avoiding deportation under the **European Convention on Human Rights 1950** than under existing domestic law relating to the granting of asylum.'

◗ **Discuss.**

How to Answer this Question

This question requires discussion of a variety of issues relating to the grant of political asylum. Students must be aware of not only the relevant domestic law and practice, but also the **Geneva Convention** as amended and a number of key decisions of the European Court of Human Rights (ECtHR).

Essentially, students should discuss the following issues:

❖ When is a political refugee entitled to asylum under the **Geneva Convention 1951**?

❖ The definition of 'particular social group' (*Fornah* (2005)).

❖ Will ECtHR decisions as to **Art 8** and **Art 3** give a better chance of asylum or a right to remain in the UK?

Answer Structure

What is an 'asylum seeker'

Geneva Convention and relevant law

A well founded fear of persecution for a particular reason is needed

Examination of cases about persecution and the reasons

Is there a 'safe third country' to which an individual can be returned?

Examination of this issue through legislation and cases

What difference, if any, has the **HRA** and the **ECHR** made to this area of law?

Examination of this issue through cases

ANSWER

In any application for asylum, the first question is whether the applicant in fact falls within the definition of a political asylum seeker. This requires considering the definitions given in the **Geneva Convention (the Refugee Convention) 1951**. The **Refugee Convention** has not been directly incorporated into domestic law but **s 2** of the **Asylum and Immigration Appeals Act 1993** states that nothing shall be laid down in the immigration rules which would be contrary to the **Geneva Convention**.

The **Convention** provides that a person is an asylum seeker when he or she has a well-founded fear of persecution for reasons of race, religion, nationality, membership of a particular social group or political opinion. There must be a sufficient causal link between the persecution and the **Convention** grounds. The focus in the question on 'political' asylum seekers might suggests that the last of these **Convention** grounds is the most relevant, although we will consider all of them because 'political asylum' is often used as a phrase covering all forms of claims to refugee status.[13]

Race as a **Convention** ground is not specifically defined. The *UNHCR Handbook* states that it applies to all kinds of ethnic groups that are referred to as races in common usage. It also suggests that serious racial discrimination interfering with fundamental rights is likely to amount to persecution. Religion has not given rise to definitional difficulties, the focus being instead on what level of interference with religious activity may amount to persecution. In *Ahmed (Iftikhar) v Secretary of State for the Home Department* (2000), the Court of Appeal held that an applicant who had suffered intense harassment due to his proselytising, which he regarded as an essential aspect of his religion, had suffered religion-based persecution. Nationality overlaps with race and is given a flexible meaning not linked to the concept of citizenship. It clearly covers the position of national minorities such as Roma.

---

13 This passage is particularly useful to the examiner as it shows knowledge, but also sets out the structure and approach the answer is going to take.

The concept of a particular social group is often difficult to pin down. What is required is that the applicant is likely to suffer persecution due to their membership of the 'particular social group'. Being a trade unionist threatened by right-wing paramilitary groups could, for example, be the basis of a claim (*R v IAT ex p Walteros-Castenda* (2000)). There is some debate as to the correct approach on which to determine the issue of what constitutes a 'particular social group'.

The ground still throws up difficult questions. Thus a series of decisions culminating in *Fornah v Secretary of State for the Home Department* (2005) held that females at risk of genital mutilation were not a particular social group because there was nothing other than the risk of persecution to link them together. Earlier cases were distinguished on the basis that once female circumcision had taken place there would be no ongoing persecution. Nevertheless, the trend appears to be in favour of a more flexible approach towards identifying a social group. In *Liu v Secretary of State for the Home Department* (2005), the Court of Appeal said that the need to identify a group should not become an obstacle course. It found that women in China who became pregnant or gave birth in breach of the one-child policy could be a social group.

'Political opinion' as a ground may be obvious such as where someone is persecuted for standing as a candidate in an election or more subtle as in *Noune v Secretary of State for the Home Department* (2000) where the Court of Appeal held that the threats and harassment suffered by a 'westernised' woman postal worker following her refusal to assist religious extremists in sending messages to Japan and the Soviet Union could be political in nature. It has been said that to qualify as political, the opinion must relate to the major power transactions taking place in that particular society. This has been given a fairly broad interpretation by the UK authorities. For example, the Asylum Policy Instructions state that a woman resisting institutionalised discrimination is expressing political opinion.[14]

The persecution need not come from a State source (*R v Secretary of State for the Home Department ex p Bouheraoua and Kerkeb* (2000)); the **Convention** provides protection from persecution by non-State agents if the authorities of the State in question are unwilling or unable to give effective protection. Persecuted Roma in Slovakia were not protected by the **Convention**, since the Slovakian authorities would offer protection (*Horvath v Secretary of State for the Home Department* (2001)).

The next issue to be determined is whether there is a 'safe third country' to which he or she may be returned under the **Dublin II EC Regulations 2003**. These provide that the European country in which an asylum seeker first made a claim for asylum should be the

14 Try and use examples to explore the law as much as possible, such as this passage does with the *Noune* case.

country to determine his application unless, under the **Geneva Convention**, that country would not be considered to be a safe third country. As far as Member States of the EU are concerned, that issue is now determined by **Sched 3** to the **IATC 2004**, which deems all countries in the European Economic Area to be 'safe' for these purposes. Though the UK courts have held that France and Germany do not apply aspects of the **Refugee Convention** appropriately (for example, *Adan and Aitseguer* (2000)), the House of Lords has also held that it is reasonable to consider these countries as safe since, in practice, they will not return applicants to face persecution in the receiving country (*R (Yogathas) v Secretary of State for the Home Department* (2002)). In any event the arguments that had succeeded in *Adan and Aitseguer* were effectively blocked by the statute. As regards States which are not members of the EEA, a judgment must be made in each case, although **Sched 3** now contains provision for further country lists to be introduced by the Home Secretary as providing safe destinations. A right, certified by the Home Secretary, to reside in one of a number of listed, allegedly safe, countries means that an asylum seeker suffers the disadvantage of being unable to appeal from inside the UK – **s 94(3)** of the **Nationality, Immigration and Asylum Act (NIAA) 2002**. Indeed the Home Secretary must now certify any human rights claim as unfounded if the applicant is to be sent to a country in the EEA.[15]

The final possibility of aid to a political asylum seeker comes from the **ECHR** and the **HRA**. Although there is no direct or implied right of asylum in either the **Convention** or the Act, **Arts 3** and **8** in particular have been used to challenge asylum and deportation decisions. Following the **HRA**, of course, asylum legislation must, so far as it is possible to do so, be interpreted in a way which is compatible with the scheduled **Convention** rights, and the officials involved, including adjudicators and the tribunals, must, as public authorities, act compatibly with **Convention** rights. UK courts must take the approach of the Strasbourg Court into account.

A number of cases, such as *Chahal v UK* (1997), have shown that **Art 3** (the right not to suffer torture or inhuman or degrading treatment or punishment) imposes an obligation of signatory States not to deport a person if there are substantial grounds for believing that they will suffer torture or some other violation of their **Art 3** rights in the receiving State. In *Jabari v Turkey* (2000), the ECtHR held it would violate **Art 3** to deport a woman to Iran where she would be subject to fierce and cruel laws on adultery.

The deportation of the seriously ill to a country where any treatment will be inadequate can, in the most serious cases, violate **Art 3** (*D v UK* (1997), where a patient in the later stages of AIDS would suffer a speedy and excruciating death due to lack of medication in the destination state). However The ECtHR limited this principle to the most extreme cases in *N v UK* (2008) approving the approach of the House of Lords in *N v Secretary of*

---

15   This passage sets out large areas of law very well by clearly explaining them in plain language.

State for the Home Department (2005) that a fully medicated AIDS patient would not suffer **Art 3** mistreatment if she were returned to Uganda, where she would not receive anti-retroviral medication.

Claimants may also seek the protection of **Art 8** (respect for private and family life). Respect for 'family life' has been invoked by deportees with strong family ties to the signatory State. There has been variable success: in *Ahmut v The Netherlands* (1996), the argument failed, but it succeeded in *C v Belgium* (1996).[16] Less serious cases of medical problems can try and invoke **Art 8** where it has been held that the need to respect for 'private life' is, arguably, applicable in respect of proposed deportation of claimants who are physically or mentally ill (*Bensaid v UK* (2001)), and there may be a lower threshold of harm than required by **Art 3**. Of course, any claim brought under **Art 8** is likely to meet a Government argument that the interference with family and private life is lawful, for a legitimate purpose and proportionate. Immigration control is accepted by Strasbourg as a legitimate purpose for interfering with private life (if it is in the economic interests of the country, for example) and so the issue tends to be resolved on the issue of proportionality and the particular facts of any case.

Of broader significance, in the case of *R (Ullah) v Special Adjudicator* (2004) the House of Lords held that the risk of violation of other **Convention** rights could affect the lawfulness of removal. The case involved alleged religious persecution and the claimants also argued that their rights under **Art 9** of the **European Convention** would be violated if they were returned. Their Lordships held as a matter of principle that **Convention** rights other than **Art 3** could be relied on. This followed from the duty of national courts to keep pace with Strasbourg jurisprudence as it evolved over time. The court found it hard to think that a person could successfully resist expulsion in reliance on **Art 9** without being entitled either to asylum on the ground of a well-founded fear of persecution for reasons of religion, or to resist expulsion in reliance on **Art 3**. However, such a possibility could not be ruled out in principle. However, successful reliance on other articles required a very strong case – to the point of saying that the right would be completely denied or nullified by the alleged breach

Through its development of **Arts 3** and **8** in particular, the **ECHR** increases the grounds on which a refugee may avoid deportation. In particular, returning someone to a country in which their **Art 3** rights are violated is, itself, a violation of the **ECHR**. Current immigration and asylum law in the UK aims to be compatible with both the **Geneva Convention** and the **ECHR**. That a deportation would violate the **Geneva Convention** or be incompatible with the **ECHR** is, for example, a ground of appeal under the **NIAA 2002**. Given that human rights claims can be used when there is no **Refugee Convention** claim and in view

---

16 By exploring cases which show variable success, such as the *Ahmut* and *C* cases show here, you show the examiner that you have a deep understanding of the law in the area.

of the different tests (such as the absence of a requirement for persecution or a ground such as race, religion, nationality etc.) it does seem clear that human rights claims extend somewhat further than the **Refugee Convention**. The two sets of rules, from the **Geneva Convention** and from the **ECHR**, now operate in tandem. Perhaps it is time for wide-ranging reform so that the **Geneva Convention** and the **ECHR** case law can be given a better degree of fit, so that the rights in the **Geneva Convention** and those in **Arts 3** and **8** of the **ECHR** are more successfully related together.

The Human Rights Act 1998 and the European Convention on Human Rights

8

INTRODUCTION

The **Human Rights Act (HRA) 1998** has at the time of writing been in force for over fifteen years (it came into force in 2000), so it is possible to make an interim but fairly tentative assessment as to its efficacy in protecting human rights and freedoms in the UK. It affords further effect to a number of the rights protected under the **European Convention on Human Rights**. It remains a controversial piece of legislation; for example, in 2006 parts of the media blamed it for weakening the UK in its 'war' against terrorism, and for the early release of criminals. The criticism was misleading, since even if the **HRA** was repealed, the UK would remain bound at international level to abide by the **European Convention on Human Rights**. The Conservative Party has stated that its policy is to repeal the Act and to replace it with a 'modern British Bill of Rights', and indeed, in March 2011 it established the Commission on a Bill of Rights to specifically look into this matter.

It is not possible at the time of writing to confidently predict what the conclusions of the Commission are going to be. One key difficulty preventing this is that its terms of reference were vague, merely saying they have been charged to investigate the creation of a Bill of Rights that incorporates and builds on the UK's obligations under the **European Convention on Human Rights**, ensures that these rights continue to be enshrined in UK law, and protects and extends liberties. Their terms are therefore very vague and generic, which merely raises more questions than it is possible to answer at this moment in time. Students need to keep a keen eye on developments in this area as the Commission are due to report back to the Government by the end of 2012.

If such proposals went ahead, such a Bill of Rights could be in place by 2014; it would presumably protect the **Convention** rights that are currently protected under the **HRA**, so the respect in which it would sharply differ from the **HRA** is unclear. In this forensic climate it is important to examine the background to the Act and to look carefully at what it can and cannot do. Its effects in fields ranging well beyond the criminal justice or terrorism ones must also be considered.

The very first edition of this book dealt in considerable detail with the so-called Bill of Rights debate pre-1998 – the advantages and disadvantages of introducing a written human rights guarantee. It also considered the advantages and deficiencies of the

European Convention on Human Rights (ECHR). It evaluated the various human rights enforcement mechanisms. The reception of the ECHR into UK law via the HRA has rendered that debate largely defunct, but knowledge of the history of the ECHR in the UK remains essential to an understanding of the background to the HRA, and the legal context that it should be placed in. Political and public support for some form of Bill of Rights grew overwhelming by the mid-1990s, but the resulting statute, the HRA, bears the hallmarks of several compromises which reflect the particular constitutional arrangements in the UK. In particular, it represents a compromise between the preservation of parliamentary sovereignty and protection for human rights.

By 2010 the debate was centred upon the effectiveness of the HRA as a human rights guarantee and the improvements in domestic human rights protection which had resulted from the introduction of the HRA and would be likely to result from it in future. Essay questions are likely to ask you to consider the way that the courts have dealt with the interpretation over the first ten years of its life of the key sections of the Act – ss 3 and 6; they are also likely to focus on gaps and inadequacies in both the ECHR and the 1998 Act. Now that the HRA has been fully in force for over ten years, some commentary on the significant early case law will be expected. The role of the judges has now come under fresh scrutiny, since they hold an important and enhanced role as human rights watchdogs, yet under the HRA lack the ultimate power of overriding legislation which breaches the ECHR.

Many different styles of essay question are possible on this large and wide- ranging topic; the following questions cover most of the significant areas of debate at the time of writing. Certain relevant issues are also touched on in most chapters, since the HRA affects every area of civil liberties law. However, it affects some much more than others: those chapters of most relevance are Chapters 1, 3, 4, 5, 6 and 7.

Checklist ✔

Students must be familiar with the following areas and their interrelationships:

- the legal protection for civil liberties before the introduction of the HRA and the former difficulties of relying on the ECHR in UK courts;

- the drive towards incorporation of the ECHR;

- the doctrine of parliamentary sovereignty;

- the key provisions of the HRA and the ECHR, especially ss 2, 3, 6, 4, 10 and 12 and Arts 3, 5, 6, 8, 10 and 11;

- key case law on the ECHR since the HRA came into force;

- key HRA cases, especially on ss 3 and 6, and especially *Ghaidan v Mendoza*, *Aston-Cantlow and Leonard Cheshire Homes*; *YL v Birmingham CC*;

- key statutes in the area of civil liberties, including the **Police and Criminal Evidence Act 1984**, as amended; the **Public Order Act 1986**, as amended; the **Terrorism Act 2000**; the **Anti-Terrorism Crime and Security Act 2001**; the **Prevention of Terrorism Act 2005** (now repealed); and the **Terrorism Prevention and Investigation Measures Act 2011**.

QUESTION 40

In terms of enhanced human rights protection, are there arguments in favour of introducing a tailor-made Bill of Rights for the UK, as proposed by the Conservative Party prior to the 2010 General Election, as opposed to relying on the **Human Rights Act 1998**?

How to Answer this Question

This is a fairly demanding question that requires quite detailed knowledge of the **European Convention on Human Rights (ECHR)**, the **Human Rights Act (HRA) 1998**, decisions on it and key **Convention** decisions. It is also necessary to say something about the possible differences between a Bill of Rights and the **HRA** in terms of enhanced human rights protection. This is a pertinent question at the present time, as the question indicates, given David Cameron's (Leader of the Conservative Party) expressed predilection for a 'British Bill of Rights', possibly to be introduced around 2014. You are not expected to discuss specific current plans for a Bill of Rights as these have not yet emerged and are not even at the preparatory stage as of yet.

This essay asks a straightforward question, and therefore you must come down on one side or the other in principle, albeit while acknowledging the force of the arguments on the other side. The essay below answers the question posed in the negative, but an affirmative answer would be entirely arguable. Further, since the detail of the plans for a Bill of Rights is not available you should acknowledge that in practice protection for rights might be weakened under it.

Issues to be discussed include:

- ❖ the various possibilities available in terms of constructing a tailor-made Bill of Rights, bearing in mind that the Conservative-dominated Coalition Government is unlikely to favour an increase in the protection given to rights, over and above that offered by the **ECHR**, despite such sentiments being expressed in the terms of reference to the Commission on a Bill of Rights;
- ❖ the exceptions to the primary rights of the **Convention**;
- ❖ the effect of the margin of appreciation in certain European Court of Human Rights (FCtHR) decisions;
- ❖ the general restrictions on **Convention** rights;
- ❖ the weaknesses of some substantive **Convention** rights, for example, **Art 14**;

❖   the (arguable) deficiencies of the **HRA** in comparison with a Bill of Rights – **HRA** cases illustrating the problems.

Answer Structure

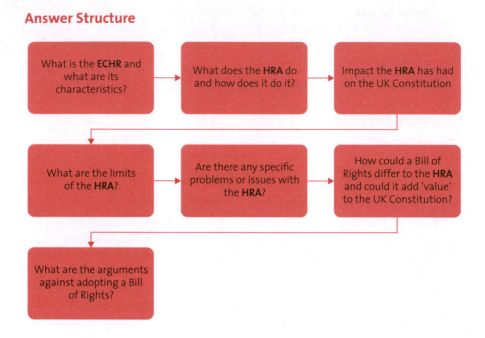

ANSWER

The **HRA** gave the **European Convention on Human Rights and Fundamental Freedoms** further effect in UK law, as will be discussed, using the mechanism of an ordinary Act of Parliament. It did not seek to entrench its own provisions or the **Convention**, and it has not introduced any new rights other than from those of the **Convention**. (It may be noted that not all of the **Convention** rights were included in **Sched 1 HRA; Art 1, Art 13** and the **Protocols**, apart from the **First** and **Sixth** ones, were excluded.) The possibility of introducing a tailor-made Bill of Rights was considered but rejected. This essay will argue that there are arguments in favour of introducing a Bill of Rights that would be unique to the UK, as proposed by the Conservative Party.[1]

The **ECHR** is a cautious document: it is not as open-textured as the **US Bill of Rights**[2] and it contains long lists of exceptions to most of the primary rights – exceptions that suggest a strong respect for the institutions of the State. These exceptions have at times

1   This background to the Bill of Rights debate shows the examiner you know what you are writing about and sets the scene for the answer.
2   Making comparisons to other law, such as this comparison to the **US Bill of Rights**, shows not just wider understanding but also serves as a useful tool to allow critique and analysis.

received a broad interpretation in the ECtHR and such interpretations are having a strong influence on domestic courts as they apply the rights directly in the domestic arena under the **HRA**. For example, **Art 10**, which protects freedom of expression, contains an exception in respect of the protection of morals. This was invoked in the *Handyside* (1976) case in respect of a booklet aimed at schoolchildren that was circulating freely in the rest of Europe. It was held that the UK government was best placed to determine what was needed in its own country in order to protect morals (application of the margin of appreciation doctrine), and so no breach of **Art 10** had occurred.

It is possible at the moment to come to some conclusions about the response of UK judges under the **HRA** to interpretations of the **Convention** rights at Strasbourg. The judges are failing to take the view that they should not apply a particular decision because it has been affected by the margin of appreciation doctrine. Arguably, this stance was taken in the post-**HRA** cases of *Alconbury* (2001), *Pro-life Alliance* (2002) and *Animal Defenders* (2008). Thus, the watering-down effect at Strasbourg of this doctrine may also be occurring under the **HRA**. The judges are also giving full weight to the express exceptions under **Arts 8–11** of the **Convention**, even where possibly Strasbourg might have decided on a different outcome. This may be said of *Interbrew SA v Financial Times Ltd* (2002), where the Court of Appeal found that on the facts of the case, no protection for a media source need be given. In *R (on the application of Gillan) v Commissioner of Metropolitan Police* (2006), the House of Lords found that, assuming that **Arts 8** and **10** were applicable, the exceptions under them were satisfied, without engaging in any proportionality analysis. The Strasbourg Court in contrast found a breach of **Art 8** when the case of *Gillan* reached it – *Gillan v UK* (2010).

Apart from the express exceptions to **Arts 8–11**, Strasbourg's interpretation of the reach of the guarantee may leave gaps or uncertainties as to the protection it offers. Now that the **ECHR** has been incorporated and the interpretative jurisprudence of the ECtHR is being used in domestic cases as a guide (**s 2** of the **HRA**), such exceptions or gaps are tending to offer judges a means of avoiding a controversial conflict with the Government, especially in the national security sphere (see, for example, the case of *Secretary of State for the Home Dept v MB* (2007)). Lord Bingham has made it clear that **Convention** rights should be interpreted domestically to offer as much as the Strasbourg jurisprudence accepts (*Ullah* (2004)). The domestic courts have succeeded in finding exceptions even to rights that appear to be largely unqualified, such as **Art 6(1)**: this was evident in *Brown v Stott* (2001) and in *Alconbury* (2001). They have done so by relying on a case at Strasbourg, *Sporrong and Lonnroth v Sweden* (1982), in which it was said that the search for a balance between individual rights and societal concerns is fundamental to the whole **Convention**. Thus, it may be argued that the domestic judiciary has explored methods of watering down the rights, that arguably would not be so readily available under a tailor-made Bill of Rights, if the provision appearing to 'anchor' the judges to Strasbourg, **s 2 HRA**, was weakened.[3]

....

3   This analysis of **s 2 HRA** shows the examiner you are able to critically consider the law.

However, the judges do have an important function under the **HRA** in giving primacy to the rights, even if, eventually, an exception to a particular right is allowed to prevail. The Strasbourg jurisprudence and the rights themselves make it clear that the exceptions are to be narrowly construed and that the starting point is always the primary right. This is in contrast to the previous position, in which the judges in some instances merely applied the statute in question (e.g. the **Public Order Act 1986**) without affording much or any recognition to the freedoms it affected. For instance, **Art 14** has had an impact on the forms of discrimination that are unlawful in situations where another **Convention** right or freedom is engaged (*Ghaidan v Mendoza* (2004), *A and Ors v Secretary of State for the Home Dept* (2004)). Strasbourg gave a lead to the UK judges in *A v UK* (2009), granting greater protection for fair trial rights than the domestic judges had done. Thus, curbing the impact of the Strasbourg jurisprudence in a new Bill of Rights would not necessarily lead to enhanced protection for rights since the judges might revert to their traditional deferential stance.

A tailor-made Bill of Rights could contain a more extensive list of rights, including social and economic rights, although it is unlikely that such rights would appeal to a Conservative-dominated government. In particular, it could include a free-standing anti-discrimination guarantee.[4] **Article 14** of the **ECHR** prohibits discrimination on 'any ground such as sex, race, colour, language, religion', but only in relation to any other **Convention** right or freedom. It has been determined in a string of Strasbourg cases since *X v Federal Republic of Germany* (1970) that **Art 14** has no separate existence, but that, nevertheless, a measure that is, in itself, in conformity with the requirement of the **Convention** right governing its field of law may, however, infringe that Article when it is read in conjunction with **Art 14**, for the reason that it is discriminatory in nature.

The **HRA** itself has limitations in terms of enhanced human rights protection. The choice of the **HRA** as the enforcement mechanism for the **ECHR** means that the **Convention** is incorporated into domestic law, but not entrenched on the US model; thus, it could be removed by the simple method of repeal of the **HRA**, as argued for currently by the Conservative Party. Moreover, the judiciary cannot strike down incompatible legislation. Entrenchment was rejected in order to maintain parliamentary sovereignty and to avoid handing over too much power to the unelected judiciary. This means that Parliament can deliberately legislate in breach of the **Convention** (**ss 19** and **3(2)**), and the incompatible legislation will be effective (**s 6(2)**). It also means that if prior or subsequent legislation is found to breach the **Convention** in the courts and cannot be rescued from doing so by a creative interpretation under **s 3**, it must simply be applied (see *H v Mental Health Tribunal, North and East London Region and Anor* (2001)), although a declaration of the incompatibility can be made under **s 4**, as it was in that instance. In *R(M) v Secretary of*

---

4   Hypothesising about future matters shows the examiner that you have confidence and ownership of the law, such as is demonstrated here by exploring what a Bill of Rights could contain.

State for Health (2003), a declaration of incompatibility was made in relation to **ss 26 and 29 Mental Health Act 1983**, but by 2007, the Government had failed to introduce remedial legislation.

The key provisions of the **Anti-Terrorism, Crime and Security Act 2001 Pt 4** were declared incompatible with **Arts 5** and **14** of the **ECHR** (protecting the rights to liberty and to freedom from discrimination) by the House of Lords in *A and Ors v Secretary of State for the Home Dept* (2004) in relation to persons detained under **Pt 4**. The Government bowed to the pressure and repealed **Pt 4**. However, the decision of the Lords did not lead to the opening of the gates of Belmarsh Prison; the Government continued for a time to rely on the incompatible legislative provisions to imprison the detainees. There was no guarantee that the Government would act to repeal the provisions. It is clear that citizens cannot always be certain of being able to rely on their **Convention** rights domestically. An entrenched Bill of Rights accompanied by a strike-down power on the US model could provide them with that certainty and, at the sacrifice of parliamentary sovereignty as traditionally understood in the UK, could therefore deliver an enhanced degree of rights protection. (It could be pointed out that there were advantages in incorporating the **Convention** as opposed to introducing a domestic instrument. In particular, if a right is violated here, since primary legislation mandates the violation, the possibility of recourse to Strasbourg is afforded encouragement.) However, a Bill of Rights need not be entrenched and it is perhaps unlikely that the Coalition Government would adopt this more radical model in relation to a new Bill of Rights.

The use of **ss 3** and **6 HRA** as the means of affording the **Convention** further effect in domestic law means that there are inherent limitations to the rights protection that the **HRA** offers. If no statute is applicable in a particular instance, and the rights-infringing body does not have a 'public function' under **s 6**, a citizen cannot obtain legal protection for his or her **Convention** right, unless there is an existing common law cause of action that can be utilised (*Campbell* (2004)). Further, even if the citizen could probably obtain redress at Strasbourg in the particular circumstances (see *Kay v Lambeth London Borough Council; Leeds City Council v Price* (2006)), redress can be denied domestically if a House of Lords precedent stands in the way.

In reaching a conclusion on the question posed, it should be borne in mind that the **ECHR** was never intended to be used as a domestic Bill of Rights. If a Bill of Rights was introduced in the UK, then it would be brought into line with the experience of most of the other European signatories. These states already possess codes of rights enshrined in their constitutions, but the majority also adhere to a general practice of incorporation of the **ECHR** into domestic law, either automatically, as in Switzerland, or upon ratification, as in Luxembourg. A domestic Bill of Rights intended to enshrine the **Convention** rights, but include certain rights of a specifically UK character, such as a right of jury trial, could potentially cure some of the gaps, defects and inadequacies of the **ECHR** and the **HRA**. However, given the unpopularity of the **ECHR** as far as the Conservative Party is concerned, it may be more likely ultimately, depending on the detail of the new Bill of Rights, that protection for rights is somewhat weakened, rather than enhanced.

QUESTION 41

To what extent do courts in the UK have to follow decisions of the European Court of Human Rights in Strasbourg?

How to Answer this Question

This question requires a detailed working knowledge of **s 2** of the **Human Rights Act 1998**. The key to successfully answering this question is to first of all set out what **s 2** says and does, and then to critically discuss some important cases that have used **s 2**. A good way to structure an answer to this question is set out in the diagram below.

Answer Structure

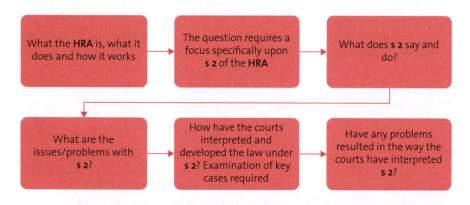

| What the **HRA** is, what it does and how it works | → | The question requires a focus specifically upon **s 2** of the **HRA** | → | What does **s 2** say and do? |

| What are the issues/problems with **s 2**? | → | How have the courts interpreted and developed the law under **s 2**? Examination of key cases required | → | Have any problems resulted in the way the courts have interpreted **s 2**? |

Aim Higher ★

If you are able to show a practical understanding of what **section 2** is and its purpose in human rights' protection in UK law then you will be able to impress the examiner.

Common Pitfalls ✗

Weaker answers will not engage with case-law.

ANSWER

The purpose of the **Human Rights Act 1998** (**HRA**) was to incorporate most of the **European Convention on Human Rights** (**Convention**) rights into domestic law. This made those rights legally enforceable in UK courts for the first time. This meant that people in the UK could rely upon the **Convention** rights in UK courts rather than only being able to argue them in the European Court of Human Rights. Some of the key provisions in the **HRA** which set out the mechanisms for how it works are contained in **ss 2, 3, 4** and **6**. This essay is only going to focus upon **s 2** as it sets out the duty of UK courts to follow the decisions of the European Court of Human Rights (ECtHR).

Section 2 of the **HRA** states that UK courts 'must take into account' decisions of the ECtHR and other relevant bodies when they are dealing with a case that concerns a **Convention** right. The key phrase here is 'must take into account'. The 'must' is very clear; it is a positive duty. The 'take into account' is problematic though as what does that mean? Does it mean the court can look at decisions of the ECtHR if it wants to? If it likes them? And not to do so if it doesn't want to? How far does this duty go?[5] That is the essence of the question that has been asked and this essay will seek to answer these questions.

In order to determine how onerous this duty is upon UK courts a detailed examination of case-law is needed as that will illustrate how the UK courts have defined **s 2** and how far reaching it is. One of the first important cases on **s 2** was *R (Alconbury Developments) v Secretary of State for the Environment, Transport and the Regions* (2001). Lord Hoffman said that whilst they were not strictly bound by the decisions of the ECtHR, in the absence of special circumstances they were under a duty to follow any clear and constant jurisprudence of the ECtHR.

In *R v Secretary of State for the Home Department, ex parte Anderson* (2002), Lord Bingham said that while the House of Lords were not strictly bound to follow the ECtHR they would not without good reason depart from decisions of the Grand Chamber of the ECtHR. This comment shows that the judiciary in the highest UK court do not feel bound by the ECtHR but that it will follow their decisions unless there is a good reason not to.[6] What exactly would or would not amount to a 'good reason' is open to interpretation. This is a similar sentiment to what Lord Hoffman referred to in the *Alconbury* case as 'special circumstances' which would need to exist for the UK courts not to follow the ECtHR.

In another key case called *R (Ullah) v Special Adjudicator* (2004), the court re-affirmed the principle set out in *Alconbury* and said the reason for doing so is that the **Convention** is an international instrument, and as such the correct and best interpretation of it is by the ECtHR which is the international body set up to interpret and apply the **Convention**. Lord Bingham in *Ullah* went on to say that UK courts should not without good reason weaken

---

5   It is acceptable to raise questions, such as these ones about **s 2 HRA**, as long as you answer them. It helps to provide the examiner with some structure.

6   This brief analysis of the *Anderson* case demonstrates that you can easily add in analysis after you have described some law.

or dilute decisions of the ECtHR. Another interesting justification by the UK courts for endorsing such an approach is that under **s 6 HRA** the UK courts are under a positive legal duty not to act incompatibly with **Convention** rights, and if they failed to follow the ECtHR then they may be breaching this duty as well. Lord Bingham also said that the UK could give more generous meanings to the **Convention** as given by the ECtHR, but he warned against such actions, saying that a uniform approach between signatory states was more desirable. His ultimate conclusion was what has become known as the 'mirror principle': that the UK should keep pace with decisions of the ECtHR over time; no more, but no less.

Some very interesting comments were given, again by Lord Hoffman, in *Secretary of State for the Home Department v AF and another* (2009). The case concerned the use of secret evidence in terrorism law. The House of Lords had previously given judgment on the relevant law. Subsequent to that the ECtHR had given a conflicting judgment in the case of *A v UK* (2009). So the question before the court in the *AF* case was what should they do? Should they follow their own previous ruling or change their mind and follow the later ruling of the ECtHR? Lord Hoffman's comments were significant in elucidating upon the judiciary's interpretation of **s 2** of the **HRA** as he said that the UK court disagreed with the ECtHR on this legal point, but given their ruling in *A v UK* the UK court were bound to follow their ruling, even though they disagreed with it. He said that even though **s 2 HRA** does not strictly bind the UK courts to ECtHR decisions he said the UK was bound by the **Convention** in international law so they reluctantly felt they had to follow the ECtHR and they duly did so. These comments were significant inasmuch as they show the UK court disagreeing with the ECtHR on a point of law but nevertheless they felt bound to follow them. This is a huge statement and illustration of the impact of **s 2 HRA**.

Further interesting comments in relation to **s 2 HRA** were given in *R v Horncastle & others* (2009). The case concerned the use of hearsay evidence and whether someone's conviction which was based largely or solely on such evidence breached their **Art 6 Convention** right to a fair trial as they may be unable to cross-examine the evidence in court. The Supreme Court believed that this would not breach **Art 6** of the **Convention**. One argument the Supreme Court were faced with was that a ECtHR decision in *Al-Khawaja* (2009) had previously ruled that such convictions would breach **Art 6**. The applicants in the case argued that the Supreme Court were bound by the ECtHR and should follow the approach the House of Lords took in the *AF* case discussed earlier. Lord Phillips rejected this argument and said that the UK courts will not follow the ECtHR if they believe the ECtHR has misunderstood, or essentially made an error, in relation to UK law. He said there will be exceptional cases where this happens and in such cases the UK courts needed to stand their own ground and this may persuade the ECtHR to re-examine the issues and change their mind in the future. Lord Phillips said that this was such a case. Subsquent to this, the Grand Chamber of the ECtHR in *Al-Khawaja* (2011) did change its mind and was persuaded by the Supreme Court's elucidation of UK law and ruled that there was no breach of **Art 6** of the **Convention**. This case was extremely important and significant in illustrating not only the limits of **s 2** of the **HRA** but also the benefit of the constructive dialogue that can ensue between the institutions as a result.

In the Supreme Court, Lord Neuberger in *Manchester City Council v Pinnock & others* (2010) reaffirmed that the UK courts would always follow the ECtHR unless it was clear that the ECtHR principles were inconsistent with some fundamental basics of UK law and the UK courts believed that the ECtHR misunderstood or were wrong about the law on such points. This case concerned the application of **Art 8** of the **Convention** principles in relation to possession proccedings by a landlord over a tenant. This essentially sums up all the previous comments from the UK judiciary in relation to **s 2 HRA** and is in accord with the application of **s 2** over time. It may perhaps be thought that the exception to this principle is the decision of the House of Lords in the *AF* case discussed above, where Lord Hoffman felt bound by the ECtHR even though he felt they were wrong. This clearly goes against the comments from cases such as *Pinnock* and Horncastle and seems out of place alongside them. However, the decision in *A v UK* (2009) which the House of Lords felt bound by in *AF* was a Grand Chamber decision of the ECtHR and the decision in *Al-Khawaja* (2009) which the Supreme Court refused to follow in *Horncastle* was not a Grand Chamber judgment, so it is important to bear in mind this crucial distinction.[7] The UK courts have often said that they will follow clear principles laid out by a Grand Chamber judgment, so the decision in *AF* may not be as out of place with the other decisions as may appear at first glance.

Two interesting cases which look at the issue of what is the extent of the duty upon UK courts to interpret and apply the **Convention** where the ECtHR has not yet expounded principles in a particular area are *Ambrose v Harris* (2011) and *Rabone v Pennine Care NHS Trust* (2012).

In *Rabone* the Supreme Court were asked to consider the extent of the duty upon health care providers in relation to voluntary patients under **Art 2** of the **Convention**. They decided that providers could be under a duty under **Art 2** in certain circumstances. In *Ambrose* the Supreme Court were asked to consider whether **Art 6** of the **Convention** was breached in relation to comments made by a suspect prior to being questioned by the police and prior to having legal assistance. The Court found no breach of **Art 6**. In *Rabone* Lord Brown looked at the comments from the court in *Ullah* discussed above and he had something to say about the 'mirror principle'. He agreed that UK courts could not offer a lower standard of protection to **Convention** right than the ECtHR, but where the ECtHR is silent on a particular matter, then he felt the UK courts should give protection to **Convention** rights and so in effect go beyond what the ECtHR has ruled up to that point – otherwise there would be a gap in protection. In *Ambrose* Lord Kerr went even

---

7   Such distinctions like this about which court made the decisions would be missed if you had not read the judgments properly. Details like this are picked up by the examiner.

further than this and said that UK courts were under a positive duty to give protection to **Convention** rights in areas where the ECtHR has not ruled upon it. Lord Brown in *Rabone* also said that UK courts should feel able to reject ECtHR decisions where they are reluctant to follow them, unless it is an authoritative decision of a Grand Chamber of the ECtHR on that specific point of law, in which case the UK courts must follow such a decision. These comments are therefore quite different to what was stated in *Ullah* and go much further.[8]

After exploring some key cases in the interpretation and application of **s 2** of the **HRA** it can be said that the UK courts are under a very strong duty to follow clear and authoritative decisions of the Grand Chamber of the ECtHR. Where decisions of the ECtHR have not been made by the Grand Chamber, then UK should also follow them, but only if they are clear and consistent and are not at odds with fundamental aspects of UK law and where the UK courts are sure that the ECtHR has understood UK law correctly. If the UK courts are not satisfied these qualities are present within decisions of the ECtHR then they should feel able to refuse to follow such decisions. That appears to be a reasonable interpretation of **s 2 HRA** so far.

QUESTION 42

Critically evaluate the provisions of the **Human Rights Act 1998** which are intended to ensure that legislation is compatible with the **European Convention on Human Rights**, and comment on their impact in practice.

How to Answer this Question

This is a question which requires a sound knowledge of **ss 3, 4** and **10**, and **Scheds 2** and **19** of the **Human Rights Act (HRA) 1998**, of some of the academic criticism generated by those provisions and of certain key cases. Close analysis of those provisions of the Act, which are in some respects quite technical, is required. This is a question which is highly likely to be set at the present time. Note that the question does not require you to consider the efficacy of the **ECHR** itself or the implications of receiving it into UK law. Also, it deliberately focuses on **s 3** and the related provisions; it does not ask you to discuss the definition of a public authority under **s 6**.

The following matters should be discussed:

- ❖ the interpretative obligation under **s 3**: its use in practice so far in key cases; *Ghaidan v Mendoza, R v A, Bellinger v Bellinger, SSHD v AF*;
- ❖ the declarations of incompatibility under **s 4**: their use in practice in key cases;
- ❖ the 'fast track' procedure under **s 10** and **Sched 2**;

----

8   It is really important to get in analysis as this does here about the recent cases in the area. Such analysis helps to lift your answer to achieve higher marks.

❖   the impact of the Act in Parliament on post-HRA legislation – s 19;

❖   evaluation of the efficacy of this aspect of the HRA scheme.

Answer Structure

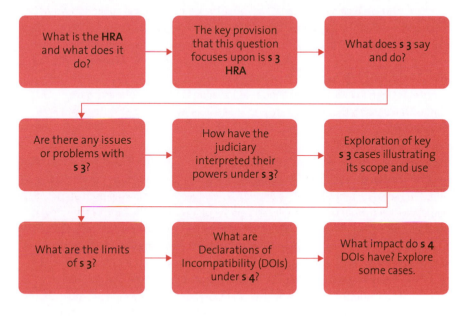

ANSWER

The **Human Rights Act (HRA) 1998** is of immense constitutional significance. The Act provides further protection for the **European Convention on Human Rights** in UK law. Once it came fully into force in 2000, UK citizens had, for the first time, human rights (in the sense of rights which may be claimed against public authorities) instead of liberties: instead of having residual freedoms they had, from 2000 onwards, guarantees of rights.

Under **s 3(1)**, primary and subordinate legislation must be given effect in a manner which makes it compatible with the **ECHR** rights; the judiciary is under an obligation to ensure such compatibility 'so far as it is possible to do so'. This goes well beyond resolving ambiguity in statutory provisions by adopting the **ECHR**-based interpretation which, of course, was already occurring in the pre-**HRA** era. As interpreted in the key post-**HRA** cases, including in particular *Ghaidan v Mendoza* (2004), *R v A* (2001), *Bellinger v Bellinger* (2003), **s 3** appears to place the judiciary under an obligation to render legislation compatible with the **ECHR** if there is any loophole at all allowing it to do so. However, they will only take a radical approach to the use of **s 3** where, as Kavanagh argues, that appears to them to be appropriate.[9]

9   This paragraph neatly summarises the mechanics of **s 3** HRA and provides some useful authority.

It is now apparent that **s 3(1)** of the **HRA** allows judges to read words into statutes (*R v A* (2001), *Ghaidan v Mendoza* (2004)) or to adopt a broad or doubtful interpretation; in *Cachia v Faluyi* (2001), the Court of Appeal held that 'action' in **s 2(3)** of the **Fatal Accidents Act 1976** should be construed as 'served process'. In *Secretary of State for the Home Department ex p Aleksejs Zenovics* (2002), the Court of Appeal added the words 'in respect of that claim' in the **Immigration and Asylum Act 1999** to the end of the provision in question. **Section 3(1)** does not, however, allow for wholesale revision of the statute: *Re S and W (Care Orders)* (2002); *Donaghue v Poplar Housing* (2001). In other words, the changes must not oppose a pervasive feature of the statute (*Anderson* (2003)). This stance was taken in *Re S and Re W* (2002); as Kavanagh argues, the courts have demonstrated that although they are prepared to read words into statutes, as in *R v A*, they will not do so, 'as a way of radically reforming a whole statute'.[10]

The judges may also be reluctant to read in words where the provisions themselves offer no reasonably ready 'avenue' to so doing. Even where such an avenue is available, the judges may be reluctant to use it. In *Bellinger v Bellinger* (2003), as Phillipson argues, it would have been more than possible, as a matter of linguistics, to interpret the single word 'female' as including a 'female' who had arrived at that gender as a result of human intervention (i.e. a post-operative transsexual). Nevertheless, the House of Lords refused to reinterpret the word in the way suggested, taking into account a range of what were essentially policy matters – the far-reaching practical effects of the change. Also Parliament had indicated that it would legislate on the subject. Kavanagh argues that the judges will take a radical approach to **s 3** where otherwise the person seeking to rely on the right in question would be left remediless, as would have occurred in *Ghaidan*. Thus, it is clear that the judges are prepared – where they view it as appropriate, taking account of the factors indicated – to use the powerful interpretative tool of **s 3(1)** to its fullest extent, even if this means twisting or ignoring the natural meaning of the statutory words or, most dramatically, reading words into statutory provisions. Thus, the judges have in some instances adopted a role which is close to a legislative one. Possibly, in so doing, they have pushed the interpretative obligation under **s 3** too far, as in *R v A*, and in that instance should instead have issued a declaration of incompatibility under **s 4**.

Section 3(2) provides that this interpretative obligation does not affect the validity, continuing operation or enforcement of any incompatible primary legislation. Thus, the **ECHR** cannot be used to strike down any part of an existing statute as unconstitutional. This is clearly an important limitation. It means that parliamentary sovereignty is at least theoretically preserved, since prior and subsequent legislation which cannot be rendered compatible with the **ECHR** cannot be struck down due to its incompatibility by the judiciary.

....

10   This passage effectively explores a series of cases about how far courts can go when using **s 3** **HRA**. A good grasp of the law like this is essential to obtaining good marks from the examiner.

If a court cannot render a statutory provision compatible with the **ECHR**, despite its best efforts, the claimant wishing to rely on the right will have to suffer a breach of his/her **Convention** rights for a period of time. This is clearly unsatisfactory; the solution chosen by the Labour Government was to include **ss 4** and **10** and **Sched 2** in the Act. **Section 4** allows certain higher courts to make a declaration of incompatibility, while **s 10** and **Sched 2** allow for a 'fast track' procedure, whereby a Minister may by order, approved by both Houses of Parliament, amend the offending primary or subordinate legislation if there are compelling reasons to do so. A number of comments may be made on this procedure. In general, executive amendation of legislation is objectionable. However, Parliamentary scrutiny of the order is provided for under **Sched 2**; Parliament will normally have 60 days to consider the order before voting on it, although in urgent cases the order can come into effect immediately, subject to later approval by both Houses. Further, the usual objections to such a procedure are arguably inapplicable since the order is intended to bring UK law into harmony with the **ECHR**, thereby raising the standard of human rights often at the expense, in effect of the executive.

Other objections to this procedure are less easily overcome. The Minister is under no obligation to make the amendment(s) and may only do so if there are 'compelling' reasons. In other words, the fact that a declaration of incompatibility has been made is not, in itself, a compelling reason. Thus, there may be periods of uncertainty during which citizens cannot rely on aspects of their **Convention** rights.[11] Further, in some instances, a declaration of incompatibility may not be obtained for some time.

Declarations of incompatibility have occurred most frequently in criminal proceedings, or in proceedings relating to State detention, although they have also occurred in civil proceedings. Many cases in which **Convention** rights are invoked in UK courts are criminal ones, or relate to matters of detention, and the question raised tends to concern an aspect of criminal procedure (see *A* (2001) and *Offen* (2001)) or the substantive issue of the right to liberty. Thus **Arts 5** and **6** are frequently invoked since they protect, *inter alia*, a fair criminal trial and the right to liberty of the person. The key provisions of the **Anti-Terrorism, Crime and Security Act 2001 Part 4** were declared incompatible with **Arts 5** and **14** of the **ECHR** (protecting the rights to liberty and to freedom from discrimination) by the House of Lords in *A and Others v Secretary of State for the Home Dept* (2005), in a constitutionally significant, and human rights-oriented decision. The Government responded by repealing **Part 4**, under the **Prevention of Terrorism Act 2005**. The **2005 Act** introduced control orders, but the process for imposing them itself had to be improved under **Art 3 HRA** to comply with **Art 6** (*SSHD v AF* (2009)).

In *H v North and East Region Mental Health Tribunal* (2001) a declaration was made in relation to **ss 72** and **73 Mental Health Act 1983**, on the basis that they infringed **Art 5(1)**

----

11   Try and get some analysis in along the way wherever possible, no matter how small. This comment upon a problem with declarations serves such a purpose.

and **(4)** of the **ECHR** since they placed the burden of proof on the patient to prove that he/she was not suffering from mental illness and so should no longer be detained. In response, the Government used its power under **s 10** to make a remedial order, amending the **1983 Act**.

It might appear that declarations of incompatibility in civil proceedings, especially those between private parties, would be less likely to occur, although if a statute affects the legal relations between private individuals (for example, employment statutes which cover private companies and their employees), **ss 3** and **4** apply. But **Convention** issues giving rise to the possibility of a declaration of incompatibility are arising in civil proceedings, either substantively under, for example, **Art 8** (*Re S and W (Care Orders) (2002)*) or procedurally under **Art 6(1)** as in *Alconbury* and in *Wilson (2003)*. *Wilson* concerned two private parties, one a large company.[12]

One problem is that if a statute governing part of the civil law is found in a lower court to be incompatible with the **ECHR**, the claimant or defendant is denied a remedy, even if their **Convention** rights have been breached.

The key weakness of this scheme might appear to be that the Government might not be willing to bring forward a remedial order under **s 10**. However, the last Labour Government in general showed a willingness to respond to declarations by bringing forward remedial legislation.

Under **s 19**, when a Minister introduces a Bill into either House of Parliament, he must make and publish a written statement to the effect either that, in his view, the provisions of the Bill are compatible with the **ECHR** rights, or that although he is unable to make such a statement, the Government wishes nevertheless to proceed with the Bill. So far, all legislation passed post-**HRA**, apart from the **Communications Act 2003**, has been accompanied by a statement of its compatibility with the rights.

In conclusion, it may be said that for the reasons discussed, the impact of the **HRA** is being realised slowly in practice. Nevertheless, it represents a radical change in the traditional means of protecting civil liberties. It has become much less likely that legislation will be introduced which has the clear effect of limiting a liberty, since such legislation might eventually be declared incompatible with the guarantees of rights under the Act (**s 4**). If such legislation is introduced, the relevant minister has to declare that a statement of compatibility cannot be made under **s 19** – something that ministers are clearly reluctant to do due to the political embarrassment which is created. The fact that only one statute has not been declared compatible with the **ECHR** indicates that this is the case. Even

---

12   This paragraph about perceived problems in civil cases demonstrates to the examiner an ability to critically consider the law and to use authority to back up such critique.

future governments less sympathetic to the **ECHR** would probably be deterred thereby from an obvious infringement of the **ECHR** guarantees. Similarly, existing legislative protection for a **Convention** right is unlikely to be repealed, since a citizen might then challenge breaches of the right under **s7(1)(a)**, so long as the right was one exercisable against a public authority. Thus, the Act, despite its complexities and limitations, represents a break with previous legislative tradition; due to the operation of **s3**, it is creating a much greater awareness in the judiciary of fundamental human rights issues. But while the operation of **s3** has had this laudable effect, it may also be argued that the judiciary should bear in mind the mechanisms of the **HRA** which were supposed to preserve parliamentary sovereignty – **ss3(2)** and **4** – and show a greater preparedness to use them. Determination to use **s3** rather than **s4** is understandable, but it keeps decisions as to what is needed in order to ensure compatibility in the hands of the judiciary.

QUESTION 43

Critically examine the implications of introducing the **Human Rights Act 1998** as the UK's human rights guarantee, giving consideration to the interpretations of **ss3** and **6** in recent cases.

How to Answer this Question

This is a reasonably straightforward essay question, which is commonly set. However, it is important that the answer should not degenerate into a list of advantages and disadvantages of the **Human Rights Act (HRA) 1998** and the **European Convention on Human Rights (ECHR)**. The implications include: a comparison with the previous situation; the changed role of judges; the impact on public authorities; the change that may be caused by **s3** in relation to interpretation of statutory provisions that raise human rights issues. A number of the significant decisions on **ss3** and **6** must be examined, indicating how far the **HRA**'s protection for the **ECHR** rights has been enhanced or diminished by them. One further implication, which should be touched on briefly, is the choice of the **HRA** mechanism as opposed to the introduction of a Bill of Rights on the US model. This has pertinence, given David Cameron's (Leader of the Conservative Party) expressed predilection for a 'British Bill of Rights', possibly to be introduced around 2013/14, although of course it would be unlikely that it would be modelled on the US Constitution.

The following matters should be discussed:

- ❖ the comparison with the pre-**HRA** position with examples of statutory provisions;
- ❖ the impact of the Act on post-**HRA** legislation – **s19**;
- ❖ the interpretative obligation under **s3** – recent case law, giving examples of its use in practice;
- ❖ the change in the judicial role;
- ❖ the impact on public authorities of **s6**; relevant **HRA** case law;

❖   the choice of the **HRA** mechanism, as opposed to entrenching the **ECHR**;

❖   an interim evaluation of the implications of relying on the **HRA** as the UK's
     human rights guarantee.

Answer Structure

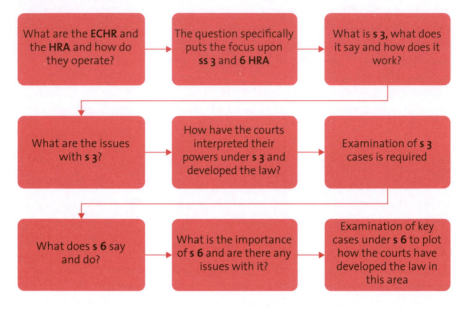

ANSWER

Until 1998, the precarious and disorderly state of civil liberties and human rights in the UK
created a strong argument in favour of the adoption of some form of Bill of Rights. The law
sought to protect certain values, such as the need to maintain public order but, in doing so,
curtailed the exercise of certain freedoms because nothing prevented it from disregarding
them. Thus, human rights (recognised as 'liberties' in the UK) had a precarious status, in
that they only existed, by deduction, in the interstices of the law. For example, the **Public
Order Act 1986** contains extensive provisions in **ss 12** and **14** that allow stringent conditions
to be imposed on marches and assemblies. They are not balanced by any provision in the
1986 Act that takes account of the need to protect freedom of assembly.

This essay will argue that the **ECHR**, as afforded further effect in domestic law by the
Human Rights Act (HRA) 1998, appears to provide a better safeguard than the previous
reliance placed upon executive reluctance to use rights-infringing provisions to the full.[13]
In contrast to the previous situation, the **HRA** now represents a minimum guarantee of

---

13   Do have the confidence to highlight what your conclusions are going to be early on. This reference to the
     success of the **HRA** helps the examiner know what is coming and serves as a useful structural technique.

freedom. The **HRA** allows Parliament to pass legislation incompatible with the **Convention** rights (see **s19(1)(b), s6(2)** and **s3(2)**), but it is notable that so far in the first decade of the **HRA** only one Bill has been presented to Parliament unaccompanied by a statement of its compatibility with the rights – the Bill that became the **Communications Act 2003**. Formally speaking, citizens of the UK post-**HRA** no longer have to rely upon the ruling party to ensure that its own legislation does not infringe freedoms. They can at least be sure that the Government has made some effort to ensure that a Bill is **Convention**-compliant before it becomes an Act of Parliament. If, despite the statement of compatibility under **s19 HRA**, statutory provisions are passed that conflict with some fundamental **Convention** guarantee, courts now have to interpret such provisions in order to bring them into compliance with the **Convention** if at all possible under **s3** of the **HRA** (see *R v A (No 2)* (2001)). They must also do so in respect of pre-**HRA** statutes.

In satisfying the obligation under **s3** they must take account of **ECHR** jurisprudence under **s2**, to determine to what extent, if at all, the rights may justifiably be curtailed and decide whether the provision in question goes further in curtailing a right than can be justified. **Section 3** goes well beyond resolving ambiguity in legislation in favour of the **Convention**-compliant interpretation and has received a fairly generous interpretation in the courts (see *Ghaidan v Mendoza* (2004)). Under **s3 HRA**, words can even be read into a statute in order to achieve **Convention** compliance (*Ghaidan* and *R v A*), so long as the changes do not oppose a pervasive feature of the statute (*R (on the application of Anderson) v Secretary of State for the Home Dept* (2002)). This stance was taken in *Re S and Re W* (2002); as Kavanagh argues, the courts demonstrated that although they are prepared to read words into statutes, as in *R v A*, they will not do so, 'as a way of radically reforming a whole statute'. The position under **s3** is in strong contrast to the prior situation, where the courts had no choice but to apply a provision of an Act of Parliament, no matter how much it might breach the **Convention** if it unambiguously expressed Parliament's intention to allow such a breach.

If, having striven to achieve compatibility under **s3**, it is found to be impossible, a court of sufficient seniority can issue a declaration of incompatibility (**s4**), although it will merely have to go on to apply the law in question (see *H v Mental Health Tribunal, North and East London Region and Another* (2001)). If a court does issue a declaration of incompatibility, the Government has so far accepted that it should act promptly to take remedial action – although it does not have to do so (**s10**).

Apart from its implications for legislation, public authorities have been greatly affected by the inception of the **HRA** due to the requirements of **s6**. Under **s6**, it is unlawful for a public authority to act in a way that is incompatible with a **Convention** right. This is the main provision giving effect to the **Convention** rights; rather than full 'incorporation' of the **Convention**, it is made binding against public authorities. In stark contrast to the previous situation, such bodies act illegally if they fail to abide by the **Convention** rights. Previously, unless forced impliedly to adhere to a particular right legislatively (for example, under **s 58** of the **Police and Criminal Evidence Act 1984**, imposing on the police, in effect, a duty to abide by one of the implied rights within **Art 6(1)**), or under the common law, they could disregard the rights in their day-to-day operations with impunity.[14]

Under **s 6**, public authorities are either 'core' or 'functional'; if the latter, they are only bound by the **Convention** in relation to their public, not their private, functions. The division between functional public authorities and purely private bodies remains one of the most controversial and difficult matters under the **HRA**.[15] Obviously its resolution has very strong human rights implications since a person affected by a rights-infringing action of a private body has no cause of action under the **HRA, s 7**. One of the early leading decisions on this matter was *Poplar Housing & Regeneration Community Association Ltd v Donoghue* (2001). Poplar was set up by Tower Hamlets as a registered social landlord specifically for the purpose of receiving its housing stock. Poplar claimed, *inter alia*, that it was neither a standard public authority (which the Court of Appeal accepted) nor a body performing a function of a public nature. As to this latter point, Lord Woolf said that an act can be 'public' for **HRA** purposes where a combination of features is present. Statutory authority for what is done can help to mark the act as being public; so can the extent of control over the function exercised by another body that is a public authority. The Court found that Poplar *was* exercising a public function in relation to the management of the social housing it had taken over from Tower Hamlets because it was so closely associated with Tower Hamlets, a core public authority.

Where no public function has been transferred, the question appears to be whether the function in question should be viewed as inherently private or public, not whether the body in question is a private or public institution (*Parochial Council of the Parish of Aston* (2003)). Focusing on the function rather than the institution is a more generous means of delimiting the concept of a public authority, and therefore may allow for a wider protection for the **Convention** rights.

A functional approach was adopted in *YL v Birmingham CC* (2007) in relation to the question of whether a private care home was a functional public authority. The majority in the Lords noted that the local authority's activities were carried out pursuant to statutory duties and responsibilities imposed by public law and the costs of doing so were met from public funds. In the case of a privately owned care home, it was noted, the manager's duties to its residents were, whether contractual or tortious, duties governed by private law. In relation to those residents who were publicly funded, the local and health authorities became liable to pay charges agreed under private law contracts and for the recovery of which the care home had private law remedies. The recovery by the

---

14   This analysis of **s 6 HRA** shows the examiner you understand the area well.

15   Such difficulties, as this one in relation to **s 6 HRA**, are not uncommon. It takes confident knowledge of the area to state this and examiners will notice this.

local authority of a means-tested contribution from the resident was a matter of public law, but was no concern of the care home. On this basis, the House of Lords held, by a 3:2 majority, that private care homes were not discharging a public function and so were not bound by the **European Convention on Human Rights**, even when looking after clients on behalf of a local authority. That was the view of Lords Scott, Mance and Neuberger. Lord Bingham and Baroness Hale dissented. Thus the *YL* case, now the leading authority, gave a restricted meaning to the term 'public function' under the **HRA**, meaning that many people cannot rely on **Convention** rights directly against a range of bodies. Prior to the *YL* case, the Joint Committee on Human Rights[16] was quite fierce in its criticisms of the approach taken by the courts in its interpretation of **s 6**, which effectively reduced human rights protection and coverage of the Act. As a result of the *YL* case, Parliament lost patience with the courts and passed the **Health and Social Care Act 2008**, **s 145** of which specifically states that certain care providers are public authorities for the purposes of **s 6**. Whilst this does offer some clarity in the area, this is restricted to care providers.

Despite this limitation, the **HRA** has created a far more active judicial role in protecting basic rights and freedoms. The open-ended nature of the terms of the **Convention** means that its interpretation is likely to continue to evolve in accordance with the UK's changing needs and social values as it is interpreted and applied by domestic judges (see *Campbell v MGN* (2004)). Incorporation of the **Convention** under the **HRA** has already had a number of advantages. Citizens may obtain redress for human rights breaches without needing, except as a last resort, to apply to the ECtHR in Strasbourg. This saves a great deal of time and money for the citizen and thus greatly improves access to human rights protection. The range of remedies available under the **HRA** is the same as in any ordinary UK court case (apart from criminal sanctions), and so includes injunctions and specific performance where appropriate, rather than simply damages. British judges are already making a contribution to the development of a domestic **Convention** rights jurisprudence (see, for example, *Lambert* (2001), *Offen* (2001) and *A and others* (2004)).

However, the interpretations given by judges to the **ECHR** have at times diluted its impact greatly. The watering-down of **Art 6** that occurred in *Brown v Stott* (2001) and of **Art 5** in *Gillan* (2006) exemplified this problem. On the other hand, the judges have also shown themselves willing to take an activist stance in protecting the right to liberty: key provisions of the **Anti-Terrorism, Crime and Security Act 2001 Pt 4** were declared incompatible with **Arts 5** and **14** of the **ECHR** (protecting the rights to liberty and to freedom from discrimination) by the House of Lords in *A and Ors v Secretary of State for the Home Dept* (2005), in a constitutionally significant, and human rights-oriented decision.

So far, this essay has indicated that the **HRA** is having an impact on the interpretation of legislation and on the operations of a large number of bodies in the UK. But there are

....

16 This reference to the Joint Select Committee shows the examiner you have undertaken wide research in the area.

limitations on its impact, which the *YL* case has exacerbated. Citizens cannot always be certain of being able to rely on their **Convention** rights domestically.

In conclusion, the **HRA** is allowing for the incremental improvement of the UK's recognition and enforcement of domestic human rights. Certain weaknesses are identifiable within the **HRA 1998** and the **Convention**, but the method chosen is a reasonable compromise between protection for human rights and parliamentary sovereignty.

> ### Common Pitfalls ✘
> Failing to discuss the key cases that determine the meaning of both **s3** and **s6**, especially *Ghaidan* and *YL*.

> ### Aim Higher ★
> It could also be noted that citizens have still at times had to seek a remedy for breach of the **ECHR** at Strasbourg (compare *Gillan* (2006) with *Gillan v UK* (2010)), the very problem that the **HRA** was supposed to address.

QUESTION 44

Critically evaluate the extent to which the **Human Rights Act 1998** is bringing about change in substantive law in the 'civil liberties' field, and the extent to which it is likely to have a further impact. Choose at least three areas of law within that field to comment on.

How to Answer this Question

This is becoming a common type of examination question, although it may appear in many forms. The question is confined to the 'civil liberties' field, and within that field you will have to be selective – and make your selection clear at the outset. In order to answer the question, it is essential that you should be able to explain and evaluate cases on selected rights of the **European Convention on Human Rights (ECHR)**, at Strasbourg and domestically, and further, to predict whether and how far UK law may have to change further in the coming years to reflect the **ECHR** rights and the relevant jurisprudence. Changes that have already occurred should be identified. When a question is phrased as generally as this one, students should avoid the temptation to refer to a long list of instances where domestic law will be likely to be challenged; it is more important to consider instances where domestic law has been challenged, and crucial to include some depth of argument and analysis of the case law. Examiners may also ask students to refer to one or more specific areas of domestic law, such as criminal law and evidence, or to refer to one or more **Convention** rights, such as privacy, expression, discrimination or torture. It is therefore essential that students have detailed knowledge of current issues concerning **Convention** rights and their status in domestic law. If the question is phrased generally, it will be necessary to be selective about the rights referred to in the answer and to make this clear in the introduction.

The following matters must be considered:

❖ the ways in which the **Human Rights Act (HRA) 1998** is able to have an impact on domestic law;

❖ the leading European Court of Human Rights (ECtHR) cases which raise issues about the UK's enforcement of human rights in key areas, for example, privacy, police powers of covert surveillance and freedom of protest;

❖ key aspects of relevant statutes, including the **Anti-Terrorism, Crime and Security Act 2001**, the **Regulation of Investigatory Powers Act 2000**, the **Terrorism Act 2000**, the **Prevention of Terrorism Act 2005** (now repealed), and the **Terrorism Prevention and Investigation Measures Act 2011**;

❖ examination of the current and probable impact of the **HRA** in the areas chosen; key post-**HRA** cases, especially in the terrorism context;

❖ evaluation – the role of domestic courts and Parliament in interpreting and giving effect to the **ECHR** rights.

Answer Structure

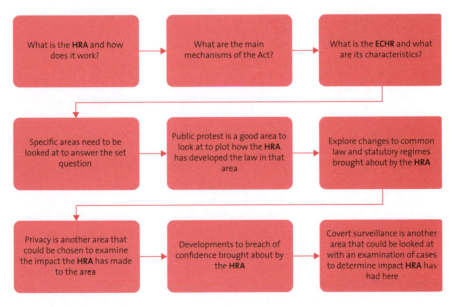

ANSWER

Under **s3** of the **HRA**, many statutes have been opened to rights-based scrutiny; some, such as the **Mental Health Act 1983** have shown themselves to be vulnerable to declarations of incompatibility issued by a higher court under **s4**. A tide of legislation in the civil liberties field apparently designed to be **Convention**-compliant has also been introduced, including, for example, the **Regulation of Investigatory Powers Act 2000**, the **Terrorism Act 2000**, the **Anti-Terrorism, Crime and Security Act 2001** (although **Part 4** required a derogation from **Art 5**) the **Prevention of Terrorism Act 2005** (now repealed) and the **Terrorism Prevention and Investigation Measures Act 2011**. Since October 2000, public authorities within the UK have been under a duty to act in compliance with the **ECHR** (**s 6 HRA**). Since the term 'public authorities' includes the courts, significant changes in UK law have occurred, since the courts must seek to ensure that current common law doctrines are in compliance with the **ECHR** rights, as discussed below.

Courts are being deluged with arguments based on the **ECHR**, and so the existing case law of the ECtHR has become a vital tool for interpretation purposes, although it is not binding (**s 2** of the **HRA**).

It should be remembered that neither the **HRA 1998** nor the **ECHR** takes the stance that human rights are absolute; each instrument has its own exceptions and limitations.[17] The key **HRA** provisions, especially **ss 3(1), 3(2), 6(1)** and **6(2)**, show that it is intended to create a delicate political balance; the rights which it contains only bind public authorities, not private bodies, and public authorities need not abide by the **ECHR** if incompatible primary legislation means that they must act in contravention of the right (**s 6(2)**). Existing legislation which contravenes the rights cannot be rendered automatically invalid by the courts, but can remain in force under **s 3(2)** although a declaration of its incompatibility is made under **s 4**. It would have been possible, although unlikely, for very little change to result from the whole exercise if the Government frequently sought to persuade Parliament to decide to take advantage of its power to legislate contrary to the rights. In fact that has only occurred once – overtly – in relation to the **Communications Act 2003**.

The **Convention** was itself a compromise document which attempted to identify core values applicable in a range of very different signatory countries: it contains no overtly economic and social rights; a number of the rights it does contain have exceptions for such matters as national security and the prevention of crime (**Arts 8–11**). **Article 14** can only operate within the ambit of another **Convention** right. The doctrine of the 'margin of appreciation' has traditionally allowed a significant leeway to States as regards the means and methods of upholding rights (*Otto-Preminger*, *Handyside*). In spite of these and other limitations, it is, however, possible to predict many fields of law which will require at least re-evaluation in the light of **Convention** rights. Since the potential areas of change in the 'civil liberties' field are so many and varied, the current and future impact on three will be examined here: privacy; police powers of surveillance; and freedom of public protest.

---

17   Insightful comments, such as this in relation to the **HRA** and **ECHR**, will impress the examiner (as long as they are correct) as it takes knowledge to make such comments.

In the field of public protest it is now clear, due to the **HRA**, that the **ECHR, Arts 10** and **11**, must be taken into account. Where protest is in question, there seems to be a preparedness evident from the decision in *DPP v Percy* (2001) and *Laporte* (2007) to look to **Arts 10** and **11**. In other words, protest is not merely treated under the **HRA** as a form of disorder, as it often was in the past, but as an exercise of freedom of expression; the freedom of expression dimension is recognised – even afforded weight. When new public order statutory provisions, such as **ss 132–138** of the **Serious and Organised Crime Act 2005**, are passed, their impact on freedom of assembly and public protest has to be considered so that the statute can be declared compatible with the **ECHR** rights under **s 19**. Clearly, it is possible that minimal interpretations of the **ECHR** requirements are being relied upon, but at least the human rights dimension of such statutes is being recognised. They are no longer considered in Parliament only in terms of their ability to curb the activities of football hooligans or late night revellers, as in the past. Thus, for example, **s 41** of the **Criminal Justice and Police Act 2001** was considered to be compatible with **Arts 10** and **11**. Clearly, the courts may take a different view when cases arise under it; if so they can use **s 3** of the **HRA** to seek to bring **s 41** into conformity with the rights if that has not already been achieved.

However, the fact that the freedom of expression or assembly dimension of a protest is recognised, does not mean that **Arts 10** and **11** are necessarily being afforded full weight. In *R (on the application of Gillan) v Commissioner of Metropolitan Police* (2006), the House of Lords found that, assuming that **Art 10** was applicable in relation to an application of **s 44** of the **Terrorism Act**, one of the exceptions under it was satisfied, without engaging in any proportionality analysis. But a different stance was taken in *Laporte* (2006) in which it was found that the **HRA** had brought about a constitutional shift in that context.[18]

There is no substantive right to privacy in either domestic law or, strictly speaking, under the **ECHR**. However, domestic law has long recognised a collection of disparate privacy-related rights, which fall within the scope of land law, tort, criminal law and a handful of statutes, including the **Data Protection Act 1998. Article 8** of the **ECHR** requires respect for family and private life, and it is this requirement which has aided in bringing about change in domestic law now that the **HRA 1998** is in force. Whilst the relevant ECtHR cases are qualified and the European Court has arguably tended towards caution in its interpretation of **Art 8**, it is clear that both respect for private life and for family life require greater protection than they had pre-**HRA** in domestic law. The case of *X and Y v The Netherlands* (1986) held that the State is under a positive obligation to ensure respect for an individual's private and family life, even where the interference comes from a non-State source, such as another private individual. *Von Hannover* (2004) made it clear

---

18 This passage about freedom of expression demonstrates to the examiner you have an ability to critically analyse the law successfully.

that this was the case. Domestically, under the **HRA**, such an individual is not bound by the **ECHR** rights, but since the Court itself is a public authority under **s 6** of the **HRA**, it has a duty to develop existing common law doctrines (in particular, in this instance, breach of confidence) compatibly with **Art 8**.

In the case of *Douglas v Hello!* (2001), it appeared that due to the influence of **Art 8, s 12** and to an extent **s 6**, a right to respect for privacy might be emerging from the doctrine of confidence. The findings in *A v B plc* (2003) confirmed that those who wish to assert 'privacy rights' will have to rely on confidence, but they can seek to rely on the Court's duty under **s 6** in relation to the development of that area of law. *Campbell* (2004) gave support to this stance and also confirmed that the doctrine of confidence had developed – partly under the influence of **Art 8** – in such a way that it had transmuted itself into an action for the protection of personal information, whether or not a pre-existing relationship of trust, imposing confidentiality obligations could be identified, as had been required in the past. **Section 12** of the **HRA** was not found to mean that freedom of expression takes priority over the right to protection of personal information where there is a conflict.

The legal basis for powers of covert surveillance and of interception has undergone a change, partly as a result of the inception of the **HRA**. In this instance, the change has been statute-based, rather than relying on judicial interpretation. There is a right to peaceful enjoyment of the home (*Sporrong and Lonnroth v Sweden* (1982), *Powell and Rayner v UK* (1990)). Invasions of the home or office, even when carried out under warrant by State officials, are open to special scrutiny (*Niemietz v Germany* (1993)). The interception of communications and covert surveillance must be carried out only in accordance with stringent safeguards and with an easily accessible method of appeal for an aggrieved party (*Khan v UK* (2000), *Klass v Germany* (1979)).[19] The **Regulation of Investigatory Powers Act 2000** was introduced in order to provide a broader statutory basis for surveillance and interception, to ensure that the 'in accordance with the law' requirement of **Art 8(2)** was met. The Act probably meets that objective. However, it arguably fails to meet the standards laid down at Strasbourg in terms of proportionality and necessity under **Art 8(2)**, since it provides such wide powers for the interception of communications and for surveillance accompanied by a low level of protection for the privacy of citizens.

The key provisions of the **Anti-Terrorism, Crime and Security Act 2001 Part 4** were declared incompatible with **Arts 5** and **14** of the **ECHR** (protecting the rights to liberty and to freedom from discrimination) by the House of Lords in *A and Others v Secretary of State for the Home Dept* (2005), in a constitutionally significant, and human rights-oriented decision. This led to the introduction of the **Prevention of Terrorism Act 2005**, which itself

---

19 You do not have to write passages of information about all cases. It is often useful to use cases to illustrate the breadth of coverage of the law, as happens here in relation to surveillance.

allowed for detention without trial, if a derogation was introduced, and for the use of non-derogating Control Orders. One such order was quashed in *Secretary of State for the Home Dept v JJ, KK etc* (2006) as incompatible with **Art 5**. The process for imposing control orders was found to require improvement to meet **Art 6** standards in *SSHD v AF* (2009). The **Terrorism Prevention and Investigation Measures Act 2011** repealed the **Prevention of Terrorism Act 2005** with its Control Order regime and replaced it with what have become known as TPIM Notices. The TPIM regime is technically very similar to the Control Order regime and the measures that can be imposed upon individuals are also very similar. The aim of the legislation was to make the measures imposed on individuals less intrusive, and therefore to make it more compatible with human rights and civil liberties. Given the similarity with the Control Order regime it is very dubious whether this aim has been achieved.

It has been argued that the **HRA** has so far had a patchy impact on certain existing areas of law. As indicated above, legislation has been introduced post-**HRA** which has been said by the Government to be in compliance with the **ECHR** and which is apparently intended to ensure that the exercise of powers by certain State bodies is human rights compliant. Such legislation includes the **Regulation of Investigatory Powers Act 2000**, which has already been discussed, and the **Terrorism Act 2000**. However, it is arguable that the **Terrorism Act**, with its extremely broad definition of terrorism in **s 1** and the **Regulation of Investigatory Powers Act**, which places 'directed surveillance' on a statutory basis but provides very meagre human rights safeguards, are based on minimal readings of the **ECHR**. Thus, it is concluded that while an awareness of the human rights dimension of legislation and of the common law is becoming apparent, especially in the very recent decisions, the pace of change is quite slow. This is largely due, it is suggested, to the readiness with which minimal interpretations of the **ECHR** rights can be adopted both by the judiciary and by the Government. Also, following *Ullah* (2006) the courts are curbed in giving greater weight to rights than Strasbourg has.[20]

QUESTION 45 --

How does the European Court of Human Rights ensure that it effectively interprets and applies the **Convention** in a way that keeps it in touch with prevailing attitudes?

How to Answer this Question

- ❖ Background to **ECHR** and ECtHR.
- ❖ Problems facing ECtHR – many different states, different values, values change over time, backlog of cases.
- ❖ Margin of appreciation.

....

20 This is a confident conclusion about the **HRA** and **ECHR** which draws together all the key arguments explored during the answer. Make sure you are able to conclude in such a confident manner.

- ❖ Living Instrument doctrine.
- ❖ More subsidiarity? Recent calls for reform in this area, backlog of cases, stepping on toes of sovereignty.

Answer Structure

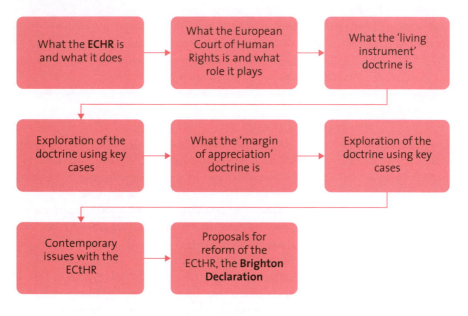

ANSWER

The European Convention on Human Rights (ECHR) is an instrument of international law and is unusual inasmuch as it contains within it the mechanisms for ensuring it is complied with. Section II of the ECHR establishes the European Court of Human Rights (ECtHR) and governs how it operates. Article 19 establishes the ECtHR and states that it has been created to ensure the observance of the engagements undertaken by the signatory states in relation to the rights in the Convention and its protocols. Article 46 ECHR states that final judgments of the ECtHR are binding upon all signatories to the Convention.

Protocols are a substantive way for the Council of Europe to keep the ECHR up to date. The ECtHR itself also helps to keep the text of the Convention relevant to contemporary pressures and issues. It does this by using special doctrines to fulfil its task of interpreting and applying the Convention. Two such notable doctrines have been given the labels of the 'living instrument' doctrine and the 'margin of appreciation'. This answer will explore these two doctrines and consider their effectiveness in keeping the application and interpretation of the Convention in line with contemporary thinking, and will conclude by considering the future of these doctrines in light of recent developments concerning the role of the ECtHR.[21]

The ECtHR have described the Convention as a 'living instrument'. The essence of this doctrine is that even though the actual words of the Convention rights themselves have not changed since their original drafting at the end of the 1940s, the *meaning* behind those words, and which the ECtHR will ascribe to them, can change over time, in order to help accommodate changes in attitudes and opinions to the rights that will necessarily take place as time progresses and different generations arrive. In other words the ECtHR can give different meanings to the Convention rights in order for them to evolve and continue to be relevant in different ages which possess different values and face different challenges as to those originally envisaged when the Convention was drafted. This is how the term 'living instrument' came about, as it refers to the analogy that the Convention is a living, breathing entity, that can evolve and change through time.

The ECtHR expressly referred to this issue in the case of *Tyrer v UK* (1978).[22] The case involved a boy aged 15 from the Isle of Man who was sentenced by a juvenile court to being birched after being convicted of assault. He complained that this amounted to a breach of Art 3 of the Convention. The UK argued that this was an effective and lawful punishment which was successful in acting as a deterrent. The ECtHR stated that the Convention had to be read in light of present-day conditions, and the court would be influenced by the commonly accepted standards of peal policy throughout the member states. By interpreting the Convention in this manner they decided that the treatment was degrading and as such did amount to a breach of Art 3. It did not matter that this was an accepted and traditional form of punishment in the Isle of Man, the relevant consideration was the application of Art 3 in present-day conditions. So whilst this

21 Providing such contextual matters as this about how the court and the convention are kept up to date demonstrates to the examiner that you have good knowledge and understanding of the area.
22 The key case of *Tyrer* is explored in some detail here. When it is relevant to do so, it is good to spend some time on key cases rather than trying to cover too many smaller cases too briefly.

treatment may not have been considered a breach of **Art 3** a number of years previously, due to the living instrument doctrine, it was a breach of **Art 3** at that time. Subsequent to this the Isle of Man changed their penal policy banning such punishment. This is an excellent illustration of the ability of the **ECHR**, through the living instrument doctrine, to effectively protect and enhance human rights protection.

Another key case illustrating the living instrument doctrine is *Goodwin v UK* (2002). The applicant was a male to female post-operative transsexual. She complained that her **Art 8** and **12** rights had been breached by the UK by not allowing her to legally change her status to a woman from a man. This prevention meant, for example, that she had to still pay National Insurance contributions until she was 65 as a man, rather than until 60, which was the rule for women, and that she could not lawfully marry a man. The ECtHR ruled in favour of the applicant, saying that the difference between social reality and legal status amounted to a clear breach of her **Convention** rights and could leave people in the same position feeling vulnerable, humiliated and anxious, and there was no evidence presented to the court that illustrated changing the law to allow gender to be changed legally would result in detriment to anyone. In reaching their decision the ECtHR expressly stated that they looked at present-day conditions across the signatory states in order to interpret the **Convention**, hence the use of the living instrument doctrine to rule in favour of transgender rights which may not have been the case a number of years previously. This case was one of the triggers to the UK introducing the **Gender Recognition Act 2004**.

The doctrine of the margin of appreciation can be summarised as a level of discretion given *by* the ECtHR *to* member states in decisions concerning breaches of **Convention** rights, with the effect being the ECtHR will not interfere with the decision of the member state. The ECtHR accepts that there is a potential breach of a **Convention** right, but they will refuse to interfere with the decision of the member state, as they believe the decision is within an accepted level of discretion that should be given to the member state (hence the 'margin of appreciation'). Whilst it is important to ensure there is a minimum threshold level of protection of **Convention** rights across all member states (that was the very purpose of the **Convention** when originally conceived) it is also important to remember the fact that the **Convention** has member states from many different countries that include a diverse range of cultures, traditions, beliefs and legal systems. The margin of appreciation came into existence as it is essential to the practical application of the **Convention** (and therefore for the ECtHR to effectively do their job) for these differences to be taken into account in certain circumstances, to ensure fairness prevails. It is important to note that the margin of appreciation will not always be available across all the rights under the **Convention**. It very much depends upon the right in question and the circumstances of the case as to whether any margin of appreciation is given to the member state.

A good starting point to explore this doctrine is the case of *Handyside v UK* (1976). The case involved publication and distribution of the 'Little Red Schoolbook', which was marketed as a sex-education book. The book was available in various member states, but when Handyside acquired the rights to sell the book in the UK, the government banned the publication of the book using the **Obscene Publications Act 1959** as they deemed it would corrupt the youth within the UK as it included within it chapters covering topics such as masturbation and homosexuality. Handyside argued this ban breached his freedom of expression rights under **Art 10** of the **Convention**, saying that it was available in other member states so the UK should not be able to ban it; the same rules should apply to all member states.

In delivering its judgment the ECtHR stated that their role was subsidiary to that of the bodies in domestic law that create and apply human rights law. Where such bodies have made careful and considered decisions in areas that affect human rights then such bodies should be given a margin of appreciation, or a level of discretion, in how they have interpreted and applied those laws. In cases such as this, involving **Art 10(2)** which specifically allows the right of freedom of expression to be restricted in certain circumstances, such as for the protection of morals, then the ECtHR would not interfere with the judgment of the domestic legal bodies. It was open for member states to apply different standards provided a minimum level of protection was afforded. As the UK had given a higher standard of moral protection in this case to protect children within their jurisdiction than other members states, then that was an acceptable decision which was within the margin of appreciation that the ECtHR would give to the UK. Individual member states were better placed than the ECtHR to determine what was acceptable according to the values and traditions that were prevailing in the countries at the time. This is an excellent example of what he margin of appreciation is, how it works, and why the ECtHR say it is necessary. It allows flexibility of application of the **Convention** rights to accommodate local conditions whilst still maintaining a minimum standard of protection.[23]

The level of discretion that the ECtHR will give to member states depends upon which article is in question and the circumstances of the case. Whilst a broad margin of appreciation was given in *Handyside*, a much more restrictive approach was taken in *Sunday Times v UK* (1979). The Attorney General obtained an injunction preventing publication of articles in the Sunday Times about the drug Thalidomide and the birth defects of some babies born by mothers who had been taking the drug. Court proceedings were taking place at the time in relation to this so the Attorney General prevented publication as he believed it would prejudice the proceedings. The Sunday Times argued this breached their **Art 10** right to freedom of expression. There was an argument that the ECtHR should give a margin of appreciation to the UK courts in this case. They said as long as the decision had been taken reasonably, fairly and in good faith,

23 This analysis of the usefulness of the doctrine shows the examiner that you are able to think critically about the law.

then the ECtHR should not interfere. The ECtHR rejected these views and said the decision was open to more in-depth scrutiny and it had to be ascertained whether the restriction was proportionate. The ECtHR decided that the ban on publication was disproportionate and amounted to a breach of **Article 10**. This case illustrates the flexibility of the margin of appreciation in that a very restrictive approach can also be taken and it also highlights the difficulties inherent in attempting to foresee exactly what approach the ECtHR will take in a particular case, given the flexible and fluid nature of the concept. Proponents of certainty and clarity will argue, however, that this fluid nature detracts from the effectiveness of it as an aid to the application and interpretation of the **Convention**.

The ability of the ECtHR to effectively interpret and apply the **Convention** has been called into question recently. Whilst the UK was chairing the Council of Europe from November 2011 to May 2012 they took the lead in holding discussions about radically reforming the role and function of the ECtHR.[24] A number of triggers caused these discussions, notably the huge backlog of cases at the ECtHR (at the time more than 150,000) and contentious decisions by the ECtHR against the UK, such as in relation to prisoners voting rights (*Hirst v UK* (2006)). The motivations for the call for change were therefore precisely due to allegations that the ECtHR is not doing its job effectively.

One of the key areas of reform being pushed by the UK was that more 'subsidiarity' was needed. Essentially the UK wanted the ECtHR to take much more a back seat role so they would not interfere as much with domestic decisions, which, the UK argued, would also help reduce the workload of the ECtHR as only the most important cases should ever reach their door. The final outcome of these discussions was the **Brighton Declaration** in April 2012. This declaration ended up being a watered down version of what the UK was originally pushing for, with subsidiarity and the margin of appreciation to be expressly mentioned in a new Preamble (rather than in the actual text of the **Convention** which the UK originally wanted) which is to be drafted by the end of 2013.

What the **Brighton Declaration** highlights is that these notions of subsidiarity and the margin of appreciation are key to the role and the effectiveness of the **Convention** and the ECtHR. Much more prominence and importance is being given to these principles which highlights their relevance. What is certain is this is a very topical and on-going debate, the end of which is still yet to be seen.

---

24 Where possible, and relevant, try to get as many references to recent developments as you can. It shows you are keeping up to date with the law and have awareness of what is happening in the world.

Index